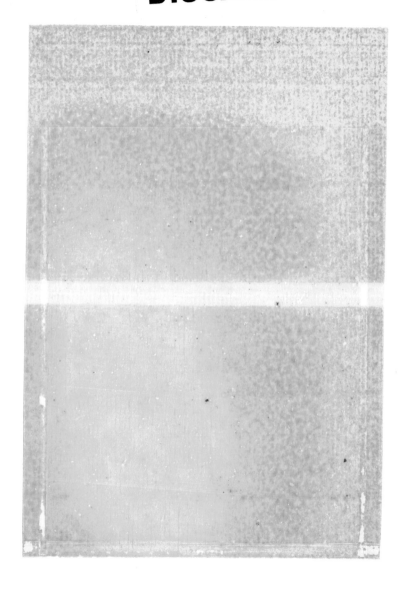

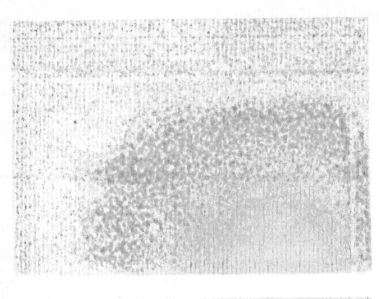

ENGLISH RECUSANT LITERATURE
1558–1640

Selected and Edited by
D. M. ROGERS

Volume 312

JOHN PERCY
True Relations of Sundry Conferences
1626

JOHN PERCY
True Relations of Sundry Conferences
1626

The Scolar Press
1976

ISBN 0 85967 324 3

Published and printed in Great Britain by
The Scolar Press Limited, 59-61 East Parade,
Ilkley, Yorkshire and
39 Great Russell Street,
London WC1

NOTE

Reproduced (original size) from a copy in the Community Library, Mount Street, London, by permission of the Librarian. In this copy the different parts are not bound in the correct order, but they are restored to correct order in the facsimile.

References: Allison and Rogers 610; STC 23530 and 10915.

TRVE
RELATIONS
OF SVNDRY

Conferences had between certaine Proteſtant *Doctours*,
and a IESVITE called *M. Fisher* (then Priſoner in *London* for the Catholique Fayth:)
togeather with Defences of the ſame.

IN WHICH

Is ſhewed, that there hath alwayes beene, ſince Chriſt, a Viſible
Church*, and in it a* Viſible Succeſſion *of Doctours &*
Paſtours*, teaching the vnchanged Doctrine of Fayth, left by*
Chriſt *and his* Apoſtles*, in all points neceſſary to* Saluation.

AND THAT

Not Proteſtants, but only Roman Catholiques haue had, and
can ſhew ſuch a *Viſible Church*; and in it ſuch a *Succeſsion* of
Paſtours and Doctours, of whome men may ſe-
curely learne what points of Fayth are
neceſſary to Saluation.

By A. C.

I beſeech you, Brethren, marke them which cauſe diuiſions and offences, con-
trary to the Doctrine you haue learned, & auoyd them. Rom. 16. v. 17.

Permiſſu Superiorum. M. DC. XXVI.

The Preface of the Publisher of these Relations.

ENTLE READER,

I haue thought good to present to thy view these Relations, together with the deféces of them; not doubting but if thou peruse and ponder them well, they will turne to thy benefit more wayes then one. First, supposing thou neuer heardst any thing of these conferences but in general, or perhaps hast heard particulers falsly related by some who are partially affected, or misinformed; thou mayest by this my labour be certified of the truth, and heerby enabled to do a worke of Charity, in freeing others from ignorance and errour, and contradicting such false rumours as thou mayst chance to vnderstand to haue bene spread abroad, whether in speach, or in print, about this matter.

Secondly, if thou be not thy selfe already resolued a right in matter of Faith necessary to saluation, thou mayest gaine no small help to-

wards

wards a found fetling of thy mynd; firft, in the true knowledge & belief of that One, Holy, Catholique and Apoftolique Church which is métioned in the Apoftles, and the *Nicene* Creed; & by meanes of it, in euery other article, & point of that true Catholique Fayth, which *S. Athanafius* in his Creed fignifyeth to be fo neceffary to faluatiō, that whofoeuer doth not hold it entire (that is, in all points)and inuiolate, (that is, in the true, vnchanged, and incorrupted fenfe, in which Chrift, & his Apoftles left it, as a facred *Depofitum*, to be kept alwayes in the Church) without doubt he fhall perifh euerlaftingly.

Thirdly, if thou be already rightly refolued, thou mayft receaue confirmation in thy Faith, and confolation, in confidering how plainly it is proued, that there is no other Church, nor confequently Fayth, which can (with any probable colour)be pretended to be truly Chriftian & Catholique, befides that which alwayes was, & yet is, the Roman, or vnited with the Roman Church, and Fayth-

Laftly, hauing once thy mind thus fetled, and confirmed in the right Roman, Chriftian Catholique Fayth, and thereby freed from waueringin vncertainty and doubtfulnes about any particuler point of Fayth, thou needft not fpend tyme in endleffe Difputes about Controuerfies of Fayth, nor be alwayes reading, and learning

(as

(as many curious people be now adayes , & neuer cōming to fetled, & well-grounded knowledg , or beliefe of all points of Fayth) but mayſt
beſtow thy tyme, as *S. Peter* coūſelleth thoſe who
be faythfull Chriſtiās, when he ſayth: *Imploying
all care, miniſter yee in your Fayth, Vertue* (by which
you may liue conformably to that Fayth *) and
in Vertue, Knowledge* (by which you may diſcerne
practically good from ill *)and in Knowledge, Abſtinence* (from all that is ill) *& in Abſtinence, Patiēce*
(in regard there will not want ſome paine to be
ſuffered , whiles you labour to abſtaine from ill)
and in Patience, Piety (or Deuotion, out of which
will ſpring ſpirituall comfort, inabling yow to
endure patiently all kind of paine *) and in Piety,
Loue of the fraternity* (or brotherhood, & vnity of
the whole Church , not ſuffering your ſelues
with a prepoſterous piety of priuate feeling deuotion, to hate, or ſeparate from the cōmon Doctrine, Sacrifice, Sacraments, Seruice, Rites or
Ceremonies of the Catholique Church *) and in
Loue of the fraternity , Charity* (or loue of God;
which charity of it be well grounded,& rooted
in your hart, it will doubtleſſe mooue you *to labour* , as the ſame *S. Peter* further aduiſeth *) by
good Workes* (and not by only Fayth, or apprehē-
ſion that your ſins be forgiuen , or that yow be
iuſt, or the children of God, or of the number of
the Elect *) to make ſure your Vocation and Election*

2. *Pet.* I.

Ibid.

* 3   *which*

Ibid.

which doing, yow shall not (as the same Apostle pro-
mifeth) finne at any tyme; and there shalbe miniftred
vnto you aboundantly, an entrance into the euerlafting
kingdome of our Lord and Sauiour Iefus-Chrift.

Some may perhaps meruaile, Why thefe Relations come out fo late, it being now long fince
the Aduerfaries haue giuen out falfe Reports,
both in fpeaches, and print? For anfwere herof,
it muft be confidered, that befides the ordinary
difficulties which Catholiques in *England* haue,
eyther to write for want of conuenient place,
tyme, commodity of bookes, and conferring
which others, or to print; there haue bene fome
speciall extraordinary impediments which haue
hindred the fame. As namely, that *M. Fisher*
was ftraightly charged, vpon his Allegiance,
from his Maiefty, that then was liuing, not to
fet out, or publish what paffed in fome of thefe
Conferences, vntill he gaue Licence; which
made both *M. Fisher*, & his friends to forbeare,
hoping (as was promifed by him who deliuered
his maiefties meffage) that *D. Whyte* and others
were not to publish any thing, vntill they meeting with *M. Fisher*, should treate, and agree, &
vnder their hands confirme what was fayd on
both fides; which his Maiefty perufing, would
grant licence to publish. The which meeting
M. Fisher expected a long while, & once went
to *D. Whytes* Houfe, to know what he would fay
about

L. K.

about the Relation which he had fet out ; but found him vnwilling to make any fuch treaty & agrement, nor would himfelffet out in print,or writing, what he thought to be the true Relatiõ, as knowing by likelihood that he could not fet out the truth,without difaduantage of his caufe, or not without impayring,or at leaft not aduancing his owne credit fo much, as he defired.

If any meruayle,why in thefe Relations fo litle is fayd of the fecõd Dayes Conference with Do-ctour Whyte,the reafon is; becaufe in a manner all the fpeach of that meeting , was betweene his Maiefty,and M. Fisher,who beareth that dutifull refpect to his Soueraigne, that he will not permit any thing fayd by him,to be publifhed now after his death , which he had fo fpecially forbidden to be publifhed in the tyme of his life.For if this caufe had not bene, it had bene alfo now publifhed as wel as the reft; there being nothing in it , which M. Fisher fhould be afhamed off, or by which any preiudice might come to the Catholique Caufe:for if there had bene any fuch matter,D. White(who in generall tearmes doth in his Preface feeke to difgrace M. Fisher,faying, he vanifhed away with difgrace)would not haue o-mitted to fet downe in particuler fome, at leaft one, blame-worthy Argument, or Anfwere.But of this, as alfo of D. Featlyes indeauouring to dif-grace M. Fifher , by obiecting falfly - fuppofed

V.ntruthes

THE PVBLISHER.

Vntruthes, Contradictions &c. more is to be sayd in another place ; and therfore not being willing to hold thee, Gentle Reader, any longer from the confideration of the firft Occafion of all this bufines, I commit thee to the Protecti-on of Almighty God.

Thy hearty Wellwifher, and feruant in Chrift. **W. I.**

THE

THE TABLE

Of the principall Contents, and Chapters of the enſuing Relations.

thode and manner, as *M. Fishers* Queftion (propofed vnto the fayd Doctours in
a former Conference) required : And much
leffe haue they, or can they, or any other fhew
fuch a vifible Proteftant Church in all Ages
and Nations, as Chrifts true Church is (in
the Prophefies, and Promifes of holy Scripture) defcribed- Whence it followeth, that
the Proteftant Church is not the true Church
of Chrift.   *pag.* 1.

** 2

VII.

CHAP.

THE TABLE.

** 3   Faultes

Faultes escaped in the printing.

In the Relations of the Conferences.

Page,	Line,	Fault,	Correction.
24	31	whome when	*dele* whome
26	5	be true	to be true
33	7	being a diuine	cōming frō a diuine
Ibid	11	this definition	ſo this definition
44	24	of fayth	of points of fayth
45	23	to be firme	be firme
49	4	*it not*	*is not*
51	1 &.2	ſo rudely	formerly
Ibid.	13	knowne	foreknowne
56	15	for *contra*	for if *contra*
Ibid.	18	What then? Is it	What then is it?
57	2	to Rome	to come
61	14	do iuſtify	do not like
64	vlt.	argument	againſt
66	15	out oppoſite	but oppoſite
70	12	vnion	vnanime

In the Anſwere to the Fisher catched. &c.

4	17	queſtions	queſtion
8	vlt.	followeth	followeth
16	12	repotteth	reporteth
23	11	ſenſe : Wherof	ſenſe wherof
39	18	deſired	deſired
59	16	heahen	heathen
60	28	with	which
67	26	pre-preſent	preſent
71	6	Proſtant	Proteſtant.

1	17	offeringes	offpringes
4	18	pages	ages
6	6	denyed not	confeſſed not
8	11	different	deficient
11	5	pretended	produced
14	31	or defend	and defend
15	8	The Proofes	Moreouer the Proofes
21	18	firſt	fifth
28	4	is of	are of
32	12	of the argument	againſt the argument
Ibid.	31	poſſeſſours	profeſſours
33	2	the M.	the ſame M.
36	7	pretenteth	pretendeth
41	21	to mooue	doth mooue
45	22	(eſpecially obſtinatly)	*dele vlt. parentheſim*

and read (eſpecially obſtinately againſt the knowne fayth of the Church) any one &c.

68   26   precept of poſitiue &c. *read*, poſitiue and negatiue precept of profeſſion &c.

69	18	infer	anſwere
74	20	*Maior*	*Minor*
84	vlt.	to be good	not to be good

96   9   do not denominate. *read*, do not (as the Name *Proteſtant* doth) denominate &c.

67   vlt.   euery piouſly diſpoſed. *read*, euery intelligent, and piouſly diſpoſed &c.

108	21	points, to take	points. To take &c.
109	29	but ſay	and ſay
117	32	,it ſeemeth	. It ſeemeth
118	1	notable	not able
119	9	hunreds	hundreds
131	29	found in	found in

THE

THE
OCCASION
OF A

Certaine Conference had betvveene
D. Francis White, *and*
M. Iohn Fisher.

T H E Occaſion of this Conference, was a certaine writté Paper, giuen by *M. Fisher*
to an Honble Lady, who deſired ſomthing to be briefly
writté, to proue the Catholique Roman
Church, & Faith, to be the *only* right.

The Copie of this Paper is as followeth.

FIRST, It is certaine, that there is
one, and but *one*, true, diuine, infal-
A

Epheſ. 4.
Heb. 11.

lible

lible Faith, without which none can please God, or attayne Saluation.

2. This *one*, true, diuine, infallible Faith, is wholy grounded vpon the authority of Gods word; and in this it differeth not only from all humane sciences bred by a cleere sight, or euident demonstration, and from humane opinion proceeding from probable arguments or coniectures, & from humane Faith built vpon the authority of *Pithagoras* his *Ipse dixit*, or the word of any other man; but also from all other diuine knowledge, had, either by cleere vision of the diuine Essence, which Saints haue in heauen, or by cleere reuelation of diuine Mysteries, which some principall persons, to wit, *Patriarkes*, and *Prophets*, and *Apostles* had on earth; and also from that Theologicall discursiue knowledge, which learned men attaine vnto, by the vse of their naturall wit, in deducing Conclu-
sions

fions, partly out of the foundations of fupernaturall Faith, partly out of principles of naturall reafon: From all thefe kindes of knowledge (I fay) that one true, diuine, and infallible Faith diffe-reth, in that it is grounded wholly vpon the authority of the *VVord of God*, as humane fallible Faith is grounded vpon the authority of the *VVord of Man.*

3.   This *VVord of God*, vpon which diuine infallible faith is grounded, is not only the word of God *Increate*, or the prime Verity, but alfo the word *Created*, or Reuelation procceding from that prime Verity, by which the truth of Chriftian myfteries, by Chrift (who is true God) was firft made manifeft to the Apoftles, and other his Difciples; partly by the exteriour preaching of his owne mouth, but chiefly by the inward reuelation of his eternall heauenly Father, and by the infpiration of the *holy Ghoft*. Secodly, It was made knowne

A 2   to

to others liuing in thofe dayes, partly by owtward preaching, partly by the writinges of the aforefaid Apoftles, and Difciples, to whome Chrift gaue lawfull miffion & commiffion to teach, faying *Teach all nations*, promifing that himfelfe would be with them all dayes, vnto the end of the world; and that his holy Spirit should affift them, and teach them, (and confequently make them able to teach others) all Truth, in fuch fort, as whofoeuer should heare them, should heare Chrift himfelf, and fo should be made *docibles Dei*, and as the Prophet foretould, *docti à Domino*, and as S. *Paul* fpeaketh of fome, *Epiftola Chrifti*, the epiftle of Chrift, written not with inke, but with the fpirit of God. Whence appeareth, that not only the Word *Increate*, but alfo the Word *Created*, may be truly fayd to be the Foundation of our Faith ; and not only that **Word** which was immediatly infpired by the

heauenly

Matth. 28..
Ioan. 16.
Luc. 10.

heauenly Father, or by the holy Ghoft, in the hartes of the Apoftles, and other Difciples, who liued in our Sauiours dayes; but alfo the Word, as well preached, as written by the Apoftles, and alfo that Word, which by the preaching and writing of the Apoftles, was by the holy Ghoft imprinted in the hartes of the immediate hearers, who were therupon faid to be the Epiftles of Chrift, as I haue already noted.

4. This *Word of God* (which I call *Created*, to diftinguish it from the word *Increate*) being partly preached, partly written, partly infpired or imprinted in manner aforefaid) was not to ceafe at the death of the Apoftles and Difciples and their immediate hearers, but by the appointment of God (who would haue all men to be faued, and come to the knowledge of the Truth,) was to be deriued to pofterity; not by new immediate reuelations, or *Enthufiafmes*, nor by

1. Tim. 2.

A 3   fending

sending *Angells* to all particuler men, but by a continuated succession of *Visible Doctours*, and *Pastors*, and lawfully-sent *Preachers* in all ages, who partly by Transcripts of what was written first by the Apostles; but cheifly by *Vocall* preaching of the same doctrine, without change, which the Pastors of euery age successiuely one from another receaued of their predecessors, as they who liued in the age next to the Apostles dayes, receaued it from the Apostles, as a sacred *Depositum*, to be kept and preserued in the Church, maugre all the assaultes of Hell-gates, which according to Chrifts promise, shall neuer preuayle against the Church Whence followeth, that not only for 400 or 500 or 600. yeares, but in al ages since Chrift, there was, is, and shalbe the true W*ord of God* preached by *visible Doctours*, *Pastors*, and lawfully-sent *Preachers*, so guided by Chrift and his holy spirit, that by them

people

people of euery Age were , are , and
shalbe sufficiently instructed in true,
diuine, infallible Faith, in all thinges
necessary to Saluation ; to the intent,
that they may not be little ones, waue-
ring, nor carried about *with euery winde* Ephes. 4.
of new doctrine; which being contrary to
the ould and first receaued, must needs
be false.

5. Wheras by this which is already
said(which if need be, may be morefully
proued) it apeareth first , that there is
one, true, diuine, infallible Faith, neceffary to saluation. Secodly, that this Faith
is wholy grounded vpon the word of
God. Thirdly, that this word of God, is
not only the word *Increate*, but also the
word *Created*, either inwardly inspired, or
outwardly preached , or written, & continued, without change in one, or other
continued succession of *Visible Pastors*,
Doctours, and lawfully-sent *Preachers*,
rightly teaching, by the direction of
A 4   Chrift,

Chrift, and his holy ſpirit,the ſaid word
of God: wheras(I ſay)all this doth moſt
euidently appeare by this which is already ſayd.

That I may proue the Romã Church
only, and thoſe who conſent and agree
in doctrine of Faith with it, to haue
that *one*, true, diuine, infallible Faith,
which is neceſſarie to ſaluation,

Thus I diſpute.

If it be needfull, that there should
be one, or other continuall ſucceſſion
of *Viſible Paſtors*, in which, and by which
the vnchanged word of God, vpon
which true, diuine, infallible Faith is
grounded, is preſerued and preached,
and no other ſucceſſion beſides that of
the *Roman Church*, and others, which
agree in Faith with it,can be shewed (as
if any ſuch were, may be shewed) out
of approued Hiſtories, or other ancient
monuments; Then without doubt, the
Roman Church on ly, and ſuch as agree
with

with it in Faith, haue that true, diuine, infallible Faith, which is neceſſary to ſaluation.

But there muſt be one, or other ſuch ſucceſſion of *Viſible Paſtors*; and no other can be ſhewed out of approued Hiſtories or ancient monuméts, beſides that of the *Roman Church* only, and ſuch others as agree with it in Faith. *Ergo.*

The *Roman Church* only, and ſuch others as agree with it in Faith, hath true, diuine, infallible Faith, neceſſarie to ſaluation.

The Conſequence of the *Maior* cannot with reaſon be denied, and if it be, it ſhalbe proued.

The *Minor* hath two partes. The firſt wherof is plaine, by that which is already ſaid, and if need be it ſhalbe more fully proued out of holy Scriptures.

The ſecond part, may be made manifeſt, firſt out of Hiſtories, ſecondly out of the confeſſion of Proteſtants.

The ſecond Argument.

If the *Roman Church* had the right Faith, and neuer changed any ſubſtantiall part of Faith : Then it followeth, that it hath now that one true, diuine, infallible Faith, which is neceſſary to ſaluation.

But the *Roman Church* once had the right Faith, and neuer changed any ſubſtantiall part of Faith.   *Ergo.*

The *Roman Church* now hath the right Faith; and conſequently *Proteſtants*, ſo far as they diſagree with it, haue not the right ſoule-ſauing Faith.

The *Maior* is euident.

The *Minor* hath two partes. The firſt is cleere out of *S. Paul*, *Rom.* 1. and is confeſſed by Proteſtants.

The ſecond part, *I proue thus* :

Yf the *Roman Church* changed any ſubſtantiall part of Faith, then there may be ſhewed the point changed, the

person

person which was the Authour of that change, the time when, and place where the change was made; & others may be named, who persisting in the ancient Faith, continued opposition against the innouation and change, as may be shewed in other like, and lesse changes , and namely in *Luthers*, and *Caluins* change.

But these circumstances cannot be shewed. *Ergo.*   No change.

If my Aduersaries name any point, which they affirme to haue beene changed. 1. This wil not suffice, vnlesse they name the other circumstances of the Author, time, place, and who persisting in the former vnchanged Faith, opposed and continued oppositiō against it, as against a Nouelty, and Heresie; as we can do in other changes, and namely in that which was by *Luther* and *Caluin*.

2.   These points, which they say

B 3   were

were changed after the firſt 600. yeares, may be shewed them to haue beene held, by more ancient approued Authors, in the ſame ſenſe, in which they are held by the *Roman Church*; which doth argue, that there was no ſuch change made.

A RE

A briefe Relation of what paſſed betweene D. White, and M. Fisher, about the foreſaid written Paper.

THI s forſaid paper paſſing from one to another, came to ſome hāds, who gaue it to D. *Francis Whyte* to an-ſwere, and to prepare himſelfe to oppugne it in a Conferéce with M. *Fisher*: who whē he wrot it, & gaue it to the Lady, did not thinke, or ſuf-pect that any ſuch great matter ſhould haue bene made of it, as after proued. M. D. *Whyte* hauing (as he cōfeſſed after to M. *Fisher*) had this paper about ten dayes in his handes, ſtudying what to ſay to it, came as he was ap-poynted to the place of meeting, and M. *Fisher* being then a Priſoner, was alſo ſent for. At the houre and place prefixed, both the one, and the other (as they were bidden) ſate downe before a few, but very Ho-norable Perſons, whoſe names I will onely (as M. *Fisher* firſt did) expreſſe in theſe enſuing letters. L. K. L. M. B. L. B. & M. B. Then D. *Whyte* drew out a copie of the aforeſaid written paper, and asked M. *Fisher* whether he wrote it. Vnto which M. *Fisher* anſwered, I wrote ſuch a thing, & if it be a true co-py. I will defend it.

Then

Then D. *Whyte* read the firſt point of the ſaid paper, in which was ſaid: *There is one, and but one, true, diuine Faith &c.* This ſaith D. *White*, is true, if Faith be vnderſtood explicite, or implicite. Which to be the true ſenſe M. *Fisher* aſſented.

Then D. *White* read the ſecond point, in which was ſaid, *That this true, diuine Faith, was wholy grounded vpon the word of God &c.* This alſo D. *White* yielded to be true.

Then D. *White* read the third point, in which was ſaid, *That this word of God, vpon which Faith was grounded, is not only the Word increate, but alſo the Word Created, to wit, the diuine reuelation made manifeſt, partly by Chriſtes outward preaching, partly by the holy Ghoſts inward inſpiration in the hartes of the Apoſtles &c.*

This point alſo D. *White* allowed, but knowing what followed in the fourth point, he asked M. *Fisher*, whether he thought that the holy Ghoſt was equally in others, as in the Apoſtles? M. *Fisher* ſaid, that the inſpiratiō of the holy Ghoſt was promiſed, & giuen both to the Apoſtles, & others, yet not in the ſame degree, nor in the ſame full meaſure; but the Apoſtles, as being after Chriſt the prime foundations of the Church, had the holy Ghoſt in ſuch high degree, and full meaſure, that they could, and did write Canonicall Scriptures. Others that were Paſtours and Doctours, had it in an inferiour degree; yet ſo, as by it they were enabled to teach infallibly, and without change, the ſubſtance of all pointes needfull to ſaluation; eſpecially when in a generall Councell, after diſcuſſion of the matter, they did conclude as the Apoſtles and Seniours did, *Viſum eſt ſpiritui ſancto & nobis*, It ſeemeth good to the holy Ghoſt, and vs. The people alſo had a meaſure of the ſame ſpirit, ſufficient to enable thē to conceiue rightly

and

and to belieue ftedfaftly the teaching of their Paftours.

D. *Whyte* did not difallow the fubftance of this anfwere, but only made a verball Obiection, faying: *The Apoftles had infpiration, Paftours and People onely illumination.*

M. *Fisher* anfwered, that both Apoftles & Paftours had infpiration and illumination, in regard the motion of the holy Ghoft, as receiued in the vnderftanding, is called *Illumination*, and as receiued in the will, it is called *Infpiration*.

L. K. bad them leaue that verball controuerfy, and proceed in the matter. D. *Whyte* excepted againft that part of the paper, wherin was faid, That the word of God was partly written, partly vnwritten, and would haue nothing to be the word of God, but what is written in Scripture.

M. *Fisher* to iuftifie that part of the paper, firft alledged that Text of S. *Paul, Hold the traditions which you haue learned, whether by our Word, or Epiftle.* 2. He made thefe two enfuing arguments (to proue that more is to be belieued by diuine Faith then is written in Scripture.)

It is neceffarie to belieue, by diuine Faith, that *Genefis, Exodus*, and other particuler Books are Canonicall, and diuine Scripture.

But this to be fo, is not affuredly knowen by the only Word written. *Ergo &c.*

Moreouer *Proteftants* hould, and belieue this propofition: Nothing is to be belieued by Chriftian Faith, but what is contayned in Scripture:

But this Propofition, is not contayned in the word written. *Ergo.* Somthing is belieued euen by Proteftants which is not contayned in the written Word, and therefore they muft admit for a ground of Faith

B 4   fome-some Word of God not written.

D. *Whyte* answered: Although at that time when *S. Paul* wrote the text alledged, some part of Gods word was not written, yet afterwards all needfull to be belieued, was written. This D. *Whyte* said, but did not, nor cannot proue, especially out of any parte of the written Word.

D. *Whyte* alledged this text, *Omnis scriptura diuinitùs inspirata, vtilis est &c.* But (as M. *Fisher* then tould him) this Text doth not proue the point which is to be proued. For this text doth not say, that all which is diuinely inspired, was written, or that *Genesis*, *Exodus*, and other particuler books, are diuinely inspired, or that nothing is to be belieued which is not contayned in scripture; but only saith, *That all, or euery Scripture diuinely inspired, is profitable*.

D. *Whyte* said: Scripture is not onely said simply to be profitable, but to be profitable, to argue, to teach, to correct, to instruct, that the man of God may be perfect: and therfore being profitable to all these offices, it may be said to be sufficient.

M. *Fisher* replyed: Although wood be profitable to make the substance of the house, to make wainscot, to make tables and stooles, and other furniture, yet hence doth not follow, that wood alone is sufficient to build and furnish a house. I will not say, that heere D. *White* was at a *Nonplus*, because I vnderstand that word *Nonplus*, doth not please him; but the truth is that to this D. *Whyte* did make no answere. And for my part I professe, I do not see what answere he could haue made to the purpose, and worthy of that Honorable, and vnderstanding Audience.

D. *Whyte* therefore without saying any thing to this instance, seemed to be weary, and giuing the paper

per to *M. Fisher*, bad him read on.

M. Fisher taking the paper, read the fourth Point, in which was sayd, *That the word of God manifested to the Apostles, and by them to their immediate hearers, was not to cease at their death, but was to be continued and propagated without change, in, and by one, or other companie of visible Pastours, Doctours, and lawfully-sent preachers successiuely in all ages &c.* All which to be true being at last graunted, or not denyed by *D. Whyte*, *M. Fisher* proposed the first of the two arguments set downe in the aforesaid Paper. viz.

If there must be in all ages one, or other continuall succession of visible Pastours, Doctours, and lawfully-sent Preachers by whom the vnchanged word of God, vpon which Faith is grounded, was preserued & preached in all ages since Christ; and no other is visible, or can be shewed, besides those of the Roman Church, and such as agree in Faith with them: Then none, but the Pastours of the Romane Church, and such as agree in Faith with them, haue that one, infallible, diuine, vnchanged Faith which is necessarie to saluation.

But there must be such a visible succession, & none such can be shewed different in Faith from the Pastours of the Roman Church.   *Ergo.*

Onely the Pastours of the Romane Church, and such as agree in Faith with them, preserue and teach that one, infallible, diuine, vnchaunged Faith which is necessarie to saluation.

D. Whyte answered, That it was sufficient to shew a succession of visible Pastours, teaching vnchanged doctrine in all points fundamentall, although not in points not fundamentall.

M. Fisher replyed saying: First, that if time permitted, he could proue all pointes of diuine Faith, to be

C   fun-

fundamentall (fuppofing they were points generally held, or defined by full authority of the Church ;) to which purpofe he did recite the beginning of this fentence of S. Auguftine : *Ferendus est disputator errans in alijs quæstionibus non diligenter digestis , nondum plena authoritate Ecclesiæ firmatis, ibi ferendus est error; non tantùm progredi debet , vt ipsum fundamentum quatere moliatur.* In which S. *Austen* infinuateth , that to erre in any queftions defined by full authority of the Church , is to fhake the foundation of Faith, or to erre in points fundamentall. But *M. Fisher* not hauing the booke at hand (and fearing to be tedious in arguing vpon a text which he had not ready to fhew) paffed on : and fecondly required D. *Whyte* to giue him a Catalogue of all points fundamentall, or a definition or defcription (well proued out of Scripture, and in which all Proteftants will agree) by which one may difcerne which be, and which be not points fundamentall.

D. *Whyte* reiected this demaund, as thinking it vnreafonable to require of him a Catalogue , or definition , or defcription of Points fundamentall , out of Scripture, in which all Proteftants will agree. But (confidering in what fenfe D. *Whyte* did vnderftand this diftinction of points fundamentall, and not fundamentall (to wit, that none could be faued who did not belieue all pointes fundamentall rightly; and that none fhould be damned for not belieuing other pointes, vnles he did wilfully againft his confcience deny, or not belieue them;) M. *Fishers* demand was both reafonable and moft neceffary : for fith all Proteftants agree in houlding it neceffarie to be certaine of their faluation; and that none can be faued, who do not belieue all points fundamentall ; and that in thefe pointes, one muft not content himfelfe with

impli-

implicite Faith, but muſt expreſſely know them; it is moſt neceſſary, that all Proteſtants ſhould out of Scripture (which they pretend to be their onely Rule of Faith) find, and conclude with vnanimous conſent certainly, what is, and what is not a fundamentall point of Faith, neceſſary to ſaluation. For whiles ſome hould more, ſome leſſe to be fundamentall, and none of them giueth (out of Scripture) a ſufficient rule by which it may be diſcerned, which is, and which is not fundamentall; how can ech particuler Proteſtant reſt aſſured, that he belieueth expreſly all points fundamentall, or ſo much as is nec̄eſſary, and ſufficient to make him aſſured of ſaluation. But to returne to the Relation. D. *Whyte*, hauing reiected *M. Fiſhers* demand, requiring a Catalogue, definition or deſcription out of Scripture (in which all Proteſtants will agree) ſaid: That all thoſe points were fundamentall, which were contained in the Creed of the Apoſtles.

  M. *Fiſher* might haue aſked him diuers queſtions vpon this anſwere. 1. What text of ſcripture taught him, that all the points contained in the Apoſtles Creed were fundamentall in the ſenſe aforeſaid? Or, That this Creed was compoſed by the Apoſtles, as a ſummary of Faith. contayning points needfull (at leaſt *neceſsitate Præcepti*) to be expreſly belieued by all men? The Church indeed ſo teacheth, but the Scripture hath not any text which doth expreſly ſay ſo, or whence by neceſſarie conſequence ſo much may be gathered; and therefore according to Proteſtant principles (permitting nothing to be belieued but *Onely* Scripture) the Apoſtles Creed ought not to be beleiued, as a rule of any point of Faith, and much leſſe a rule containing all principall and fundamentall points of Faith.

  2. M. *Fiſher* might haue asked, Whether *Onely*

the

the words of the Creed are needfull to be held, as a sufficient foundation of Fayth, or the Catholique sense?
If onely the wordes; then the *Arrians*, and other condemned Heretikes may be sayd to haue held all the
fundamentall points sufficient to Saluation; which is
contrary to the iudgement of Antiquity, and is most
absurd. If the Catholique sense; then the question
must be, who must be iudge to determine which is the
catholique sense? and whether it be not most reaso-
nable, and necessary, that the Catholique Church it
selfe, rather then any particuler man, or Sect of men,
should teach the true sense? When especially, the holy
Ghost was promised to the catholique church (and
not to any particuler man, or Sect of men, differing in
doctrine from it)to teach it all Truth.

Ioan. 14. &
16.

    3.   M. *Fisher* might haue asked, whether all points
fundamentall were expressed in the creed, or not? If
they be not, by what other rule shall one know, what
is a point fundamentall? If all which is fundamentall
be expressed in the creed,then to belieue only Scripture, or to belieue that there is any Scripture at
all,is not fundamentall, or necessary to Saluation;
but to belieue the catholique church (and consequently the truth of all such doctrines of Fayth,
which she generally teacheth, or defineth in her generall councells) is fundamentall. So as, we may say
with S. *Athanasius*, Whosoeuer will be saued, must belieue the catholique Fayth (that is, the Fayth taught
by the catholique church) and this not only in part
or in a corrupt sense, but in all points, and in catholique sense. For as the same S. *Athanasiu*s saith, vnles one
belieue the said Catholique faith (*integram inuiolatamq̨;*)
entiere and inuiolate, without doubt he shall perish
euerlastingly. All these questions M. *Fisher* might
                            haue

haue asked, but he at that prefent only asked, Whether all articles of the Creed, were held by D. *Whyte* to be fundamentall ?

To which Queftion D. *Whyte* anfwered, That all was fundamentall.

M. *Fisher* asked, Whether the article of chrifts defcending into hell, were fundamentall?

D. *Whyte* faid, Yes.

Why then (faid M. *Fisher*) did M. *Rogers* affirme, That the Church of England is not yet refolued, what is the right fenfe of that Article ?

It was anfwered, that M. *Rogers* was a priuate man. M. *Fisher* replyed: That his Booke in the title profeffeth to be fet out by publique authority. To which M. *Fisher* might haue added, That the Booke fo fet out by publique authority, beareth title of the Catholique, or Vniuerfall doctrine of the church of England; by which addition is fhewed a difference betwixt this book of M. *Rogers*, and fome others, which were obiected to be fet out by licence of the catholique fide : for thefe our books are only licenced to come out in the name of fuch, or fuch a priuate author, and as books declaring his priuate opinions: but this of M. *Rogers* was authorized, and graced with the title of the Catholique doctrine of the church of England, and therfore ought by Proteftants to be more refpected, then other priuate mens books.

M. *Fisher* not thinking it neceffary to preffe this difference, returned againe to D. *Whytes* firft anfwere to the maine argument, in which he hauing faid, That it was fufficient to fhew a vifible fucceffion of fuch as held points fundamentall, did implicitely grauntit neceffary, that a fucceffion fhould be fhewed of fuch vifible Paftours as did hold all points, which

Rogers in his doctrine of the Church of England. Art. 3.

C 3 at

at leaft himfelf held to be fundamentall, or neceffary
to faluation . Whereupon M. Fisher bad D. Whyte
name a continuall companie, or fucceffion of vifible
Proteftants (different from the Romane Church
which they call Papifts) holding all points which
he accounted fundamentall .

D. Whyte expiefly graunted, That he could not
fhew fuch a vifible fucceffion of Paftours and Doctours (differing in doctrine from the Romane
church) who held all points which he accounted
fundamentall. Which his ingenuous confeffion , I
defire the Reader to note , applying it to the aigu-
ment which M. Fifher propofed, fhewing that Onely
the Roman church hath had fuch a fucceffion . For
if, as the argument vigeth, one fuch fuccefsion hath
bene, and none differing in doctrine from the Roman can be fhewed by D. Whyte (being accounted
a prime Proteftant Contioueifit, who may teach fuch
as D. Featly, as was lately proteffed by D. Featly himfelf) we may abfolutely conclude, that no fuch vifible
fucceffion was of Proteftants, fo faire as they differ in
doctrine from the Roman church, and confequently
till they affigne fome other (which they can neuer do)
they muft acknowledge the Romane to be the only
church, or at leaft a church which hath had a vifible
fuccefsion , teaching the vnchanged Faith of chrift
in all ages , in all points, at leaft fundamentall : which
being acknowledged, worthily might M. Fisher aske
(as he did aske) D. Whyte, Why Proteftants made a
fchifme from the Romane church ? and why Proteftants did perfecute Romane cathol.ques, contrary
to the cuftome of the ancient Fathers , who ftill kept
vnity with other churches, although in their opinion
holding errours ; (vntill the catholique church by
full

full authority defined them to be errours in Faith) and that after such definition of the church (which was yet neuer made againft the Romane church) they would ftill obftinatly perfift in errour; as appeareth in *S. Cyprians* cafe. To thefe demaunds made by *M. Fisher*, *D. Whyte* anfwered ; We do not perfecute you for Religion. About which anfwere I defire the gentle Reader to obferue, that *M. Fisher* asked two Queftions. 1. Why *Proteftants* made a fchifme from the Romane church ? 2. Why *Proteftants* did perfecute Romane catholiques?

To the firft of thefe queftions being about Schifme, *D. Whyte* anfwered not a word, and yet this was the moft important Queftion, fufficient to fhew Proteftants to be in a damnable ftate, vnles they repent and returne to vnity with the Roman church. For on the one fide, it cannot be denyed, but that fchifme or feparation of ones felfe from church-Vnity, is a moft damnable finne, which cannot be made lawfull for any caufe, nor cannot without repentáce, & returning to Vnity, be wafhed away, euen with martyrdome it felfe, as the ancient Fathers confeffe : And on the other fide it is euident (& euen confeffed by fome Proteftants) that *Proteftants* did feparate themfelues from the Romane Church, which is confeffed to be the mother Church, and which cannot be fhewed to haue feparated it felfe from a former church yet extant, as the true church of chrift muft alwayes be vifibly extant; Neither can there be fhewed any other reafon, why Proteftants did make, and continue this their feparation, then were, or might haue bene alledged by Heretiques, and Scifmatiques of ancient times, feparating themfelues from the catholique Roman church : For fetting afyde all temporall ref-

C 4   pects,

pects, which doubtles were (but were very infufficient and vnworthy) caufes why fome did firft, and do yet continue this feparation ; there cannot be imagined any pretended caufe which may not be reduced to thefe two heads : to wit, corruption of *Manners*, or corruption of *Doctrine*. Corruption of *manners*, is not a iuft caufe to make one leaue the Faith, Sacraments, and rites of the church, our Sauiour hauing fufficiently forewarned what is to be done in this cafe, when he faid ; *Vpon the chaire of Moyfes the Scribes and Pharifees haue fitten ; all therefore that they fay vnto you, obferue, and do, but according to their works do not*. For by this is fhewed that the feparation which in other places of Scripture is commanded, is not meant fo, as if it were to be made by neglecting or contradicting the doctrine of lawfully authorized Paftours, or by corporally abfenting ones felfe from communicating with them in neceffary Sacraments, and church Rites, but only fpiritually to departe from the imitation of their ill manners. The fecond, to wit, corruption of *Doctrine*, pertayning to the common Faith of the catholique Church, neither did, nor can happen to the whole vifible church : chrift hauing promifed, that the holy Ghoft fhalbe alwaies with it, to teach it all Truth ; and that Hell-gates fhall neuer fo preuaile againft it, as to ouerthrow in it the fundation of all goodnes, to wit, true Faith. And for other errours in fuch queftions as are not determined by full authority of the faid catholique church, S. *Auftens* rule is to be obferued, whom when he faith, *Ferendus eft difputator errans*: neither muft one for the errour of a few, leaue the fociety and communion of all ; neither muft one or a few, pre-
fuming

Matth. 23.

Aug. de Verb. apoft. Ser. 14.

fuming vpon their owne priuate reading, and interpreting of scripture, or their priuate spirit (which is
or may be the comō pretext of all Heretiques) censure
& condemne the doctrine, or practise of the vniuersall
Catholique Church to be erroneous: which to doe, is
by *S. Bernards* sentence, *Intollerable Pride*, and in *S. Austens* iudgment, *Insolent madnes*.

The beginning therefore and continuance of the
Schisme, and separation of the Protestants from the
Catholique Romane Church (in which euen, as
Caluin confesseth, there was made a discession & departure from the whole world) is very damnable,
and altogether inexcusable. Which perhaps was the
cause why D. *White* passed ouer that part of the Question (touching this Schyfme) with silence, and onely
answered, as is aboue said, to the other parte saying:
We do not persecute you for Religion.

To which answere M. *Fisher* replyed, saying: You
do vs wrong, for my self being a prisoner was neuer
taxed with any state matter, but do suffer for Religion. L. M. B. made another answere, saying:
You of your side, did first persecute *Protestants*.

M. *Fisher* answered, that we Catholiques hold all
points, in which Protestants differ from vs in doctrine of faith to be fundamentall, and necessary to
be belieued, or at least not denyed, and so may haue
cause to punish them who deny, or contradict. But
Protestants, who belieue catholiques to hold right
in all points which themselues esteeme fundamentall, haue no reason to persecute vs, for supposed errours in points not fundamentall, which Protestants
do not account damnable. For better cleering wherof
M. *Fisher*, asked D. *White*, whether he thought errour
in a point not fundamentall to be damnable?

D   D. *White,*

*Caluin l. Ep.
epist. 141.*

D. *White*, faid, No, vnles one hold it againft his confcience.

M. *Fisher* asked, How one could hould an errour againft his confcience?meaning that one could not inwardly in his confcience belieue that be true, which he knew in his confcience to be an errour.

D. *Whyte* anfwered, That by peruerfity of will he might hould an errour againft the knowne truth. Which anfwere is true, if he meane, that one who knoweth the truth at this inftant, may after by peruerfity of Will, incline the Vnderftanding to hold the contrary errour. But that, at the fame inftant, he fhould know the truth actually, and yet actually hold, in the fame inftant, the contrary errour in his confcience, or inward knowledg, is more then I think any Philofopher can explicat. For this were to know, and not know, and to belieue two contraries, Truth, and Errour, about the fame obiect in the fame fubiect, the inward confcience at one, and the fame inftant, which is impoffible.

M, B. meruayling at D. *Whites* anfwere asked, him againe the fame queftion, faying: May one be faued that holdeth errour in points of Faith, not fundamentall, fuppofing he hould not againft his confcience?

D. *White* fayd; Yes.

Thofe (faith M. B.) who fuffering for confcience hould errour in Faith againft their confcience, are worthy to be damned.

M. *Fisher* hauing obferued, that D. *White* had infinuated, that one might be damned for holding errour in points of Faith not fundamenall, in cafe he hould them againft his confcience, faid; If it be damnable to hold errours in points not fundamentall, in
safe

eafe one hold them willfully againft his confcience:
à fortiori, it is damnable to hold the like errours wilfully and obftinatly, againft the known iudgment,
and confcience of the Church. For as S. *Bernard* faith:
Quæ maior fuperbia, quàm vt vnus homo iudicium fuum præ-
ferat toti Congregationi? What greater pride, then that
one man fhould preferre his iudgment(or confcience)
before the iudgment (and confcience) of the whole
Church?

D. *Whyte* faid, he remembred that fentence of *S.*
Bernard: but it is not remembred that he gaue any good
anfwere, either to that fentence, or to the argument
confirmed by it. Neither indeed can he giue any good
anfwere, in regard it is certaine, that the iudgment &
confcience of the whole Church (or Congregation
of fo many faithfull, wife, learned, and vertuous men,
aflifted by the promifed Spirit of truth) is incompara-
bly more to be refpected, and preferred before the
iudgment, and confcience of any priuate man; as appeareth by that of Chrift our Sauiour, who (without
excepting any who pretendeth to follow his confcience, and without diftinguifhing the matter in
which he pretendeth to follow it, into points fundamentall, & not fundamentall) abfolutely affirmeth,
He that will not heare (that is, *beleiue* and *obey*) *the Church,*
let him be to thee as an Heathen & Publican.

Hence *Proteftants* (who preferre their priuate Iudgment and Confcience before the iudgment and
confcience of the Catholique Church, in interpreting
Scriptures, or otherwife) may learne, in what ftate
they remaine, fo long as they do thus, being by the
Cenfure of *S. Bernard*, extremely *Proud*, and in the
iudgement of *S. Auften* infolently *madde*, and by the
fentence of Chrift himfelfe, to be accounted no better

Bern. ferm. 5.
de refurrect.

Matt. 18.

then *Heathens* and *Publicans*.

It feemeth that D. *Whyte* did not deeply ponder this point, or els was willing to paffe ouer it (as a Cat ouer hote coales) and fo he betooke himfelfe to oppugne another part of M. *Fishers* paper, in which is fayd, that; *No company of vifible Paftours deliuering vnchanged doctrine, could be shewed in all ages, befydes thofe of the Romane Church .*

D. *Whyte* denyed this to be true, and (notwithftanding he had before faid that he could not fhew any companie differing in doctrine from the Roman Church, holding in all ages all fundamentall points) faid, that both the Greeke Church, and the Proteftant Church had fuch a fucceffion of vifible Paftours : which two fayings, how D. *Whyte* will reconcile, pertayneth to him to declare.

M. *Fisher* replyed , and tould him that the Greeke Church changed, and erred in a point of Faith, to wit, about the *holy Ghoft*. A like, or greater change he might, and in likelyhood would, haue tould him to haue bene in many points held by the Proteftant Church , if he had not bin interrupted by L. K. who asked, *Whether notwithftanding that errour of the Greeke Church, Ignorant men might not be faued?*

M. *Fisher* anfwered to L. K. his queftion, faying: Some ignorant men may be excufed from actuall finne, in holding that errour, as, through inuincible ignorance, one holding fome errour againft the holy Trinity it felf, may be excufed. Yet for other actuall finnes, they might be damned for want of meanes neceffary for remiffion of them. This anfwere was meant by M. *Fisher* of fuch ignorant men, who (although by inuincible ignorance excufed from the actuall finne of pofitiue Infidelity , Herefy & Scifme) wanted

wanted true fupernaturall Faith, Hope and Charity, out of which an act of true Contrition fpringeth; or wanted the true, and lawfull vfe of the Sacrament of Pennance, & Prieftly Abfolution; which being need-full to obtaine pardon of finne, may eafily be wanting to fuch people as commit other finnes againft the light of nature, or againft thofe good motions of Grace, which now and then Almighty God giueth to all forts, who confequently (through this their owne fault) are not illuminated with true fupernaturall Faith, but are permitted ftill to remaine in Infidelity, or Herefy, or Schifme, or in a negatiue difpofition of want of all Faith, deuotion, and defire of vnion with God, and fuch good men who truly ferue god in his true Church: of which fort of ignorant people, it is to be doubted there be but to many in all (efpecially In-fidel, Hereticall, or Schifmaticall) Countries. But hence doth not follow, neither did M. *Fisher* euer meane to affirme, that all ignorant Græcians, Prote-ftants, or of any other fort of Schifmatiques, Here-tiques, or Infidels are damned; for if on the one fide this their ignorance be inuincible, fo as to excufe them from the actuall finne of their Schifme, Herefy, and Infidelity; and on the other fyde, they by Almighty Gods fpeciall grace, be preferued from other actuall mortall finne, and by the fame grace be excited ex-traordinarily to Faith, Hope, Charity, and to true Contrition for all finne, they may be faued: But this being extraordinary, no man ought ordinarily prefume, or rely on it, efpecially fo, as to neglect the ordinary meanes, knowne to be in the vnity of the Catholique Roman Church.

After this D. *White* excepted againft another point of M. *Fishers* paper, in which was fayd: *That the Roman*

Church

*Church had still held vnchanged doctrine of Fayth in all points
&c.* And for inftances of change made, he obiected
*Tranfubftantiation, Images, Communion vnder one kind, Sa-
crament of pennance &c.* Thefe points he flieghtly began to touch, but did not (as the paper required) name
when, and by whome the change was made in thefe
points, but fayd; It was not needful to fhew thefe circumftances. As for example (fayth he) the Pharifies
held errour, in faying, that the gold of the Altar was
more holy then the Altar, which was a change in doctrine, & yet you cannot fhew when, and by whome
this change was made.

To this *M. Fisher* anfwered, that although he could
not on the fuddaine tell when, and by whome this
Change was made; yet he did not doubt but that with
ftudy he might find it out. And fo indeed, he might
haue named the Author of the Sect of Pharifies, who
firft brought in that error, and the time when that Sect
began, which is inough. For we do not preffe *Proteftants* to tell the very day, or houre in which euery
one of our fuppofed Errors were brought in; but to
name the firft Author of any erroneous doctrine, or
of any Sect of men who were fpecially noted for
teaching fuch a peculiar doctrine, and about what
yeare, or Age that Sect of men, firft began; and
who they were, who then noted them to teach fuch
doctrine, contrary to the formerly receaued Fayth of
the vniuerfall Church; as muft be, and is vfually noted, when efpecially any fuch notorious matters as
thofe which D. *White* obiected, were by any man,
or any fect of men, taught contrary to the formerly
receaued Faith of the vniuerfall church.

Sith therfore, the aforefaid circumftances are
vfually noted in other fuch kind of changes, and that
it is

it is morally impoffible , that fuch great changes and
fo vniuerfally fpread ouer the world, fhould be made
ether in an inftant, or in fuccceffion of time, and that
not one, or other writer would haue made mention
of the change, and when, where, and by whome it
was made, as they do of all other fuch matters; D.
White (who obiected fuch great changes of doctrine
to haue beene made in the Roman church, accufing
hereby greuioufly her, which confeffedly was once
the true Mother church,)is obliged and bound, not
only to proue this his accufation, by fhewing the for-
fayd circumftances, in good Authors, if he will not be
accounted an vnnaturall and falfe calumniator of
his true Mother-church: but he muft alfo fhew another continually vifible church, which neuer did admit any fuch change in doctrine of Faith, if he will
not impioufly deny the truth of the Prophefyes and
Promifes of Scripture, wherby we learne, that Hell
gates fhall not preuaile againft the church: And that
Chrift himfelf, and his holy fpirit will alwaies be with
the church teaching it, and confequently enabling it
to teach vs all truth, and making it the pillar and
ground of truth, and confequently free from all error
in matters of Fayth.

But D. *White* can neuer proue his accufation by
fhewing out of good Authors the aforefayd circumftances of the change of the Roman church , in doctrine of Fayth, nor can fhew any other continually
vifible church, which did not admit change in doctrine of Fayth. Let him therfore confider , whether
it be not better to recall his falfe vnnaturall accufation of his Mother the Roman church , being forry
for it, with purpofe here after humbly to heare, belieue, obey, and followher doctrine and direction,

rather

rather then to incurre, not only the foresayd censure of men, but also of christ himselfe, who sayth; *He that will not heare the Church , let him be to thee as an heathen & Publican:* that is, cast out of the fauour of God, and all good men, both in this present life, and also, if he do not in time repent, in the future eternall life.

These be the chiefe points which I haue gathered out M. *Fishers* first Relation , which he shewed to D. *Whyte* with an intét that he should put him in mind if any thing were not remembred, or misremembred: But the Doctour at that time did not, nor could truly say, that any thing was falsely related; only he sayd. 1. That himselfe did not remember a point or two, which both M. *Fisher* and M. B. did perfectly remember to haue bene so as is here related. 2. He sayd, that something more was sayd then is related , which M. *Fisher* did not deny, but was willing to add any thing, that D. *Whyte* could put him in mind of, or that himselfe should after remember: and so being put in remembrance made by D. *Whyte*, to wit, Whereas M. *Fisher* vpon some occasion or other, had sayd, *That although a generall Councell* might erre in the premisses, yet not in the Conclusion, D. *Whyte* obiected, saying: That in all sciéces the conclusió is no more certayne, thé the Premisses, & therfore if the premisses in a general councell be fallible, the conclusion cannot be infallible. To which M. *Fisher* answered, saying ; Although in sciences which depend only vpon the light of Nature, the conclusion cannot be more certaine then the premisses; yet in a generall councell, assisted by the holy Ghost, in the finall conclusion, or definitiue sentence, the conclusion is alwayes infallible, although sometimes the premisses be fallible.

And M. *Fisher* had great reason to answere in
this

this manner. Indeed if to define a matter of Fayth were to conclude the same by way of difcourse out of Principles, as the Argument doth fuppofe ; then if Councels might erre in the Premiffes they might like-wife erre in their Conclufion , and definitiue fen-tence. But this fuppofition is falfe, Infallibility in de-fining , being a diuine Affiftance , not to inferre one thing out of another by way of connexion and con-fequence, but to decree and declare what is conforme to the word of God, by way of authority , binding the Church fo to belieue. And this definition is euer infallible, though all the arguments the Councell bringes by way of difcourfe in proofe of the defini-tion eyther before or after the fame is made, be not still demonftratiue.

Another obiection M. *Fisher* hath fince that time remembred (to wit)that D.*White* alleaged fomething out of *Abulenfis* in *Matt.* 7.19. which M. *Fisher* differred to make anfwere vnto, vntil he might fee the Author himfelf, hauing had experience inough , how falfely many Minifters cite Authors, and how falfe their Note-Bookes be. Now M. *Fisher* hath feene the booke, and findeth the words cited by D. *White* to contayne two parts; one, as contrary to D. *white* as the other feemeth contrary to M. *Fisher*, & that the whole difcourfe of *Abulenfis* in that place, sheweth that euen that part which feemeth contrary to M. *Fisher*, doth nothing preiudice M. *Fishers* caufe, as will appeare to any that will duly ponder all that is there fayd of the Authority of the Church, in defining what bookes be, and what be not Canonicall. For *Abulenfis* exprefly declareth, that all, and only thofe bookes are to be ac-counted Canonicall, which the church doth define to be canonicall : and the reafon why he did (in his pri-

uate

uate opinion) thinke one , or two Bookes not to be
canonicall, which we do now hold for canonicall, is,
for that the Church had not then so cleerely defined
them to be Canonicall , as it hath done since *Abulensis*
wrot that passage: as there are diuers other Bookes held
for Canonicall, euen by *Protestants*, which haue not
beene so esteemed by some of the Ancient Fathers, in
regard the church had not then so clearely defined
them to be canonicall , as it hath done in after times.

A third obiection was made by D. *White* about *the*
worship of Images , which D. *white* would needs affirme to be an *Innouation*, *and grosse Error of Papists:*
Which M. *Fisher* denied, and sayd, that the worship
(meaning the same worship which is due to the Prototypon) is not giuen by vs to the Image it selfe.
This obiection D. *White* vrged no further the first
day; but the next day of meeting, he vrged those words
of *Bellarmine*, *Datur veneratio ipsi imagini*. M. *Fisher* an-
wered, that *Bellarmine* did not meane that the same
worship, which was due to the *Prototypon*, was giuen
to the Image it selfe, but an inferior degree of worship,
and that also for the *Prototypons* sake .

Then D. *White* betooke himselfe to *Suares* , saying:
That *Suares* did hold, that the same worship which
was giuen to the *Prototypon* , was giuen to the Image.
M. *Fisher* answering, sayd: You do not vnderstand our
Authors : For, sayd M. *Fisher* , they that seeme to giue
most, giue the least to Images ; for those that say that
one and the same worship is giuen to the Image, and
that which is represented by it, hold the Image to be
incapable of any part of worship , and so the whole to
pertayne to the thing : Wheras others who distinguish
one honour to be due to the thing, and another farre
inferior to be giuen to the Image , giue something, as

M. Fi-

M. Fisher explicated in the example of the refpect one beareth to the picture of his friend, which although it be not capable of that friendly refpect, and affection which by looking vpon it, he exciteth in himfelfe towards his friend reprefented by it; yet is it capable of an inferiour degree of refpect, as to be fet in a more worthy and eminent place &c. then it fhould be, if it were the picture of fome other, who were not ones friend.

Thefe be the chiefe Paffages of this Conference, between *D. White,* and *M. Fisher,* fo far as hath come to my notice, who haue vfed fo much diligence in inquiring the truth of this matter, as I haue no doubt, but for fubftance I haue not omitted any thing that may much import, confidering what the occafion, and fubiect of the Conference was; to wit, that Paper written by *M. Fisher,* in which he proued the *Roman Church,* and thofe who agree in Fayth with it, to be that Company, of whome euery one muft learne what is the truth, in all points and queftions of Fayth neceffary to faluation: which paper not being fubftantially confuted, as it was not, by any thing fayd by *D. White,* or any other at that time or after, *D. Whyte* is yet obliged to make a better anfwere, if he meane to giue fatisfaction either to Catholiques or Proteftants in this moft important point of a perpetually vifible church, of which all forts muft learne true, diuine, infallible Faith, neceffary to Saluation.

1927630

F I N I S.

A
RELATION
OF THE
Conference between a certain B. & M. Fisher,
defended against the said B. his Chaplayne.

The Preface.

ENTLE Reader, I think it needful to let thee vnderſtand, that whereas the Chaplaine of a certayne B. ſayth: (in the Preface of his Anſwere to a Relation of what paſſed betweene the ſaid B. and *M. Fisher,*) *That the Ieſuite ſpread abroad papers of this Conference, which were full of partiality to his cauſe, more full of calumny againſt the B.* the truth is, that the Ieſuite did not at all, ſo much as in fpeach, & much leffe in papers publifh this, or either of the other two Confe-rences, which he had with *D. White,* vntill he was forced vnto it, by falfe **R**eports giuen out about them, to his priuate difgrace, and to the preiudice of the Catholique Caufe. Neither then did he fpread papers abroad, but only deliuered a very few Copies to fpeciall friends; and this not with intent to ca-lumniate either the B. or the Doctor, or to make the papers common, but to enable his friends to anfwere and coun-termaund fuch falfe Reportes, as they had heard, or might heare. Which being fo, I do not fee, how the Chaplaine can free himfelf from the faults of partiality and Calumny, wherof he doth accufe the Iefuite, vnles he do (by fome other proofs better then his owne, or his Mai-fters bare affirmation) proue, that the Iefuite fpread fuch papers; fhewing alfo particulerly wherein he did relate par-tially

tially to his caufe , and calumnioufly a-
gainft the B. I fay *relate*, in regard I do
not at this prefent promife to examine
exactly all doctrines infinuated in the
Iefuits Relation, and impugned by the
Chaplaine (as neither hauing fufficient
leyfure, nor commodity of Bookes requifite for fuch a worke;) but the Relation to haue bene fincere and true , free
from partiality, more free from calumny , I vndertake to defend. For which
purpofe I thinke beft to fet downe the
Iefuits Relation (for the moft part as I
find it in the Chaplains printed Copie)
in greater letters , and in a leffer letter
the Chaplains chiefeft exceptions , and
my anfwere vnto them.

I thinke the Iefuite himfelf for his
owne particuler refpect , could be content to let paffe this partiall and calum-
nious Cenfure of his Relation, fuffering
it patiently as one of the ordinary per-
fecutions , which he, and others at this

E 4   day

day endure for the Catholique Faith,
and for that peculiar order of life which
he profeſſeth , vnder the name of the
Society of IESVS; comforting himſelf
with the exáple of Chriſt his Apoſtles,
Act. 5. 41. who reioyced that they were thought worthy
to ſuffer Contumely , for the name of Ieſus .
In this reſpect I ſay, I ſuppoſe the Ieſuite
himſelf could be content, that nothing
were ſaid to the Chaplaines Cenſure:
But conſidering the hurt which may
come to the common cauſe by his vniuſt diſgrace, I haue thought it neceſſary
to defend the ſincerity and truth of his
Relation, and ſome of the chief heads of
doctrine conteined in it , to the intent
that hereby men may be moued better
to truſt what he hath written hereto-
fore, or may write hereafter, in defence
of the Catholique Faith & Church; &
leſſe truſt his Aduerſaries, who without
iuſt cauſe do ſo much endeauour to ca-
lumniate his perſon, or writinges .

M.

M. Fishers *Relation of the Confe-*
rence, betvveene a certaine B.
and himselfe.

T H E occasion of this Conference was, for that it was
obserued, that in a second
Conferéce with *D.VVhite,*
all the speach was about
particuler matters, & little or nothing
about a Continuall, Infallible, Visible
Church, which was the chief and onely
point in which a certaine Lady required satisfaction, as hauing formerly
setled in her mind, that it was not for
her, or other vnlearned persons to take
vpon them to (a) iudge of particulers,
without depending vpon the Iudgment
of the true Church.

(*a*) To wit
absolutly &
to rely vpō
theirpriuate
iudgment;
so, as to ad-
uenture Sal
uation vpō
it alone, or
chiefly.

F   This

(b) The Chaplaine noting the word, *Infallible*, to be fometimes put in, fom times left out, taxeth *M. Fisher* of fpeaking diftractedly But I note herein, that *M. Fisher* fpake moft aduifedly, and with precife care of pūctuall Truth: for when he fpeaketh of what was obferued, or defired by the La. he putteth in theword

This La, therefore hauing heard it graunted in the firft Conference, that there muft be a continual, vifible Company euer fince Chrift, teaching vnchanged doctrine, in all points Fundamentall, that is, in all points neceffary to Saluation, defired to heare this confirmed, and proofe brought to shew which was that Continuall, (b) Infallible, Vifible Church, in which one may, and out of which one cannot, attaine Saluation. And therefore hauing appointed a time of meeting betwixt a certaine B. and my felfe, and thereupon hauing fent for the B. and me, before the B. came, the La. & a friend of hers came firft to the roome where I was, & debated before me the aforefaid Queftion, and not doubting of the firft part, to

Infallible, becaufe he knew it was an infallible Church which fhe fought to rely vpon. But when he fpeaketh of what D. *Whyte* or L. K. graunted, he leaueth it out, becaufe they did not mention the word *Infallible,* but onely granted a vifible Church in all ages teaching vnchanged doctrine, in all matters neceffary to Saluation.

to wit, That there muſt be a Continuall
Viſible Church as they had heard grā-
ted by *D. VVhite, L. K. &c.* The Queſtion was, which was that Church? The
La. friend would needs defend, that not
only the Romane, but alſo the Greeke
Church was right. I told him, that the
Greeke Church had plainely changed,
and taught falſe in a point of doctrine
concerning the Holy Ghoſt, and that
I had heard ſay, that euen his Maieſty
should ſay, *The Greeke Church hauing
erred againſt the Holy Ghoſt, had loſt the
Holy Ghoſt.* The La. friend not knowing
what to anſwere, called in the Bishop;
who ſitting downe firſt (c)excuſed himſelf as one vnprouided, and not much
ſtudied in Controuerſies, and deſiring
that in caſe he should faile, yet the
Proteſtant Cauſe might not be thought
ill of, it hauing a hundred better Schollers to maintaine it then he. To which
I ſaid, there were a thouſand better

F 2　　　　ſchollers

(c) The Chaplaine taxeth the Ieſuite, as if in this par-cell he did inſult: and ſaith it was the B. his modeſty to vſe this ex-cuſe, and to ſay *there were a hundred ſchollars better then he.* But I do not ſee any Inſultation, but a ſimple & true nar-ration of what was ſayd: Ney-ther do I ſee leſſe mode-ſty in the Ieſuits pre-ferring a thouſand before him-ſelf, then in the B. his preferring a hundred be-fore himſelf.

schollers then I, to maintaine the Catholique cause.

Then the Question about the Greek Church being (d) propo- sed, I said as before, that it had erred. The B. said, that the er- rour was not in a point (e) Fun- damentall.

Wherupon I was forced to repeate, what I had formerly brought against D. VVhyte con- cerning points fundamentall, first (f) reading the sentence of S. Au-

(d) The Chaplaine tel- leth, that the Iesuite sayd, that what the B. would not acknow- ledge in this, he would *wring & extort from him:* But these words, of *wringing & extorting* the Iesuite neuer vseth, euē to his meanest Aduer- saries, & therfore not likely to haue vsed thē to the B. but at most, that he would euince, by argument, or such like.

(e) The Chaplaine saith, *the B. was not so pe- remptory: his speach was, that diuers learned men, & some of your owne are of opinion (as the Greeks expressed themselues) it was a question not simply fundamentall.*

But the Iesuite cannot remēber the B. to haue said these words; yet if he did, the Iesuite did not much misse of the chiefe point of the B. his meaning, which was by the distinction of Faith funda- mentall and not fundamentall, to defend the error of the Græcians not to be such (although held against the knowen definitiue sen- tence of the Church) as doth hinder saluation, or exclude them from being members of the true Church. About which see more hereafter.

(f) The Chaplains corrupt Copie hath *righting*, insteed of *reading* the sentence of S. Austen. The whole sentence is set downe by the Chaplaine thus: *This is a thing founded: An erring Disputer is to be borne with.*

withall in other questions not diligently digested, not yet made firme by full au-
authority of the Church; there errour is to be borne with . But it ought not to
goe so far that it should labour to shake the foundation it selfe of the Church:
S. August. Ser. 14. de verbis Apost. cap. 12.

S. *Augustine; Ferédus est dis-*
putator errans &c. Out of
which is (g) proued that
all pointes defined by the
Church are (h) fundamé-
tall .

Secondly, I required to
knowe, what points the
Bishop woulde account
(i) funda-

(g) Out of this place we may
gather, that all points defined
are fundamental. *All points defined*
are (as S. Aussten speaketh) *made*
firme by full authority of the Church.
But all points made firme by
full authority of the Church are
fundamentall, in such sense as
the Iesuite taketh the word *fun-*
damentall, that is (in S. Austens
language) such as cannot be denyed, or doubtfully disputed
against, without shaking the
foundation of the Church. For

denying or doubtfully disputing against any one , why not against
another, & another, and so against all; sith all are made firme to vs
by one and the same diuine reuelation, sufficiently applyed by one
and the same full authority of the Church : which being weakened
in any one, cannot be to firme in any other.

(h) By the word *Fundamentall*, is vnderstood not only those *Prime*
Credibilia, or prime Principles, which do not depend vpon any former grounds, for then all the Articles of the Creed were not (as both
the B. and D. *White* say they are) fundamentall points ; but all which
do so pertaine to supernaturall, diuine, infallible, Christian faith (by
which Faith Christ the only prime foundation of the Church, doth
dwell in our hearts, (1. *Cor.* 3. 11.) & which Fayth is to the Church
the substance, basis, and foundation of all good things which are to

F 3   be hoped

be hoped for, *Heb.* 11.) as that (they being once confirmed, or made firme by full authority of the Church)if they are wittingly, willingly and efpecially obftinately denyed or queftioned, al the whole frame and in a fort the foundation it felf of all fupernaturall diuine Chriftian Faith is fhaken.

(i) The Chaplaine granteth, that there are *quædam prima Credibilia,* or fome prime Principles, in the bofome whereof, all other Articles lay wrapped and folded vp; So as euery point of the Creed is not a prime Foundation, and therefore the B. himfelf did not vnderftád the word fundamentall fo ftrictly, as if that which in one refpect is *a foundation,* may not in another refpect (to wit, as included in, and depending vpõ a more prime Principle)be accoũted *a fuperftruĉture.*

(i) fundamétall? He faid; All the points in the (k) Creed were fuch.

I afked, how then it happened that M. *Rogers* fayth, that the English Church is not yet refolued what is the right fenfe of the Article of *Chrift his defcending*

(k) If the B. meane, that *Onely* thofe points are fundamentall, which are expreffed in the Creed of the Apoftles; I meruayle how he can afterwards account Scriptures, wherof no expreffe mention is made in the Creed, to be the foundation of their Faith. But if he meane, that not only thofe are fundamentall which are expreffed, but alfo all that is infolded in the Articles of the Creed; Then not Scriptures *onely,* but fome at leaft of Church-*Traditions* vnwritten may be accounted fundamentall, to wit, all thofe that are inwrapped in thefe two Articles, *I believe in the holy Ghoft, The holy Catholique Church:* as all thofe are, which being firft reuealed by the holy Ghoft vnto the Apoftles, haue byn by fucceffiue Tradition of the Church (affifted by the fame holy Ghoft) deliuered vnto vs; one of which is,
That

That the Bookes of Scriptures themselues be diuine, and infallible in euery part: which is a foundation so necessary , as if it be doubtfully questioned, all the Faith built vpon Scripture falleth to the ground. And therefore I meruayle how the B. can say, as he doth afterwards in the Relation, That Scriptures Onely , and not any vnwritten Tradition, was the foundation of their Faith .

descending into Hell ? The B. sayd, that M. *Rogers* was but a priuate man. But (said I,) if (*l*) M. *Rogers*, writing as he did by publique authority be accounted onely a priuate man , in what Booke may we find the (*m*) Protestãts publique Doctrine?

The B. answered; That to the Booke of Articles (*n*) they were all sworne: and

(*l*) The reason why the Iesuite did specially vrge M. *Rogers* booke, was for that it was both set out by publique authority, and beareth the Title *Of the Catholique doctrine of the Church of England*. Our priuate Authors are not allowed (for ought I know) in such a like sort, to take vpon them to expresse our Cath. doctrine in any matter subiect to question .

(*m*) By Protestants publick doctrine in this place, the Iesuite meant, as he vnderstood the B. to meane , onely of English Protestants; for the words going before making mention only *of the English Church*, do limit the generall word, *Prote-*

stants, to this limited sense .

(*n*) This Answer hath reference to that sense which the question had of *Onely English Protestantes*, and not of all English Protestants, but of such as the B. and others are , who by office are teachers of Protestant doctrine, who do either sweare to the booke of Articles, or by subscribing oblige themselues to teach that, and no contrary
doctrine:

doctrine. But if the Chaplain (to difcredit the Relation) will needs inforce a larger extent of the fenfe, contrary to the meaning of him that made the anfwere, and him that asked the Queftion, who vnderftood one another in that fenfe which I haue declared; he muft know, that although none do fweare or fubfcribe befides the Englifh clergy to the Book of Articles , yet all who wilbe accounted members of, or to haue communion with one and the fame Englifh Proteftant church, are bound eyther to hold all thofe Articles, or at leaft not to hold contrary to any one of them, in regard the Englifh Proteftant church doth exclude euery one from their church by Excommunication *ipfo facto*, as appeareth in their book of Canons. *Can. 5. Who shall hold any thing contrary to any part of the faid Articles*.

So as, in this refpect I do not fee, why any one who pretendeth to be of one and the fame Proteftant communion with the church of England, can be fayd not to be obliged to hold one, and the fame doctrine which is in the *book of Articles*, not onely as the chaplaine fayth, *in chiefeft doctrines* (which like a chewidell point may be enlarged to more by thofe who agree in more, and ftraitned to fewer by thofe who agree in fewer points) but abfolutly in all points, and not to hold contrary to any one, or any the leaft part of any one of them. Such a fhrew (as it feemes) is the church of England become, (no leffe then the chaplaine faith, the church of *Rome* to haue bene) in denying her bleffing, and denouncing *Anathema* againft all that diffent (although moft peaceably) in fome particulers , remote inough from the foundation, in the Iudgment of the purer fort, both of forraine and home-bred *Proteftants*.

(o) The Chaplaine faith, *The Church of England grounded her pofitiue Articles vpon Scripture &c.* True; if themfelues in their owne caufe may be admitted for competent Iudges; in which fort fome other Nouellift will fay,

and the (o) Scriptures only, not any vnwritté Tradition was the foundation of their Fayth .

I asked ,

say,that he groundeth his positiue Articles vpon scriptures ; and his Negatiue refute not only our Catholique , but also Protestant doctrines. As for example , *Baptizing of Infants*, vpon this Negatiue ground, *it not expressely* (at least euidently) *affirmed in Scriptures, nor directly* (at least not demonstratiuely) *concluded out of it*. In which case I would gladly know, what the Chaplaine would answere, to defend this doctrine to be a point of Faith, necessary (for the saluation of poore Infants) *necessitate medij*, as all Catholique Deuines hold?I answere with S. Austen, *aug. l.1.contra Cresc.c. 31. Scripturarum à nobis tenetur veritas, cùm id facimus quòd vniuersa placet Ecclesia , quam earundem scripturarum commendat authoritas:* We hold the verity of Scriptures, when we do that which pleaseth the whole Church, which the authority of the same scriptures doth commend. But what answere the chaplaine can make, I cannot easily guesse,vnles with vs he acknowledg authority of church-tradition to be necessary in this case.

I asked,how(*p*)he knew Scripture to be Scripture, and in particuler *Genesis*, *Exodus &c.* These are belieued to be Scripture,yet not proued out of any place of Scripture . The B. said, That the Bookes of Scripture are principles

(*p*) The Iesuite did not aske this question as doubting of the diuine authority of Scripture , but to make it seene, that beside scripture, which the B.sayd was the *Onely* foundation of Faith, there must be admitted some other foundation , to wit, *Vnwritten* Tradition,and this of infallible authority,to assure vs infallibly that these Bookes are diuine; which to be diuine is one point infallibly belieued by diuine Faith , and yet cannot be infal-

libly proued out of *Onely* Scripture; therefore *Onely* Scripture cannot be sayd (as the B. said) to be the *Onely* foundation of Fayth, or of euery point belieued by Faith. I hope the Chaplaine (who is so carefull

carefull to auoyd all fufpition of being familiar with impiety, as he
would haue no queftion moued about this point vpon any termes
or pretence) will not be fo impious as to fay, That to belieue thefe
bookes to be diuine fcripture, is not a point of diuine Faith; or that
this point (being fo important as it is, to be moft firmely belieued) is
belieued by diuine Faith, without any ground or foundation; or without a fufficiet infallible, &diuine foundatiō of Gods word, written
or vnwritten. Sith therfore this is a point of Faith, & hath a foundation, yea an infallible foundation; it is not againft either art, or
equity, or piety (for confutation of Error, and confirmation of
Truth) to enquire what particuler foundation of Gods word, written or vnwritten, doth affure vs infallibly, that thefe particuler
bookes containe the fole, and whole truth of God, belieued by chriftian Fayth. Neyther need any be troubled, or endangered by this
queftion, but fuch as not finding any fufficient foundation in gods
word written, do pertinacioufly refolue, not to belieue any thing to
be Gods word which is not written. Thofe that belieue that there is
a word of God, partly written and partly vnwritten (according to
that of *S. Paul* (2. *Theß.* 2.) *Hold the Traditions whether by our word or
Epiftle*) do eafily, without too much turning in a wheele, or circle,
anfwere the queftion. See the Reply to M. *Wotton* & M. *White* in
the Introduction (of which mention is made in the Relation,)
where this, and diuers other important matters pertayning to the
drift of this Conference, are handled at large.

(*q*) The Chaplaine faith, that fome body tould him, *that the B. vntied the knot*; But why doth not the Chaplaine tell how he did vntie the knot ? It feemeth the knot was not well vntied, when the Iefuite had a Reply fo ready, as is infinuated, by his only going againe and reading ples to be fuppofed, and needed not to be proued. Againft this I read what I had formerly written in my Reply to M. *Iohn White*; wherin I plainly in shewed, that this (*q*) Anf-were

were was not good; and that no other Anſwere could be made but by admitting ſome Word of God vnwritten, to aſſure vs of this point.

in the Book which he had ſo rudely writen. Although a *Præ-cognitum* in faith need not be ſo cleerly knowne as a *præcognitum* in ſcience; yet there muſt be this proportion, that as *primum præcognitum*, the firſt thing fore-knowne in a ſcience, muſt be *primò cognitum*, firſt knowne, &

From muſt not need another thing pertayning to that ſcience to be *priùs cognitum*, knowne before it: So if in Faith, the Scriptures be the firſt and only foundation, and conſequently the firſt thing knowne, *primùm præcognitum*, it muſt be in Faith *primò cognitum*, firſt knowne, and muſt not need any other thing pertayning to Faith to be *priùs cognitum*, knowne before it; & ſo Church-Tradition, which is one thing pertayning to Fayth, could not (as the Chaplain ſaith it is, and as indeed it is) be knowne firſt, and be an Introduction to the knowledge of Scripture. Moreouer like as ſciences which ſuppoſe a principle proued in a higher ſcience, cannot haue certainty of that principle, but either by hauing ſeene that principle euidently proued by other principles borowed of that higher ſcience, or by giuing credit to ſome that haue ſeene, or haue by ſucceſſion receiued it from others that haue ſeene it euidently ſo proued: So Faith cannot haue certainty of her firſt principles, but either by ſeeing proof from the knowledg of the Bleſſed, which ordinarily no má now ſeeth, or by giuing credit immediatly to ſome who haue ſeene, as to Chriſt who cleerly ſaw, or to the Apoſtles to whom cleere reuelation (I ſay cleere *in atteſtante*) was made; or by giuing credit to others who by ſucceſſion haue had it from the firſt ſeers. In which laſt caſe the certainty of theſe principles can be no greater then is the authority of that ſucceſſion. If it be meerely humane and fallible, the ſcience and Faith is humane and fallible. Neither can either ſcience or Faith be diuine and infallible, vnleſſe the authority of that ſucceſſion be at leaſt in ſome ſort diuine and infallible.

The

The chaplain therefore, who (as it feemeth) will not admit church-Tradition to be in any fort diuine and infallible, while it doth introduce the beliefe of fcriptures to be diuine bookes, cannot fufficiently defend the Faith introduced of that point to be infallible, vnles he admit an infallible impulfion of the priuate fpirit *ex parte fubiecti*, without any infallible fufficiently applied reafon *ex parte obiecti*, which he feemeth not, nor hath reafon to doe : for this were to open the gap to Enthufiafms of all vpftart Anabaptifts, and would take away due proportion of Obiect and Subiect, and the fweet order of things which diuine prouidence hath appointed. It may be, that if he would but confider the Tradition of the Church, not only as of a Company of fallible men, in with fort the authority of it is but humaine and fallible, but alfo as it is the Tradition of a Company; which (by it owne light) theweth it felf to be affifted by Chrift and his holy Spirit, farre more cleerely then Scripture (by it owne light) doth fhew it felfe to be the infallible word of God; he would find no difficulty in that refpect to account the authority of Church-Tradition to be infallible, and confequently not only able to be an Introduction, but alfo an infallible motiue reafon or at leaft condition *ex Parte obiecti*, to make both it felf, and the bookes of Scripture appeare (infallibly, though obfcurely) to our foule difpofed and illuminated by Gods fpirit, to haue in them diuine and infallible authority, and to be worthy of diuine and infallible credit, fufficient to breed in vs diuine and infallible Fayth.

Neither do I fee why the Chaplain may not confider the Tradition of the prefent Church thefe two waies, as well as the prefent fcriptures printed and approued by men of this age. For if the fcriptures printed and approued by men of this age muft be confidered, not onely as printed or approued by men, in regard the credit giuen to them thus confidered can be no more then humane; but alfo as printed, and by authority of men affifted by Gods fpirit approued to be true copies of that which was firft written by the Holy Ghofts Pen-men, before we can giue infallible credit vnto them; I fee no reafon, why the like twofold confideration of the Tradi-

tion

tion of the prefent church may not be admitted, efpecially when as the promife of Chrift and his holy Spirits continuall prefence and affiftance (*Luc.* 10. 16. *Math.* 28. 19. 20. *Ioan.* 14. 16.) was made no leffe (but rather more) exprefily to the Apoftles and their fucceffours, the lawfully-fent Paftours and Doctours of the Church in all ages, in their teaching by word of mouth ; then in writing, or reading, or printing, or approuing copies of what was formerly written by the Apoftles.

Perhaps the Chaplaine will aske mee, how I know that any church or company of men of this age, or any age fince the Apoftles, haue promife of chrift and his holy fpirits affiftance ? I anfwer that I know it both by Tradition and Scripture (confidered in the twofold manner aforefaid) both which without any vitious circle, mutually confirme the authority of ech other (as a Kings Embaffadors word of mouth, and his Kings letter beare mutuall witneffe of ech other) ; And I do not want other both outward and inward arguments or motiues of Credibility, which are fufficient not only to confirme the Fayth of belieuers, but alfo to perfwade well difpofed Infidells, that both the one and the other were fent from God, and that one is the infallible word of God, fpeaking in and by his Legats, the lawfully-fent preachers of the Church ; The other, the infallible word of God fpeaking in, and by his letters the holy fcriptures, which he hath appointed his faid legats to deliuer and expound vnto vs, and which among other things do warrant that we may heare and giue credit to thefe Legats of Chrift, as to Chrift the King himfelf.

From this the La. called vs, & defiring to heare, (*r*) whether the B. would grant the Roman Church to be

(*r*) The Chaplain faith : *As it is true, that this queftion was asked, fo it is falfe, that it was asked in this forme, or fo anfwered.* I anfwer that the Iefuite doth not fay that the La. asked this queftion in this, or any other precife forme of words,

G 3

of words, but onely faith, fhe was defirous to heare, whether the B. would graunt the Roman Church to be the Right Church: which to haue ben her defire the Iefuit is fure, as hauing particulerly fpoken with her before, and wifhed her to infift vpon this point.

Secondly, he is fure, that fhe did not propound the queftion in that precife forme infinuated by the Chaplayne, vz. whether the Romane Church be a true Church; as if fhe meant to be fatisfied with hearing the B. fay, that the Rom. church is a true church, and the Greek church another, and the Proteftant another. This, I fay, could not be her Queftion, for that fhe was perfuaded that all thefe were not true and right, and that there was but One Holy Catholique church; and her defire was to heare, whether the B. would graunt the Rom. church, (not only that which is in the Citty or Dioceffe of Rome, but all that agreed with it) to be it?

Thirdly, what precife forme of words the La. did vfe, the Iefuite did not remember perfectly, and therefore did not aduenture to fet downe; but by the B. his Anfwer which he perfectly remenbred, & fo fet downe in thefe words (*It was*) he thinketh that her queftion was, whether the Roman church was not the right church? (vz. once, or in tyme paft, before *Luther* and others made a breach from it?) To which queftion fo vttered, or fo vnderftood (as it feemes by the Anfwere, and the enfuing difcourfe made by the B. it was vnderftood) the B. might truely (& certainly did) anfwere, as is related (to wit) not, *It is*; but, *It was*: vz. once, or in tyme paft the right Church; for fo the Chaplaine doth heere confeffe *pag*. 37. *The time was &c. that you and we were all of one belief*. Out of which anfwere it may be the B. fufpected that the La. would inferre: If once it were the right, what hindereth it now to be? fith it did not depart from the Proteftant Church, but the Proteft. Church departed from it. And therefore (as in the Text) he was willing to graunt, that the Proteftants made a Rent or diuifion from it &c.

(*s*) The

to be the right Church? The B. graunted, *That it was.* Further he(s) granted, that Proteſtants made a Rent or Diuiſion from it.

Moreouer he ſaid, he would ingenuouſly acknowledge, that Corruption of māners was not a ſufficient Cauſe to iuſtifie their departing from it.

But (ſaid he) beſides Corruption of manners, there were Errours in doctrine, which whē the Generall Church would not reforme, it was lawfull for particuler churches to reforme themſelues .

I asked

(s) The Chaplaine (hauing told vs that the B. could be hartily angry,) ſaith: *The B. neuer ſaid nor thought, that Proteſtants made this rent. The cauſe of the ſchiſme is yours &c.* I anſwere, that the Ieſuite is ſure ; that whatſoeuer the B. thought (which may be was as the Chaplain now expreſſeth, to wit, that we had giuen cauſe to the Proteſtants to do as they did;) yet he did ſay (either *ijſdem* or *æquipollentibus verbis*) iuſt as is in the Relation. For the Ieſuite did in freſh memory take ſpeciall notice of this paſſage, in regard it concerned a moſt important point, which being vrged by him in the firſt Conference againſt D. *White* in theſe words, *Why did you make a ſchiſme from vs ? Why doe you perſecute vs?* the Doctour ſlipped ouer that of the ſchiſme without denying it to haue ben made by them, or laying the cauſe to vs, and only anſwered to the other, ſaying, *We do not perſecute you for Religion.* The Ieſuite therefore, I ſay, did, as he had reaſon, take ſpeciall notice in freſh memory, and is ſure he related at leaſt in ſenſe, iuſt as was vttered by the B.

And I aske the Chaplain, what reaſon the B. had to diſcourſe ſo long as he did, endeauoring to ſhew what reaſon Proteſtants had to make that rent or diuiſion, or (if he like not theſe words) that *diſceſſion,* (to vſe Caluins phraſe) or *departure,* not only from the church of Rome, of Rome, but alfo (as *Caluin, lib. Epiſt. ep.* 141.)confeſſeth, *à toto mundo,* *from the whole world* ; if he had not (as the Iefuite related) confeſſed that Proteſtants, being once members of the Roman Church, feparated themfelues from it, as the world knowes they did, when they got the name of Proteſtants, for proteſting againſt it. Now for the Chaplains afcribing the Caufe of the fchifme to vs, in that *by excommunication* we thruſt them from vs ; he muſt remember, that befoꝛe this, they had diuided themfelues by obſtinate holding and teaching opinions contrary to the Roman Fayth, and practiſe of the Church, which in *S. Bernards* iudgment (*ſerm. de reſur.*) is moſt great pride. *Quæ maior fuperbia &c.* What greater pride, then that one man (*Luther* for example) ſhould prefer his Iudgment, not only before a thoufand Auſtens, and Cyprians, and King Harry-Churches ; but before the whole Congregation of all chriſtian churches in the world? which in *S. Aaſten* his Iudgment is moſt infolent madnes ; for, *contra id diſputare &c.* to difpute againſt that which the vniuerfall church doth practiſe, is, faith *S. Auſten,* moſt infolent madnes .

What then? Is it, not onely by way of doubtfull difputation, but by folemne and publick & proteſtation, to condemne the generall practiſe of the church as fuperſtitious, and the doctrine as erroneous in Fayth, yea as hereticall and euen Antichriſtian ? All this confidered, the B. hath no caufe *to be hartily angry,* either with the Iefuite for relating, or with himfelf for granting Proteſtants to haue made a rent or diuiſion from the Rom. church ; but might with a fafe confcience yet further grant, as one did (was it not He?) to an Honorable perſon, *That it was ill done of thoſe, who did firſt make the ſeparation.* Which is moſt true, both in regard there can be no iuſt caufe to make a fchifme and diuiſion from the whole Church (for the whole Church cannot vniuerfally erre in doctrine of Fayth, and other iuſt caufe there is none) and alfo for that thofe who firſt made the feparation (*Luther* and his Affociates) gaue the firſt caufe in manner aforefayd to the Rom. church to excommunicate them, as by our Sauiours warrant fhe might, when they would not heare the church, which did both at firſt ſeeke to recall them from their nouell opinions,

nions, and after their breach did permit, yea inuite them publikely
with fafe conduct to Rome to a Generall Councell, and freely to
fpeake what they could for themfelues. And I make no doubt, (fo
farre is the Rom. Church from being caufe of continuance of the
fchifmes, or hinderance of Re-union) that it would yet (if any
hope may be giuen that Proteftantes will fincerely feeke nothing
but truth and peace) giue them a free hearing, with moft ample &
fafe conduct; which is more then euer we Englifh catholiques
could obtayne, although we haue made offers diuers times to come
to publique Difpute, firft in Queene *Elizabeth* her dayes, and alfo in
his Maiefties that now is; only requiring the Princes word for our
fafety and equality of Conditions of the difpute. Vnto which offer
our Aduerfaries neuer did, nor euer will giue good Anfwere : As
one faith; *Honeftum refponfum nullum dabunt præter vnum quod numquam
dabunt; Regina* (Rex) *fpondet, Aduola. Camp. in rat. Acad. red.*

I (t) asked; *Quo Iudice,*
did this appeare to be fo?
Which queftion I asked,
as not thinking it equity
that Proteftants in their
owne Caufe should be Ac-
cufers , Witneffes, and
Iudges of the Romane
Church .

       I alfo

(t) This queftion the Iefuite
made chiefly againft that part
of the B. his laft fpeach, in
which he faid, *There were errours in doctrine*; for if the B.
meant (as the Iefuite vnderftood him to meane) that there
were errours of doctrine of
Fayth in the Generall Church,
neuer did any lawfull & competent Iudge fo cenfure, neither can it fo be. No power in
Earth or Hell it felf can fo far
preuayle againft the Generall
Church of Chrift, built vpon a Rock, as to make it, or the paftours
thereof erre generally in any one point of diuine truth. Chrifts promifes ftand (*Matth.* 16. & 28. *Luc.* 22. *Ioan.* 14. & 16.) and will
neuer permit this, no not in Antichrifts dayes. Particuler Paftors &

and Churches may fall into Herefy or Apoftafy, but the whole Church cannot. It may fometyme not exprefly teach, or know all diuine truthes, which afterwards it may learne by ftudy of Scriptures and otherwayes; but it neuer did, nor can vniuerfally, by its full authority teach any thing to be diuine truth, which is not; and much leffe, any thing to be a matter of Fayth which is contrary to diuine truth, either expreffed, or inuolued in Scriptures rightly vnderftood. So as no reformation of Fayth can be needfull in the Generall Church, but only in particuler Churches; in which cafe alfo when the need is onely queftionable, particuler Paftours or Churches muft not take vpon them to iudge, and condemne others of errour in Fayth, but as *S. Irenæus* intimateth, muft haue recourfe to that Church which hath more powerfull Principality, the Church of *Rome*, and to her Bifhop being Cheife Paftour of the whole Church, as being Succeffour to *S. Peter* : To whom Chrift promifed the Keyes, (*Matth.* 16.) For whom Chrift prayed, that his Fayth might not faile: (*Luc.* 22.) and whom he charged to confirme his brethren; and to feed and gouerne the whole flock, lambes and fheep (*Ioan.* 21.) people and Paftours, fubieds and fuperiours; which he fhall neuer refufe to do in fuch fort, as that this negled fhalbe a iuft Caufe for any particuler man or Church to make a fchifme or feparation of himfelf and others, from the whole Generall Church, vnder pretence of Reformation either of manners, or of Fayth.

Proteftants therefore did ill in firft deuiding themfelues from the Generall Church, and do ftill ill in continuing deuided from it. Neither can thofe Proteftants be excufed from intolerable pride & infolent madnes, who prefume to be Accufers, Witneffes, Iudges, & Executioners of the fentence pronounced by themfelues againft the Church in Generall, and againft the principall and Mother Church, and the B. of Rome, which is, and ought to be their Iudge in this cafe. For although it be againft equity that Subieds and Children fhould be accufers, witneffes, iudges and executioners againft their Prince and Mother in any cafe; yet it is not abfurd that in fome cafe the Prince or Mother may accufe, witneffe, iudge, and (if need be) execute

execute Iuſtice againſt vniuſt or rebellious ſubiects, or euill children.

I alſo asked; Who ought to iudge in this caſe? The B. ſayd : (*u*) A Generall Councell.

I told him, that a Generall Councell (to wit of *Trent*)had already iudged, not the Roman Church, but the Proteſtant, to hold

(*u*)It is true, when the Queſtion is about the Generall Fayth of the church, the matter may be made moſt firme, if the church in a Generall Coū-cell with the full authority of her cheif Paſtour,and all other Paſtours (whome all people muſt obey(*Rom. 13. Hebr.13.*) decree , what is to be held for diuine truth, by *Viſum eſt ſpiritui ſancto & nobis (Act. 15.*) and by adding *Anathema* to ſuch as reſiſt this Truth. For if this be not firme and infallible,what can be ſo firme and well foun-ded in the church, which vnder pretext of ſeeming euidēt Scripture or demonſtration, may not be ſhaken, and called in queſtion by an erring diſputer? For if all Paſtours being gathered togeather in the name of chriſt, praying *vnanimiter* for the promiſed Aſſiſtance of the Holy Ghoſt,making great and diligent ſearch and examination of the Scriptures,and other grounds of Fayth, and hearing ech Pa-ſtour declare what hath been the ancient Tradition of his church, ſhall in fine conclude and decree in manner aforeſaid, what is to be held for diuine truth: If(I ſay) the Councell in this decree may erre,and may be controlled by euery particuler , or any particuler vnlearned, or learned man, or church, pretending euident text of Scripture or cleere demonſtration (*ſupple, Teſte & Iudice ſeipſis* ;)what can remaine firme or certaine vpon Earth,which may not by a like pretence be cōtrolled, or at leaſt(by one or other)called in queſtion?

A Generall councell therefore being lawfully called , continued and confirmed,is doubtles a moſt competent iudge of all contro-uerſies of Fayth. But what is to be done, when a Generall councell

cannot

cannot be called, as many times it cannot by reason of manifold impedimēts, or if being called, all will not be of one mind; (As among Proteſtants and others, who admit no Infallible meanes, rule, or iudge beſide *Onely Scripture*, which ech man will interprete as ſeemeth beſt to his ſeuerall priuate Iudgment or ſpirit, it is ſcarſe to be hoped that all, or the maior part will euer ſo agree, as to remaine conſtant in one and the ſame mind :) Hath chriſt our Lord in this caſe prouided no meanes, no rule, no iudge, which may Infallibly determine and end controuerſyes, & procure vnity and certainty of belief being ſo neceſſary for the honor of God, and the good of his church? Muſt people for want of ſuch a iudge, rule or meanes, continue not only moneths and yeares, but whole Ages in vncertainty and diſiunity of Fayth, and in perpetuall Iarres about euen maine matters of diuine truth ? There is no earthly Kingdome that (in caſe matters cannot be compoſed by Parlament, which cannot be called vpon all occaſions, and at all tymes) hath not beſide the lawbookes, ſome liuing Magiſtrates and iudges, and aboue all one viſible King, the higheſt Magiſtrate and Iudge, who hath authority ſufficient to end controuerſies, and procure peace and vnity, and certainty of Iudgments, about all temporall affayres : And ſhall we thinke that chriſt the wiſeſt King hath prouided in his kingdome, which is the church, onely the Law-bookes of Holy Scriptures, and no liuing viſible Magiſtrats and Iudges, and aboue all *One cheife Magiſtrate*, and iudge, ſo aſſiſted with his ſpirit and prouidence, as may ſuffice to end controuerſies, and breed vnity and certainty of Fayth, which neuer can be while euery man may interprete Holy Scripture, the Law-booke as he liſt ?

(*x*) The chaplain ſaith, *that the B. ſaid not only ſo, but that it was no Generall Councell.* I anſwere, that if the B. ſaid ſo, it was onely for want of memory that the Ieſuite did not relate it ſo: for the Exceptions which the B. did or hold Errour. That ſaid the B. was not a (*x*) lawfull Councell. So, ſayd I, would the

can

can make againſt the lawfulneſſe or generallneſſe of the Councell of *Trent*, may be made by *Arrians* againſt the councell of *Nice*. It is not neceſſary to the lawfulneſſe and generallneſſe of a Councell that all Biſhops of the world be actually preſent, and actually ſubſcribe or yield aſſent;but that ſuch promulgation be made as is morally ſufficient to giue notice that ſuch a Councell is called,and that all may come if they will,and that a competent number, at leaſt the maior part,of thoſe which be preſent,yield aſſent to the decree.

(*y*)the *Arrians* ſay of the Coũcell of *Nice.* The B. would not admit the caſe to be like,pretending that the Pope made Biſhops of (*z*)purpoſe for his ſide: but this the B. proued not. In

(*y*) As Proteſtants do thinke that the councell of *Trent* is not lawfull, for hauing (in their Iudgment) departed from the letter & ſenſe of Scripture: ſo did the *Arians* thinke of the councell of *Nice.* And as Proteſtants do iuſtifie that ſome were ſent from the Pope to *Trẽt*, and that the Pope was Preſident: So doubtleſſe did the *Arians* miſlike, that at *Nice* the Pope had Legats, who did carry his meſſages, and one of them in his place ſate as Preſident .

(*z*)The Chaplain ſaith, that the B. did not ſay, *that the Pope made Biſhops of purpoſe &c.* I anſwere,that the Ieſuite doth not ſay that the B. expreſly ſaid ſo; but that (by inſinuation)he did pretend ſo much, which in effect the chaplaine ſeemeth to graunt,when he ſaith (*pag.* 40.) the B.ſaid,*the Pope made himſelf a ſtrõg partie in it.* For although theſe words may be taken in another ſenſe , yet they may alſo be taken in that ſenſe which the Ieſuite (by the circumſtances of the B. his ſpeach) did then vnderſtand,and expreſſe in his Relation : for that a great number of Italian Biſhops, which the Chaplain ſaith the B. alledged as a proof,may very well import , that the B.cõceiued the Pope to haue made more *Italian* Biſhops then of other Countryes, of purpoſe to haue a ſtrong faction. But this proof was ſo weake, as the

Ieſuite

Iefuite might well fay, it was no proofe, nor worthy of anfwere, or of looking into the book for it ; it being only a fuimife of Aduer-faries, who are apt to interprete euery thing to the worft. *Italian* Bifhops might be more, as being neerer, (as in Greeke Councells more *Grecians* were prefent) without any factious Combination with the Pope, in any other fort then all the Cath. Bifhops in the world, who are as much vnited with the Pope for matters of Fayth, defined in the Councell, as any *Italian* Bifhop.

Neither can the B. proue, that any Catholique French, or Spa-nifh, or of any other Country, or the fchifinaticali Greekes did agree with Proteftants in thofe points which were defined in the Coun-cell, efpecially after it was confirmed by the Pope. For they all, euen *Grecians*, did, & do at this day vnanimoufly oppofe Proteftâts, as ap-peareth by the Cenfure of *Hieremias* the Grecian Patriarch. So as if fuch a free Councell as the B. and others wifhed, were gathered out of Eaft and Weft, Proteftants (doubtles) would be condemned for Heretiques, and their negatiue refutes and denialls of ancient Arti-cles, for Herefies, by more then the double maior Part compared to thofe who would take their part. For although (as all Heretiques vfe to do) Proteftants perfwade themfelues, Scriptures to be euident for their opinions, and that with euident demóftrations they fhould be able to conuince all the world, that they teach truth, and nothing but truth ; yet they would find innumerable others as learned (to fay no more,) and as well ftudyed in Scripture, and skilfull in ma-king demonftrations, who are of another mind.

(*a*)I meruaile, in what fort the B. will defcribe fuch a Gene-rall Councell ; and how it fhould be gathered ; and what Rules are in it to be obferued, which are morally likely fo to be obferued as to make an end of côtrouerfies, better then our catholique Generall councels.

In fine, The B. wished, that a lawfull (*a*) Generall Councell were called to end Controuerfies. The perfons prefent faid, The King

King was enclined ther-unto, and therefore we Catholiques might do well to concurre.

I asked the B. whether he thought, a Generall Councell might erre? He said,it might.If a Generall Councell may erre, what neerer are we then (fayd I) to Vnity after a Councell hath determined? yes (faid he) although it may erre yet we shall be bound to (b) hold it, till another come to reuerse it.

After this,we all rising, The La.asked the B. whether she might be faued in the Roman Fayth? he anfwered,

(b) The Chaplaine faith, that the B. added a Caution(which the Iefuit omitteth)faying: *The determination of a Generall Councell erring,was to stand in force, and haue externall obedience at least yielded to it, till euidence of Scripture,or a demonstration to the contrary made the errour appeare, and vntill thereuppon another Councell of equall authority did reuerse it.* I anfwere, that added Caution(which eyther was not then added, or not remembred by the Iefuite) maketh the B. his Anfwere far worfe, then as the Iefuit did relate. For whereas the Iefuite relateth onely thus, *Although it may erre*; this caution maketh the cafe to be, *that it doth actually erre*. And whereas the Iefuite relateth, *That we (not knowing whether it do erre or not, but only that it may erre,) are bound to hold it till another come to reuerse it*; this caution doth put the cafe fo, as if the determination of a Generall Councell actually erring, were (not *ipfo iure* inualide,but) fuch as is to ftand in force, & to haue externall obedience at leaft yielded vnto it, till(not onely morall certainty,but) euidence of Scripture,or a demonftration to the contrary make the errour appeare;and after the errour appeareth, yet we muft continue
this

this yeilding of obedience : And how long? Vntill thereupon a Councell (and not euery Councell, but) of equall authority do reuerse it, which perhaps will not be found in a whole Age. Verily I can not belieue, that the B. vpon better aduisement will allow this Caution, or giue any thankes to his Chaplain for setting it downe, but will commend the Iesuite for relating his speach more truely, and at least lesse disgracefully.

(c) Heere againe the Chaplain taxeth the Iesuite saying, *That the B did not answer thus in particuler.* But the Iesuite is sure he did; and it appeareth to be so by the Iesuits wordes who said to the La. *Marke that.* Vnto wered , Shee (c) might.] bad her mark that. She (sayd the **B.**) may be better saued in it, then you. D. White

which the B. replied saying, *She may be better saued in it then you;* which Reply sheweth that the B. had said, that she in particuler might be saued in the Roman Fayth. Otherwise, if his first Answere had ben as the chaplaine would now make, the B. should haue said, *The ignorant may be saued in it, but neither you, nor she.* But the Iesuite is sure that this Answere of the B and Reply of the Iesuite (*Marke that*) was iust as he related, without any such addition, as now the chaplain doth relate ; and that if such a Caueat were added, it was after the end of the conference, and not in the Iesuits presence.

Out of this last passage the Chaplain obserueth that Catholiques take aduantage, and make vse of the argument. drawne from Protestants granting, *That one liuing and dying a Rom Catholique may be saued;* accounting it secure so to liue and die, euen by confession of Aduersaries. The force of which argument he endeauoureth to weaken by saying, that although Protestants grant it to be possible, yet they say withall that it is not secure, but hard &c. But he must remember, that when Protestants graunt, that in the Rom. Fayth and Church there is ground sufficient, and consequently possibility of saluation; this is a free confession of the Aduersaries argument themselues, and

therefore

therefore is of force againſt them, and is to be thought to be extorted from them by the force of truth it ſelf. But when Proteſtants do ſay, that ſaluation is more ſecurely and eaſily had in Proteſtant Fayth & Church, then in the Romane; this onely is their partiall priuate opinion in their owne behalf, which is of no weight, eſpecially when Romane Catholiques farre more in number, and farre more ſpread in place, and of much longer continuance in tyme, and for vertue and learning at leaſt equall, or rather much exceeding Proteſtants, do confidently, and vnanimouſly, and with authority and reaſon proue, that (according to the ordinary Courſe of Gods prouidence) *Out of the Cath. Romane Church, there is no poſsibility of ſaluation.* And therefore, who will not thinke it ſafer to adhere to the Cath. Romane Fayth and Church , in which all both Catholiques and beſt learned Proteſtants do promiſe poſſibility of ſaluation without doubt, then to the Proteſtant Church, ſith all Roman Catholiques do threaten damnation to all who obſtinately adhere vnto it; and dye in it ? The which threat, doth not proceede out of malice, or want of Charity, but is grounded in Charity ; as are the like threats of Chriſt our Sauiour, and Holy Fathers , who knowing that there is but *One True Fayth* , and *One True Church* , out of which there is no ſaluation , do out of their Charitable care of our ſoules good , ſo commend to vs the beliefe of that Fayth, and the cleauing to that Church, as they pronounce, *He that ſhall not belieue , ſhall be condemned.* (*Mar.* 16.) and, *He that will not heare the Church,* and haue it for his Mother, *is to be accounted as a Heathen and Publican* (Matth. 18.) and cannot haue God to be his Father; accounting it more charity to forewarne vs by theſe threats, of our perill , that we may feare and auoide it, then to put vs in a falſe ſecurity, and ſo to let vs runne into danger, for want of foreſight of it.

Thoſe examples which the Chaplaine giues of the *Donatiſts* giuing true Baptiſme in the opinion of all, and Proteſtants holding a kind of *Reall Preſence* not denied by any , are nothing like our caſe. For in theſe caſes there are annexed other reaſons of certainly knowne perill of damnable ſchiſme and hereſie , which we ſhould

I　　incur

incurre by cōſenting to the Donatiſts deniall of true Baptiſme to bē among Catholiques;and to the Proteſtants denyall, or doubting of the true ſubſtantiall preſence of Chriſt in the Euchariſt. But in our caſe there is confeſſedly no ſuch perill of any damnable Hereſy, ſchiſme,or any other ſinne,in reſoluing to liue and die in the Catholique Rom. Church: and in caſe ſome Proteſtants ſhould ſay,that there is perill of damnation in liuing and dying Roman Catholiques; the authority of them that ſay there is perill, being ſo few (in compariſon of thoſe who ſay there is none ,) and ſo paſſionate and partially affeĉted men, who are in this their ſaying contradiĉted by their owne more learned brethren,ought not to be reſpeĉted more then a Scarre-crowe. But the authority of thoſe who allow ſaluation to ſuch as do liue and die Roman Catholiques, being ſo many, ſo ancient,ſo vertuous,ſo learned, and ſome no way partially affeĉted, out oppoſite to the Romā Church, ought to be accoūted of exceeding great weight,& may worthily perſwade any wiſe man that it is moſt ſecure to liue and dye a Roman Catholique, and conſequently that in ſo important a matter this moſt ſecure courſe of liuing and dying in the Roman Church , ought in all reaſon to be choſen, and that ſo pretious a Iewell as the Soule is , ought not to be left to the hazard of looſing heauen, and falling into hell, by relying vpon ones ownes opinion, or the opinion of thoſe few new Proteſtant Doĉtours,who acknowledg that their whole congregatiō may erre:& much more therfore may they thinke that ech member therof may be deceiued, in following his owne, or any other mans opinion .

(*d*) Heere the Chaplain taxeth the Ieſuite for falſly relating D. *Whites* Anſwer, and ſaith he hath ſpoken with D. *White,* who auowes this, & no other Anſwere: *He was asked in the Conference, whether Papiſts errours were fundamentall? To this he gaue anſwere*

D. White(*d*), ſaid I , hath ſecured me , that none of our errours are damnable, ſo long as we hold them not againſt our Cōſcience, and

anſwere by a diſtinction of perſons,which held and profeſsed the errours ; Na-
mely,that the errours were fundamentall reductiue, by a reducent , if they
who imbraced them did pertinaciouſly adhere vnto them, hauing ſufficient
meanes to be better informed: Nay further, that they were materially in the
kind and nature of them,leauen,droſse,haye, and ſtubble; yet he thought with-
all, that ſuch as were miſled by education, or long Cuſtome , or ouer-valuing
the ſoueraigntie of the Romane Church , and did in ſimplicity of heart im-
brace them,might by their generall Repentance, & faith in the merits of Chriſt
attended with Charity and other vertues, finde mercy at Gods hands. But that
he ſhould ſay,ſignanter & expreſsè , that none of yours or your fellowes er-
rours were damnable,ſo long as you hold them not againſt your Conſcience,that
he vtterly diſauowes &c .

To this the Ieſuite anſwereth; firſt,that he did not in this his Relation ſay,that D.*White* did *ſignanter*, and expreſly ſay theſe preciſe
words,*None of yours,or your fellowes errours are damnable*. Secondly, he
ſaith,that D. *White* did not *ſignanter*, and expreſly make this preciſe
Anſwere which now he maketh, nor ſcarſe any part of it ; as appeareth by the Relation of the firſt Conference made by the Ieſuite in freſh memory,and conferred with D. *White* himſelf,who did
not at that time contradict it in this point .

Thirdly,the reaſon which moued the Ieſuite to ſay,that D.White
had ſecured him,as is ſaid in this Relation , was for that D. White in
the ſaid firſt Conference graunted, that there muſt be one or other
church ,continually viſible, which had in all ages taught the vnchanged Fayth of Chriſt in all points fundamentall ; and being vrged to aſſigne ſuch a church,D. Whyte expreſſely graunted that he
could not aſſigne and ſhew any church different from the Roman,
which held in all ages all points fundamentall. Whence the Ieſuite
gathered his opinion to be,that the Roman church held and taught
in all ages vnchanged Fayth in all fundamentall points, and did
not in any age erre in any point fundamentall. Whereupon the Ieſuite asked, whether errours in points not fundamentall were damnable ? D. White anſwered, they were not , ſo long as one did not
hold them againſt his conſcience ; which Anſwere he repeated
againe

againe to M. B. asking the fame queſtion. Out of all which, the
Ieſuite did collect, that D. Whites opinion was, that the Roman
church held all points fundamentall, and only erred in points not
fundamentall, which he accounted not damnable, ſo long as one
did not hold them againſt his conſcience: and thereuppon the Ieſuit might well ſay, that D. White had giuen ſecurity to him, who
holdeth no Faith different from the Roman, nor contrary to his
owne conſcience.

As for D. Whites ſaying he could diſcerne but ſmall loue of truth,
and few ſignes of grace in the Ieſuite, I will let it paſſe as the cenſure of an Aduerſary, looking vpon the Ieſuite with eyes of diſlyke,
which is not to be regarded further then to returne vpon him (not a
like cenſure, but) a charitable wiſh, that he may haue no leſſe loue
of truth, nor fewer ſignes of grace, then the Ieſuite is thought to
haue, by thoſe who know him better then D. White doth.

(e) The Chaplain noteth, that and I hold none againſt
the B. was confident, and had my Coſcience. The Lady
reaſon of his confidence. For asked, Whether she might
ſayth he, *To belieue the Scripture*
and Creed in the ſenſe of the An- be ſaued in the Proteſtant
cient Primitiue Church; to receiue Fayth? Vpon my (e) ſoule
the firſt fowre Generall Councells
ſo much magnified by Antiquity: To (ſaid
belieue all points of doctrine generally receiued, as fundamentall, in the
Church of Chriſt, is a Fayth, in which to liue and dye, cannot but giue ſal-
uation. And I would fayne ſee, ſayth the chaplain, any one point
maintained by the church of England, that can be proued to depart from the foundation.

To which I anſwer, firſt, that if to ſay thus be a ſufficient cauſe of
confidence, I meruayle why the chaplain maketh ſuch difficulty to
be confident of the ſaluation of *Rom. Catholiques*, who belieue all
this in a farre better maner then Proteſtants do: neyther can they be
proued

proued to depart from the foundation so much as Proteſtants do, who denying infallible authority to all the Paſtours of the cath. church aſſembled in a Generall councell, do in effect deny Infallibility to the whole catholique church, which is bound to heare & belieue what is defined, and to practiſe what is preſcribed by her Paſtours in a generall councell, and ordinarily doth ſo belieue and practiſe.

Secondly I aske, how Proteſtants, who admit no certaine and infallible meanes and rule of Fayth, beſide onely Scripture, can be infallibly ſure that they belieue the ſame entier ſcripture and creed, and the foure firſt Generall councels &c. in the ſame vncorrupted ſenſe which the Primitiue Church belieued? What text of ſcripture doth tell, that Proteſtants who now liue, do belieue all this, or that all this is expreſſed in thoſe particuler Bibles, or in the writings of the Fathers or Councells which now are in the Proteſtants handes, or that Proteſtants do rightly vnderſtand the ſenſe of all which is expreſſed in their bookes according to that which was vnderſtood by the Primitiue Church, and the Fathers which were preſent at the foure firſt Generall Councells? Or that all, and onely thoſe points which Proteſtants do account to be fundamentall and neceſſary to be expreſly knowne by all, were ſo accounted by the Primitiue Church? I ſuppoſe, neither the B. nor the Chaplain can produce any text of ſcripture ſufficient to aſſure one of all this: And therfore he had need to ſeeke ſome other Infallible rule and meanes, by which he may know theſe things infallibly, or els he hath no reaſon to be ſo confident, as to aduenture his ſoule, that one may be ſaued liuing and dying in the Proteſtant Fayth.

(ſaid the B.) you may . Vpon my (*f*) my Soule , ſayd I , There is but one ſauing Fayth, and that is the Roman.

(*f*)Heere I note, that the Ieſuite was as confident for his part, as the B. for his; but with this difference, that the B. had not ſufficient reaſon of his Confidence as I haue declared; But the Ieſuite had ſo much reaſon both our of

Vpon

I 3

expreſſe

expreſſe ſcriptures and Fathers, and the infallible authority of the Church, that the B. himſelf then did not, nor his Chaplaine now doth not, taxe the Ieſuit of any raſhnes : but the Chaplain expreſly graunteth that, There is but one ſauing Faith, and the B. did(as was related) graunt that the La. might be ſaued in the Rom. Fayth; which is as much as the Ieſuite did take vpon his ſoule. Onely the chaplain ſaith, without any proofe, that we haue many dangerous errours: but he neither tels vs which they be, nor why he thinketh them dangerous, but leaueth vs to look to our owne ſoules, and ſo we do, and haue no cauſe to doubt; becauſe we do not hold any new deuiſe of our owne, or any other man, or any thing contrary, but all moſt conformable to ſcriptures interpreted by Vnion, conſent of Fathers, and definitions of Councells.

Which being ſo, the B. and his chaplaine had need to looke to their ſoules, for if there be but one ſauing Fayth, as the Chaplain graunteth, (and he hath reaſon, becauſe *S. Paul* ſayth (*Epheſ* 4.) *Vna fides*, One Fayth: and *S. Leo*, (*ſerm. de Natiuit.*) *Niſi vna eſt fides, non eſt*, vnleſſe it be *One*, it is not Fayth) and this *One Fayth* was once the Roman, which alſo yet is (as the B. graunteth) a ſauing Fayth ; (or elſe he ought not to haue granted, that one may be ſaued liuing & dying in it:)I ſee not how they can haue their ſoules ſaued without they entirely imbrace this Fayth, being the Cath. Fayth, which as *S. Athanaſius* (*in Symb.*) affirmeth, vnles one hold entiere(that is euery point of it,)and inuiolate, (that is, belieuing all in right ſenſe, and for the true formall reaſon of diuine reuelation ſufficiently applied to our vnderſtäding by the Infallible authority of the Cath. Church propoſing to vs by her Paſtours this reuelation) without doubt he ſhall periſh for euer. In which ſort if the B. and his chaplain did belieue any one Article, they(finding the ſame formall reaſon in all, and applyed ſufficiently by the ſame meanes to all) would eaſily belieue all. But ſo long as they do not belieue all in this ſort, but will, as all Heretiques do, make choyſe of what they will, and what they will not belieue, without relying vpõ the Infallible authority of the Cath. Church, they cannot haue that *One Soule-ſauing Fayth,*

Fayth, which all good Catholique Chriftians haue, in any one article of Fayth. For although they belieue the fame truth, which other good Catholiques do in fome Articles, yet not belieuing them for the fame formall reafon of diuine reuelation, fufficiently applyed by Infallible Church-authority, but either for fome other formall reafon, or at leaft not for this reafon fufficiently applyed, they cannot be fayd to haue one and the fame Infallible diuine Fayth which other good catholique chriftians haue, who do belieue thofe Articles, not for any other formall reafon befide the diuine reuelation applyed fufficiently and made knowne to them(not by their owne fancie, or the fallible authority of humaine deductions,) but by the infallible authority of the church of God, that is of men infallibly affifted by the Spirit of God, as all lawfully called, continued, and confirmed Generall councells are affifted.

Whence I gather, that although euery thing defined to be a diuine truth in Generall councells, is not abfolutly neceffary to be exprefly knowne and actually belieued (as fome other truthes are) by all forts; yet no man may (after knowledge that they are thus defined) doubt deliberatly, and much leffe obftinatly deny the truth of any thing fo defined. For, euery fuch doubt and denyall is a breach from that one fauing Fayth, which other good chriftians haue, in regard it taketh away infallible credit from the church; and fo the diuine reuelation being not by it fufficiently applyed, it cannot according to the ordinary courfe of Gods prouidence breed infallible belief in vs; for as S. *Paul Rom.* 10. *faith, How shall they belieue vnles they heare, how shall they heare without a Preacher, how shall they preach* (to wit infallibly) *vnles they be fent,* to wit, from God, and infallibly affifted by his fpirit? And if a whole Generall councell defining what is diuine truth be not belieued to be fent, and affifted by gods fpirit, and confequently of Infallible credit, what man in the world can be faid to be of infallible credit? or if fuch a Councell lawfully called, continued, and confirmed may erre, in defining any one diuine truth, how can we be Infallibly certaine of any other truth defined by it? for if it may erre in one, why not in another and another,

ther, and fo in all? or how can we(according to the ordinary courfe)
be infallibly affured, that it erreth in one, and not in another, when
it equally, by one and the fame authority, defineth both to be diuine
truthes? for if we leaue this to be examined by any priuate man, this
examination not being infallible had need to be examined by another, and this by another, without end, or euer coming to infallible
Certainty, neceffarily required in that One Fayth which is neceffary
to faluation, and to that peace and Vnity which ought to be in
the Church? It is not therefore (as the Chaplain would perfwade)
the fault of councells definitions (but the pride of fuch as will pre-
ferr, and not fubmit their priuate Iudgments)that loft, & continueth
the loffe of peace and vnity of the Church, and the want of certainty in that one aforefaid foule-fauing Fayth:the which how far
it doth extend is indeed (as the Chaplain *pag. 73.* confeffeth) no
work for his penne, but is to be learned of that one Holy Catholique, Apoftolique, alwayes Vifible, and Infallible Roman Church,
of which the La. once doubting, reftethnow fully fatisfied, that in it
fhe may learne all truth neceffary to faluation, and that out of it
there is no ordinary meanes fufficient to teach her the right way of
faluation. And therefore the Iefuit might well fay, as he did in the
Relation, that the La. was by this & a former conference, fatisfied of
the truth of Roman Religion.

(g) The Cha-
plain vpon this
laft claufe faith,
that he is fure
fhe wilbe bet-
ter able to anf-
wer for her co-
ming to church
thē for her lea-
uing the church
of England, &
fol-

Vpon this, and the precedent Conference, the Lady refted fully fatif-
fied in her Iudgment (as she tould a
friend) of the truth of the Roman
Churches Fayth: Yet vpon frailty, &
feare to offend the King. she yielded
to goe to (g) Church; for which
she was after very forie, as fome of
her friends can teftifie.

Iowing the fuperftitions and Errours of the Church of Rome. But
he neither proueth, nor can proue that it is lawfull for one (perfwaded efpecially as the Lady is) to goe to the Proteftant Church,
which were to halt on both fides, to ferue two Maifters, to diffemble with God and the world, to profeffe outwardly a Religion
in confcience knowne to be falfe; neyther doth he, or can he proue
any fuperftition or errour to be in Romane Religion; but by prefu-
ming with intolerable pride to make himfelf, or fome of his fellowes iudge of Controuerfies, and by taking authority to cenfure
all to be fuperftition and errour, which futeth not with his fancy,
although it be generally held or practifed by the vniuerfall church,
which in *S. Auguftins* Iudgment, is *moft infolent madnes.*

 I befeech fweet Iefus, to giue grace to euery one
that offendeth in this fort, to fee, repent, and get
pardon of their faults paft, and light of true Fayth
in tyme to come ; for obtayning whereof they
had need to pray to God for it, and with a great
defire to feeke after it, and with humility to fubmit their will and Iudgment to thofe whom God
hath appointed to teach it ; To wit, fuch Doctours and Paftours as by a vifible continuall fucceffion, haue without change brought it from chrift
and his Apoftles, euen vntill thefe our dayes; and
fhall by a like fucceffion carry it along, euen vntill
the end of world. The which fucceffion not being
found in any other church, differing in doctrine from
the Romã Church, I wifh the Chaplain & his Lord,
and euery other man carefully to confider; whether
it be not more Chriftian and leffe brainfick, to thinke
that the Pope, being S. Peters fucceffour, with a Generall Councell fhould be Iudg of Controuerfies, &
that the Paftorall Iudgment of him (vpon whom as
vpon a firme rock Chrift did build his Church, and *Ephef.* 4. 11.
K   for

Matt. 16. 18.
Luc. 22. 32.
Ioan. 20. 18.

for whofe Fayth Chrift prayed, enioyning him to confirme his brethren, and to whofe care and gouernent Chrift committed his whole flock of lambes, and fheep) fhould be accounted Infallible, rather then to make euery man that can read Scripture Interpreter of Scriptures, Decider of Controuerfies, Controller of Generall Councels, and Iudge of his Iudges: Or to haue no Iudge of Controuerfies of Fayth, to permit euery man to belieue as he lift, as if there were no Infallible certainty of Fayth to be expected on earth; The which were to induce infteed of *One fauing Fayth*, a *Babylonicall Confufion* of fo many Fayths as phantafies, or no true chriftian Fayth at all. From which euills fweet I E S V S deliuer vs. Amen.

F I N I S.

AN

ANSWER TO A PAMPHLET,

INTITVLED:

THE FISHER CATCHED IN HIS OWNE NET.

IN VVHICH, BY THE VVAY, IS SHEVVED, That the Proteſtant Church was not ſo viſible, in al *Ages, as the true Church ought to be: and conſequently, is not the true Church.*

Of which, men may learne infallible Faith, neceſſarie to Saluation.

By A. C.

MATTH. 28. verſ. 19,20.
Going, teach al Nations, baptizing them, &c. Behold, I am with you AL DAYES, *euen to the conſummation of the World.*

EPHES. 4. verſ. 11, 14.
Chriſt gaue ſome Apoſtles, *and ſome* Prophets; *otherſome* Euangeliſts, *and otherſome* PASTORS *and* DOCTORS, &c. *that we be not Children,* WAVERING *and* CARRIED ABOVT *with euerie winde of Doctrine, &c.*

M. D. C. XXIII.

THE PREFACE.

G Entle Reader , although I doubt not, but al that be wise and iudicious especially if they duly consider the occasion and state of the question, lately treated (in a Conference betwixt D.White and D. Featly Ministers; and M. Fisher and M. Sweet Iesuits) wil easily discerne (euen by that false Relation, which is set out in print by a Protestant) that the Protestants Cause hath not gained any thing : Neuerthelesse , because those who be partially affected, or of meane capacitie, may (as it is to be doubted diuers doe) conceiue and speake amisse of this matter , to the disgrace of the Catholike Cause, and the preiudice of their owne and other mens soules : I haue thought it needful to set out a true Relation of the occasion, progresse, and issue of that Conference, and this in such sort, as diuers falsehoods of the Protestant Relator, may be easily pereeiued, and the weakenesse of the Protestants Cause may be euidently discouered; which is also so bad, as it seemeth it cannot be supported, but by setting out such lying Relations ; the sight and consideration whereof, maketh me more easily beleeue that to be true which I haue read , viz. That a decree was made by Diuines in Geneua, defyning it lawful to lye for the honor or credit of the Gospel ; and that conformably to this decree , an English Minister being told that one of his Pewfellowes had made lyes in stead of proofes of his Protestant Religion, did answer , saying : He cannot lye too much in this cause. It must needes be a weake and bad cause , that needeth to be supported by such weake and bad shifts. I for my part wil not promise , to haue perfectly remembred and

Eudaimon Iohannes in defens.p.H.Garn.

D.Bishop against Rob. Abbots.

A 2   set

The Preface.

*set downe euery word that paffed in this Conference, efpecially
spoken by by-standers; nor to haue ftriɛtly obferued the precife order of euerie paffage: but for the fubftance, and truth of
the matter that I doe relate, I affure, that there fhal not be
found any falfehood, vnleffe it be in fome of thofe Parcels;
which I doe not relate of my felfe, but out of the Proteftant
Relator : whofe Relation ordinarily as I doe not contradiɛt,
vnleffe it be vpon neceffarie occafion ; fo I doe not intend to
approue : but fimply relating what it faith, I wil leaue it to
others to iudge, what they thinke fit of it. Onely this I wil
fay, That euerie one may beleeue it fo farre, as it relateth any
thing, which may aduantage the* Catholique Defendants,
and their Caufe, or difaduantage the Proteftant Difputants,
*and their Caufe. For it is certaine, that no man wil lye for
the aduantage of his Aduerfarie, or his Caufe; nor for his
owne difaduantage. But in fuch things as it hath fet downe
aduantagioufly for the* Proteftant Difputant, *or his Caufe,
there is iuft reafon to fufpeɛt it ; in regard I am toid, that
D.* Featly *himfelfe (who is faid to be the Author) hath confeffed, That more is faid in the Relation, then was faid in the
Conference it felfe; and I am fure fomething is left
out, which was faid, and fomething mif-reported.
This being premifed, by way of Preface,
I wil begin to difcourfe of the
matter it felfe.*

CHAP. I.

About the firſt occaſion of the Conference, in which is ſhew-
ed, that Maſter Fiſher *did not ſeeke it , or prouoke his*
Aduerſaries by any challenge vnto it , nor did intend to
haue it ſo publike, as by his Aduerſaries fault it proued

The Proteſtant Relator of this Conference, ſetteth downe
the occaſion in theſe words.

"EDWARD BVGGS Eſquire, about the age of
" 70. yeeres, being lately ſicke, was ſolicited by
" ſome Papiſts then about him, to forſake the
" Proteſtant Faith, telling him : There was no
" hope of ſaluation, without the Church ; there was no
" Catholike Church but theirs; and to beleeue the Ca-
" tholike Church, was the Article of his Creede ; and
" by it, could no other Church be meant but the Church
" of Rome, becauſe it could not be proued by al the
" Proteſtants in the Kingdome, that they had any
" Church before *Luther.*

" This Gentleman being much troubled in his mind
" with theſe and the like ſuggeſtions, who al his life
" time had beene, and profeſſed himſelfe a Religious
" Proteſtant, became now more ſicke in mind then
" body.

" After his recouerie, being much troubled in mind
" with theſe former ſuggeſtions of the Popiſh Prieſts,
" he repayred to Sir *Humfrey Lynd* Knight; who, by rea-
" ſon of his alliance, and long acquaintance with him,
" gaue the beſt ſatisfaſtion that he could to his ſaid Cou-

A 3   " ſin

" fin Mafter *Buggs*, who feemed to take content in fuch
" his Conference, and to be wel fatisfyed by him, in
" al points.

" But the Popifh Priefts and Iefuits not defifting to
" creepe in further, where they had once made a breach,
" perfeuering ftil in queftioning him, where his Church
" was before *Luther*.

" Whereupon hee repayred againe to Sir *Humfrey*
" *Lynd*, and required fome further fatisfaction of him,
" concerning that demand. And thereupon Sir *Humfrey*

A very weake and Infufficient fatisfaction, as is fhewed hereafter.

" *Lynd* told him, it was firft in Chrift and the Apo-
" ftles, confequently alfo confpicuous in the Primitiue
" Church, for 600. yeeres after Chrift, after which time
" fome errors crept into the Church, as difeafes into a
" mans body, fo that the Church which *Luther* & we ac-
" knowledge, was in general the fame Chriftian Church,
" as his body was the fame fubftantial body being now
" wel and lately ficke, though different in the quali-
" ties, &c.

How farre this parcel of the Relation is true or falfe,
I wil not ftand to difcuffe, as not yet knowing how, or
by whom, the aforefaid Gentleman came firft to doubt
of his Church, and confequently of his Religion; yet I
haue fome caufe to doubt, that it is not altogether true,
efpecially in that he faith : *The Popifh Priefts and Iefuits*
" *not defifting to creepe in further where they had once made*
" *a breach, perfeuering ftil in queftioning him : where his*
" *Church was before Luther?* For I doe not thinke that
many (if any at al) Priefts or Iefuits, did firft put this
doubt into the old Gentleman his head, nor perfeuered
in queftioning him about it. And for Mafter *Fifher* in
particular, I know certainly that hee neuer faw this old
Gentleman, much leffe did he fpeake to him, in any matter of Religion, til that time, when Sir *Humfrey Lynd*
firft

firſt met Maſter *Fiſher*. The which meeting is mentioned in the Proteſtant Relation, ſaying thus :

" And after his returne to London,the ſaid Sir *Hum-*
" *frey Lynd* going to Maſter *Buggs* his houſe in Drury
" lane, to vſit him, found Maſter *Fiſher* the Ieſuit there,
" where after ſome debates about Religion, and the vi-
" ſibilite of the Church , Maſter *Fiſher* called for Pen
" and Inke , and ſet downe this queſtion *in terminis*,
" thereby adding vnder his hand, that he would anſwer
" vpon it negatiuely, as challenging and expecting Op-
" poſers; deliuering alſo the Paper into the hands of the
" ſaid Sir *Humfrey Lynd* ; who vpon view of it,anſwe-
" red : That it was an Hiſtorical queſtion , and not ſo
" proper for diſputation. But Maſter *Fiſher* vrging it,
" Sir *Humfrey* told him : If he would goe to D. *Whites*,
" where formerly he had beene, the ſaid D. would eaſi-
" ly reſolue thoſe doubts , which being refuſed by the
" Ieſuite, the ſaid Sir *Humfrey* did then returne him his
" Paper againe, and ſo left him.

In this parcel ſome thing is omitted, ſome thing miſreported, as wil appeare by this which followeth :

A certaine Catholike Gentleman,comming to Maſter
Fiſher, told him : That the aforeſaid old Gentleman was
deſirous to heare D. *White* and him diſpute ; and therefore deſired to know, whether he would think it conuenient to vndertake a meeting with D. *White*. M. *Fiſher*
told him expreſly , that hee neither might , nor would
make any challenge to D. *White*; but , ſaith hee : If
D .*White* doe challenge me, I wil not refuſe.

And ſome reaſon M.*Fiſher* gaue to the Gentleman, to
let him ſee, that it was not fit that he ſhould be a Chal-
lenger in ſuch a buſineſſe : whereupon the Gentleman,
for feare of miſ-deliuering M.*Fiſhers* mind , did intreat
M.*Fiſher* to deliuer his owne anſwer to a Proteſtant
Knight,

Knight, Sir *Humfrey Lynd*, who was imployed by the
said old Gentleman, to moue D.*White* to come to such a
meeting. M. *Fisher* hauing some acquaintance in the
house where the old Gentleman was, said : He would
that night be there, and if the Knight would come, he
should heare the same answer. So M. *Fisher* came, and
Sir *Humfrey* (being aduised by the said Catholike Gentleman, of M. *Fishers* intention to be there) also came.
And after some speeches, the question was moued, Whether M.*Fisher* would speake with D.*White* about the visibilitie of the Church ? He answered as before : *That*
he would not challenge D. White ; *but if D.White would*
challenge him to treate of that matter, he would not refuse.
It was answered : That it was not meant in the nature of
a challenge, but to haue a quiet meeting, to satisfie the
old Gentleman : and so Sir *Humfrey* wished M. *Fisher* to
set downe the questions. Then M. *Fisher* hauing heard
wherein the Gentleman did chiefely doubt, set downe
these two questions :

Whether there must not bee in al ages a visible Church,
of which, al forts must learne that one infallible faith
which is necessary to saluation ?

Whether the Protestants Church was in al ages visible,
especially in the ages before Luther : and whether the
names of such visible Protestants in al ages, may be
shewed out of good Authors?

The first question being read before Sir *Humfrey* and the
old Gentleman, and some others, they said : That it was
out of question, that such a visible Church as the question mentioned, must needes bee granted ; whereupon
M.*Fisher* tooke his Pen, and subscribed to the first question, these words :   *It is granted.*
Which being supposed; M.*Fisher* read the second question,

on, and was contented it should be the onely Question, for so Sir *Humfrey* desired.; who also bad M. *Fisher* choose, whether he would be the Disputer or Answerer. M. *Fisher* said, It would be requisite both to dispute and answer. Yet Sir *Humfrey* vrging him to choose the one or other part, M. *Fisher* said, *I wil answer*; and so he tooke his Pen, and writ in the Margent briefely, what answer he meant to make to the whole Question, and said: *I wil answer, that it was not*; to wit, so visible as the Question required.

This Paper, in which these Questions were, Sir *Humfrey* tooke, but with intent, that onely one, that is, the second, should be disputed on. Then question being made about the Place, Sir *Humfrey* named D. *Whites* house. M. *Fisher* said, he had no reason to goe to the Doctors house; in regard, the last time he was there, it was giuen out, and made a general report, That M. *Fisher* would haue killed D. *White* in his house. And therefore, saith M. *Fisher*, I wil not goe, vnlesse himselfe inuite me: but if he inuite, I wil goe. Sir *Humfrey* doubted, that D. *White* would not inuite M. *Fisher:* and so, for want of agreeing about the Place, M. *Fisher* verily thought, that no meeting would be at al: yet he did not take againe the Paper, in which the Questions were; but eyther left them with Sir *Humfrey*, or the old Gentleman: yet without any minde at al, to make any challenge, as he had more then once expressed.

" About two dayes after (saith the Protestant Rela-
" tor) M. *Buggs* repayred to Sir *Humfrey Lynd*, and en-
" treated him (for his satisfaction) to giue M. *Fisher* a
" meeting, saying: That M. *Fisher* had againe told him,
" That he would maintaine what he had set downe; and
" that our Diuines could not proue our Church visible,
" before *Luthers* time. Whereupon Sir *Humfrey* told
B " him,

" him, That D. *White* and D. *Featly* were to dyne with
" him on Fryday following ; and if, after Dinner,
" M. *Fisher* would come thither, with foure, or six at the
" most, they should be admitted for his fake and his
" Wifes, who (by reason of such follicitation) were
" troubled in their mindes ; and fatisfaction should be
" giuen, as occasion required. And these were the true
" causes of the meeting.

What to fay to this Parcel, I know not, becaufe it was
priuate, betwixt Sir *Humfrey* and the old Gentleman.
But there were other more remarkable paffages, omitted
by the Proteftant Relator, which I thinke fit to fet
downe. As firft, That M. *Fisher* comming to the old
Gentleman, the next day, or next but one, after the Queftion was fet downe ; found him ftill defirous, to haue
the meeting goe forward : and then it may very wel be,
that M. *Fisher* might fay ; *He would maintaine what he*
had fet downe, and that Proteftant Diuines could not proue
the Proteftant Church vifible , before Luthers *time.* But
what in particular he faid, he doth not remember. Onely
he is fure he made no challenge ; and fo the old Gentleman did wel vnderftand : who told M. *Fisher*, That it
was intended onely to be a friendly and a priuate meeting at Sir *Humfrey* his owne houfe : and that D. *White*
would bring with him one to affift him, as M. *Fisher*
fhould bring with him one to affift him ; and befide,
fome foure more, whom they thought good, to be Witneffes ; and two Writers, to fet downe on each part
what was faid : and that Fryday next fhould be the
day.

M. *Fisher* hearing this equal offer, did not refufe : but
(to prepare the mind of the old Gentleman, to be better
able to make benefit of what fhould be faid about it)
writ, and deliuered vnto him a Paper, fhewing briefely
and

and plainely, how the true vifible Church of Chrift muft be fo vifible in al Ages, as that the names of fome principal Members thereof, in euerie Age, may be fhewed out of good Authors.

A true Copie of which Paper, I thinke fit here to fet downe; in regard it may ferue others, as wel as this old Gentleman, to vnderftand, Why Catholiques doe ordinarily fo much preffe Proteftants, to name (if they can) Proteftant Profeffors, in al Ages, as Catholiques doe in printed Bookes ordinarily fet downe, a Catalogue of the Names of the chiefe Paftors, and other principal Members of the Catholique Roman Church, in al Ages.

A Copie of the firſt Paper, which M. Fifher writ, and deliuered to the old Gentleman, before the meeting.

1. It is certaine, There is one, and but one true infallible Faith; without which, none can pleafe God, nor confequently, attaine eternal Salnation. | Eph. 4. Heb. 11.

2. This one infallible Faith cannot be had (according to the ordinarie courfe of Gods prouidence) but by hearing Preachers and Paftors of the true vifible Church, who onely are lawfully fent and authorized to teach the true Word of God. | Rom. 10. v. 14,15. Eph. 4. 11.

3. As therefore this one infallible Faith hath beene, and muft be, in al Ages: fo there muft needes be, in al Ages, Preachers and Paftors of the true vifible Church; of whom, al forts of people haue in time paft (as appeareth by Hiftories) learned, and muft in al future times, learne the faid infallible Truth. | Ofe. 2. v. 19,20. Ifa. 59. 20. Matth. 18. 20. Eph. 4. v. 11.

4. Hence followeth, That if Proteftants be the true

viſible Church of Chriſt; al ſorts of men, who in euerie Age haue had the aforeſaid infallible Faith, haue learned it, by hearing Proteſtant Preachers, whoſe names may yet be found in Hiſtories; as the names of thoſe are found, who in euerie former Age did teach and conuert People of ſeueral Nations vnto the Faith of Chriſt.

5. Hence further followeth, That if there cannot (as there cannot) be found in Hiſtories, Names of Proteſtant Preachers, who in al Ages did teach al ſorts of faithful People, and who conuerted ſeueral Nations vnto the Chriſtian Faith: Hence followeth, I ſay, That Proteſtants are not the true viſible Church of Chriſt; neyther are their Preachers lawfully ſent, or ſufficiently authorized to teach; nor People ſecurely warranted, to learne of them that one infallible Faith, without which none can poſſibly pleaſe God, nor (if they ſo liue and dye) be ſaued.

If any Proteſtant wil anſwer; let him ſet downe Names of Proteſtant Preachers in al Ages, who taught People Proteſtant Doctrine in euerie ſeueral Age; or confeſſe, there were no ſuch before *Luther*; or, at leaſt, not in al Ages to be found in Hiſtories.

After this, M. *Fiſher* let the old Gentleman ſee a little printed Booke, in which was a Catalogue of viſible Roman Profeſſors in al Ages: wiſhing him to vrge his Miniſters, to ſhew (if they can) a like Catalogue of their Proteſtant Profeſſors. And it is very likely, that this Booke (as alſo the foreſaid Paper) was by this old Gentleman carryed to Sir *Humfrey* : from whom, about two or three dayes before the meeting, a Paper was ſent to M. *Fiſher*, contayning the former Queſtion; and another like Queſtion propoſed to him, to diſpute vpon : the contents whereof were as followeth.

" The

" The queſtion propoſed by M. *Fiſher*, in which he
" vndertaketh to maintaine the negatiue, is ſet downe
by him in *hæc verba*:

" *Whether the Proteſtant Church was in al ages viſi-*
" *ble, eſpecially in the ages going before Luther : and*
" *whether the names of ſuch viſible Proteſtants,in al*
" *ages,can be ſhewed and proued out of good Authors?*

" To this vniuerſal demand (requiring rather an Hi-
" ſtorical large volume then Syllogical briefe diſputes,
" we anſwer, That although:

1. " Diuine infallible Faith is not built vpon
" deduction out of humane Hiſtorie, but diuine
" Reuelation,as is confeſſed by the Schoolemen,and ex-
" preſſely by *Bellarmine*, *Hiſtoriæ humanæ non faciunt*
" *fidem niſi humanam.*

2. " And this queſtion is grounded vpon vncertaine
" and falſe ſuppoſals : yet wee requite this Proponent,
" putting him to his owne taske in his owne defence,
" by propounding to him the like queſtion: *viz.*

" *Whether the Romiſh Church, (that is, a Church hol-*
" *ding the particular entire doctrine of the now Ro-*
" *maniſts, as it is compriſed in the Councel of* Trent)
" *was in al ages viſible, eſpecially in the firſt* 600.
" *yeeres ; and whether the names of ſuch viſible or*
" *legible Romaniſts in al ages can be ſhewed and pro-*
" *ued out of good Authors ?*

" We wil anſwer negatiuely,That no ſuch Church or
" Profeſſors can be ſhewed.

This Paper being deliuered to M. *Fiſher*, he writ a ſecond Paper, to explicate the meaning of his queſtion,

B 3   to to shew an equal method of proceeding in the Disputation.

A Copie of a second Paper, written by M. Fisher
before the meeting.

M. *Fisher* being requelted thereunto, for satisfaction of a Gentleman, propounded two questions :

1. The first, Whether there must not be in al ages a visible Church, of which al sorts are to learne the infallible Faith, necessary to saluation?

2. The second, Whether the Protestant Church was in al ages visible, especially in the ages going before *Luther*; and whether the names of such visible Protestants in al ages can be shewed, and proued out of good Authors?

To the first question, Sir *H.* and others that were present, assented ; so as it was subscribed with these words, *It is granted :* and so M. *Fisher* was content, that his second question should be the only question. Then Sir *H.* hauing left it to the choice of M. *F.* whether he would answer, or dispute : M. *F.* did choose to answer, and defend the negatiue part. So as it lyeth vpon Sir *H.* and those whom he shal choose, to make his party good, to proue out of good Authors the affirmatiue ; to wit : *The Protestants Church was in al ages visible, especially in the ages before* Luther. *And likewise, they must set downe the names of such visible Protestants in al ages, as was demanded.* When Sir *H.* or his friends shal haue performed this their taske, M. *Fisher* wil performe what is required in the Paper sent vnto him by Sir *H.* in the same sort and sense, as he requireth Sir *H.* and his friends to performe their taske.

For auoyding therefore of al mistaking, and consequietly,

quently , needleſſe and fruitleſſe Diſputes, M. *F.* in his
queſtion requireth :

1. That names of men in al ages be ſet downe, whom
Sir *H.* and his friends conceiue to haue bin Proteſtants.

2. That thoſe men whoſe names they ſet downe , be
ſhewed out of good Authors, to agree in holding ſome
points of Faith, in which Proteſtants differ from the
Romane Catholikes.

3. That Sir *H.* or his friends wil defend againſt M.
F. that the ſame men held no other points of Faith, one
differently from another , and from the preſent Proteſtant Doctrine (contayned in the 39. Articles , vnto
which al Engliſh Miniſters are ſworne) for otherwiſe
they cannot make one and the ſame Proteſtant Church.

In this ſort and ſenſe, when Sir *H.* or his friends ſhal
haue ſhewed a viſible Proteſtant Church in al ages, then
M. *F.* or his friends wil in a like proportionable ſort and
ſenſe, ſhew, proue and defend a viſible Romane Church
in al ages.

This Paper was deliuered to the old Gentleman, and
was confeſſed to haue beene receiued by the Doctors
before the diſputation , and before the meeting. The
time and manner of which meeting is ſet downe by the
Proteſtant Relator, in manner following :

" The 27. of Iune, 1623. M. *Fiſher*, M. *Sweet*, Ieſuits,
" and ſome others with them , came to Sir *H. Lynds*
" houſe, in a little dyning roome, where they found the
" aforeſaid M. *Buggs*, his wife and children, and others
" of Sir *H.* friends, that had then dined with him, toge-
" ther with ſome others alſo : whoſe comming in, as
" the ſaid Sir *H.* did not expect ; ſo he could not with
" ciuilitie put them forth his houſe , but did inſtantly
" cauſe his doores to bee locked vp , that no more
" might enter : notwithſtanding which his command,
                                                          ſome

" fome others alfo came in fcattering, after the confe-
" rence began.

In this parcel it is to bee confidered, how great care
M. *Fifher* had to haue the meeting fecret, and how wel
he obferued the fore-appointed conditions : in which he
was fo punctual, that after he had his number, of one
Affiftant, and foure Witneffes, and a Writer, he would
not fo much as tel a Gentleman of his acquaintance(who
had by other meanes vnderftood of the meeting, and the
place of meeting)at what houre the meeting fhould be;
whereas on the contrary part, fo much fpeech was made
of it, by fome of the Proteftant fide, that (befide the
number appointed to bee Auditors) many Proteftant
Gentlemen and Gentlewomen, and fome Noblemen,
and many Minifters, did repaire to Sir *Humfrey* his
houfe, which M. *Fifher* found to be fo filled, as he complained to Sir *Humfrey* of the inequalitie of that Audience, compared with the few he brought; which Sir
H. could not denie, but excufed himfelfe in fuch manner as he could, faying : He could not helpe it, &c.

CHAP. II.

About that which paffed in the Conference it felfe.

" **D**Octor *White* and Doctor *Featly*,being inuited to
" dinner(faith the Proteftant Relator)by Sir *Hum-*
" *frey Lynd*, and ftaying a while after, had notice giuen
" them,that M. *Fifher*,and M. *Sweet*,Iefuits,were in the
" next roome, ready to conferre with them, touching a
" Queftion fet downe by M. *Fifher*, vnder his owne
" hand, in thefe words : *viz.*

" *Whether the Proteftants Church was in al ages vifible,*
and

" *and especially in the ages going before Luther.* 2. *And*
" *whether the names of such visible Protestants, in al*
" *ages, can be shewed and proued out of good Authors* ?

" This Queftion being deliuered to the parties aboue
" named, and it being notified vnto them, that there
" were certaine perfons who had beene follicited, and
" remaining doubtful in Religion, defired fatisfaction
" efpecially in this point; they were perfwaded to haue
" fome fpeech with the Iefuites touching this point:
" the rather, becaufe the Priefts and Iefuites doe dayly
" caft out Papers, and difperfe them in fecret ; in which
" they vaunt, That no Proteftant Minifter dare encoun-
" ter with them in this point.

Any man reading this parcel, would be induced to
thinke, that D. *White* and D. *Featly* had neuer had notice before, for what end they were inuited to Dinner,
or for what end they were to meet with the Iefuites: but
that they were on the fuddaine fummoned to this Conference, without any preparation, or knowledge of the
Queftion. Which not to be fo, is euidently conuinced,
partly, by that which is alreadie faid, partly, by that
which I am after to fay.

2. This Relator would make his Reader beleeue, that
M. *Fisher* vnder his owne hand had fet downe the words
of the Queftion, diftinguifhed with the expreffe figure
of 2. Which is not fo, for M. *Fisher* did not write any
fuch figure of 2. in the middle of the Queftion, nor did
not meane to make any more then one only entire Queftion, as Sir *Humfrey* himfelfe had defired.

3. He feemeth willing to perfwade, that Priefts and
Iefuites doe dayly caft out Papers, which is not true.

" At the beginning of this meeting, when the Difpu-
" tants were fet (faith the Proteftant Relator) D. *Featly*

C " drew

" drew out the Paper, in which the Queſtion aboue re-
" hearſed was written, with theſe words in the Mar-
" gent, *viz. I wil anſwer, that it was not*; and deman-
" ded of M. *Fiſher*, Whether this were his owne hand?
" which after he had acknowledged, D. *Featly* began as
" followeth:

D. *Featly.* " συν Θεῷ To this vniuerſal demand, re-
" quiring rather an Hiſtorical large Volume, then a Syl-
" logiſtical briefe diſpute, we anſwer:] And then he
read out of a Paper (which this Relator would make
men beleeue to haue beene ſaid *memoriter*) the ſame
in effect, which was written before the meeting, to
M. *Fiſher*.

1. " That although diuine infallible Faith is not
" built vpon deduction out of humane Hiſtorie, but
" vpon diuine reuelation, as is confeſſed by your owne
" Schoole-men, and expreſſely by Cardinal *Bellarmine*,
" *Hiſtoriæ humanæ faciunt tantum fidem humanam, cui*
" *ſubeſſe poteſt falſum*: Humane Stories and Records
" beget onely an humane Faith, or rather Credulitie,
" ſubiect to error; not a diuine and infallible Beleefe,
" which muſt be built vpon ſurer ground.

2. " Although this Queſtion be grounded vpon vn-
" certaine and falſe ſuppoſals: for a Church may haue
" beene viſible, yet not the names of al viſible Profeſ-
" ſors thereof now to be ſhewed and proued out of
" good Authors: there might be millions of Profeſ-
" ſors, yet no particular and authentical Record of
" them by name: Records there might be many, in
" ancient time, yet not now extant, at leaſt for vs
" to come by: Yet we wil not refuſe to deale with
" you in your owne Queſtion, if you, in like man-
" ner, wil vndertake the like Taske in your owne
" defence, and maintaine the Affirmatiue in the like
                                    " Queſtion,

" Queſtion , which we now propound vnto you here
" in writing.

> " *Whether the Romiſh Church , (that is, a Church hol-*
> " *ding the particular entire doctrine of the new Ro-*
> " *maniſts, as it is compriſed in the Councel of* Trent)
> " *was in al ages viſible , eſpecially in the firſt* 600.
> " *yeeres ; and whether the names of ſuch viſible or*
> " *legible Romaniſts in al ages can be ſhewed and pro-*
> " *ued out of good Authors ?*

Here the Relator omitteth to tel how M.*Fiſher* cauſed
the two Papers,written and giuen the old Gentleman,as
is aboueſaid, to be publiquely read : by the firſt whereof,it appeared why he had propounded ſuch a Queſtion:
by the ſecond, the true ſence and meaning of the Queſtion was explicated, and a conuenient Method of proceeding was preſcribed, with due proportion to be obſerued on both ſides.

Then D. *Featly* beginning to argue (in this place,
and not in the end of the Diſputation, where the Proteſtant Relator placeth it) did ſay : M. *Fiſher,* I wiſh, I
warne, I command, I coniure you,to anſwere truely and
ſincerely, in the ſight of God, and as you wil anſwere it
at the Day of Iudgement. To this M. *Fiſher* ſaid: I willingly accept your warning, and I wiſh you to obſerue
the like.

About this time M. *Sweet* propounded theſe Conditions to be obſerued.

1. That al bitter ſpeeches ſhould be forborne.

2. That nothing ſhould be ſpoken, or heard, but to
the purpoſe.

Which ſecond he did propound, to preuent impertinent digreſſions.

Ne-

Neuerthelesse, after this, D. *Featly* made a long digression, altogether impertinent to the Question which he
was to dispute of : for in stead of prouing a Protestant
visible Church, and naming visible Protestants in al ages,
he made a vaine and vnseasonable bragging offer, to dis-
proue the Roman Church in diuers particular points (as
are rehearsed by the Protestant Relator) which he read
out of a Paper. Whereunto as he was speaking, M. *Sweet*
according to the second Condition, before propounded,
answered, *That those things were then impertinent, and nothing to the purpose.* But M. *Sweet* did not say, as the Re-
" lator reporteth, *They are Scholastical points, not Funda-*
" *mental.* Neyther was there any such Syllogisme then
made, as the Relator annexeth.

D. *Featly* hauing ended his long digression, M. *Fisher*
" said (as the Protestant Relator telleth:) After you
" haue proued your Church visible in al ages, and na-
" med the Professors thereof, I wil satisfie you in your
" particulars.

D. *Featly.* " In the meane while, name but one Fa-
" ther, but one Writer of note, who held the particulars
" aboue named for fiue hundred yeeres after Christ. To
" which instant demand of D. *Featly* (saith the Relator)
" nothing was answered.

But neyther was this said, neyther was it needful to
answer. First, for that M. *Fisher* formerly answered, That
he would satisfie al particulars, after the visibilitie of the
Protestant Church, in al ages, was shewed, as the present
Question required. Secondly, becaufe to dispute of
these particulars, was vnseasonable, and not to the prefent purpose: as likewise was that other motion, made
by Sir *Humfrey Lynd* to M. *Sweet*, to dispute of *Tran-
substantiation* out of S. *Augustine.* To which motion,
being (as I said) vnseasonable, M. *Sweet* answered wel,
accor-

according to his fecond Prouifo,faying : *That is not now to the Queſtion.*

   " Then D. *Featly* faid (faith the Proteſtant Relator)
" there are two meanes onely to proue any thing by ne-
" ceſſarie inference, to wit, a Syllogifme, and an Induc-
" tion; other formes of Argument haue no force,but as
" they are reducible to thefe. I proue the vifibilitie of
" our Church by both, and firſt,by a Syllogifme.

  No,faith M. *Fiſher,* you muſt not onely proue it to be vifible, but fo vifible,as the names of Proteſtant Profeſ-fors in al ages may be ſhewed out of good Authors.

   " To this, D. *Featly* faid : There are two *Quæres* in
" your Queſtion: Firſt,Whether the Proteſtants Church
" were in al ages vifible ? And fecondly, Whether the
" names of fuch vifible Proteſtants can be ſhewed ?

  No, faid M. *Fiſher ,* my Queſtion is meant to be but one entire Queſtion : and fo, to cut off al needleſſe wrangling (made by D. *White* and D. *Featly* about the Aduerbe *Vtrum, Whether,* and the Copulatiue *Et, And,* as if Grammar Schollers had beene difputing , rather then graue Diuines,who were not to ſtand vpon rigor of Grammar, efpecially iń this cafe, where the fence of the Speaker is plaine, and may wel ſtand with Grammar) M. *Fiſher* faid : The Queſtion being mine, it pertaineth to me to tel the meaning ; and my meaning was, onely to make it one Queſtion : *viz.*

Whether the Proteſtants Church were fo vifible, as the names of vifible Proteſtants, in al ages, may be ſhewed out of good Authors ?

  Wherefore, if you wil difpute, you muſt difpute in my fenfe, and muſt conclude the Affirmatiue : *viz.* The Proteſtant Church was fo vifible,as the names of the

Pro-

Profeſſors in al ages may be ſhewed out of good Authors. Proue this, or proue nothing.

D. *Featly.* " That Church, which is ſo viſible, as the
" Catholique Church ought to be, and as the Popiſh
" Church is pretended by M. *Fiſher* to be, is ſo viſible,
" that the names of the Profeſſors thereof may be pro-
" duced and ſhewed, in al ages, out of good Authors.

" But the Proteſtant Church is ſo viſible, as the Ca-
" tholique Church ought to be, and as the Popiſh
" Church is pretended to be.   *Ergo*

M. *Fiſher.* " I denie the *Minor.*

  Minor probate.

D. *Featly.* " That Church, whoſe Faith is eternal,
" and perpetual, and vnchanged , is ſo viſible, as the
" Catholique Church ought to be , and the Popiſh
" Church is pretended by M. *Fiſher* to be.

" But the Faith of the Proteſtant Church is eternal,
" perpetual, and vnchanged.   *Ergo*

To this, M. *Fiſher* anſwered : firſt excepting againſt the Word, *Eternal* ; ſaying : Faith is not eternal, or *ab æterno.*

It is true, ſaid a Miniſter who ſate by ; Faith is not eternal, but euiternal.

Neyther ſo, ſaid M. *Fiſher* ; for it is not to be for euer in Heauen.

It is eternal (ſaid D. *White*) *in Predeſtination.*

So (ſaid M. *Sweet*) D. *White* himſelfe may be ſaid to be eternal : and he might haue added, this preſent Diſputation may be ſaid to be *Eternal.*

D. *Featly.* " You haue a purpoſe, M. *Fiſher*, to cauil :
" you know my meaning wel enough, by the terme *Per-*
" *petual* ; to wit, that Chriſtian Faith, which hath conti-
" nued from Chriſts firſt publiſhing it, til this preſent,
" and ſhal continue vntil his ſecond comming, &c.

                                                    If

If this were said by D. *Featly* (which is doubted) he should haue confidered, how he and D. *White* cauilled vpon the word *Whether*, and *And*, when they knew M. *Fisbers* meaning wel enough ; yea, after they had heard him plainely explicate his meaning : Whereas M. *Fisber* onely put them in minde to speake properly, like Scholers, and did not cauil or reply, after D. *Featly* did explicate his meaning. But to returne to the argument.

D. *Featly.* " That Church which holdeth this Faith, " you beleeue shal be so visible, that the names of the " Professors thereof may be shewed in al ages.

" But the Proteftant Church holdeth this perpetual " Faith.   *Ergo*

M. *Fisber.* " Your argument is a fallacie, called *Petitio principij.*

D. *Featly.* " A demonftration, *a causa*, or *a priori*, is " not *Petitio principij.*

" But such is my argument.   *Ergo*

" Is it not a founder argument, to proue the visi- " bilitie of the Professors from the truth of their " Faith ; then as you, the truth of your Faith from " the visibilitie of Professors ? Visible Paftors argue " not a right Faith. Heretikes, Mahumetans, and " Gentiles, haue visible Professors of their Impie- " ties : yet will it not hence follow, that they " haue a right beleefe. On the contrarie, we know " by the Promises of God in the Scripture, That " the Church which maintayneth the true Faith, " shal haue alwayes Professors, more or lesse, vi- " fible.

M. *Sweet.* " You ought to prooue the truth of " your Church *a posteriori*, for that is to the Queftion, " and not *a priori*.

D. *Feat*~

D. *Featly.* " Shal you prefcribe me my Weapons?
" Is not an argument *a priori,* better then an argument
" *a poſteriori?* &c.

" To this, M. *Fiſher* faid : A proofe *a poſteriori* is
" more demonſtratiue then *a priori.*

Thus farre the Relator ; who hath here added much
more then was faid : and in particular, thofe formal
words which he reporteth M. *Fiſher* to haue faid : *viz.*
A proofe a poſteriori *is more demonſtratiue then* a priori,
M. *Fiſher* did not fpeake : perhaps he might fay, That a
proofe *a poſteriori* doth better demonſtrate to vs then
a priori: not meaning in general to preferre a Logical
demonſtration *a poſteriori* before that which is *a priori;*
but that fuch a proofe *a poſteriori,* as he in this prefent
Queſtion required, and as the Queſtion it felfe exacted,
would better demonſtrate or ſhew to al forts of men,
which is the true Church , then any proofe which
D. *Featly* or D. *White* can make *a priori,* to proue the
Proteſtant Church to be the true Church, as ſhal be
ſhewed when need is, hereafter : at this prefent it may
fuffice to fay to that which D. *Featly* now obiecteth a-
gainſt the proofe taken from viſibilitie,That although al
kind of viſible Profeſſors doe not argue right Faith,yet
want of viſible Profeſſors argueth want of Chriſts true
Church. For fuppoſing it to be true , which euen
D. *Featly* himfelfe here faith (according to the Proteſtants Relator) *viz. We know by the Promiſes of God in*
the Scripture, that the Church which maintaines the true
Faith , ſhal haue alwayes Profeſſors, more or leſſe, viſible :
and (as M. *Fiſher* further proued in one of the forefaid
Papers,giuen to the old Gentleman before this meeting)
ſo viſible,as their names in al ages may be ſhewed out of good
Authors. Suppoſing alfo out of D. *Whitaker,contra Dur.*
l.7. p.472. That whatfoeuer is fore-told by the ancient

Prophets, of the propagation, amplitude, and glory of the Church, is moſt clearely witneſſed by Hiſtories : and ſuppoſing laſtly out of D. *Iohn White*, in his *Way. p.* 338. That things paſt cannot be ſhewed to vs, but by Hiſtories. Suppoſing al this (I ſay) it is moſt apparant, That (if there cannot be produced (as there cannot) names of Proteſtants, or of any other Profeſſors of Chriſtian Faith, in al ages, out of Hiſtories, to whom Gods Promiſes agree, beſide thoſe which are knowne Roman Catholikes) not Proteſtants, nor any other, but onely the Roman Catholikes are the true Church of Chriſt ; which teacheth the true Faith, and of which al ſorts are to learne infallible Faith, neceſſarie to Saluation.

But as for the argument, which D. *Featly* wil needes perſwade vs not to be *Petitio principij*, but *Demonſtratio a priori : viz.*

That Church, whoſe Faith is eternal, and perpetual, and vnchanged, is ſo viſible, as the Catholike Church ought to be, and as the Popiſh Church by M. *Fiſher* is pretended to be.

But the Faith of Proteſtants Church is eternal, perpetual, and vnchanged.

Ergo, The Proteſtants Church is ſo viſible as the Catholike Church ought to be, and the Popiſh Church is pretended by M. *Fiſher* to be.

This argument, as it is ſet downe, is ſo farre from being a Demonſtration (whoſe propertie is to conuince the Vnderſtanding) as it is not a probable or Moral perſwaſion : For I am verily perſwaded, that no wiſe man (not alreadie poſſeſſed with Proteſtant opinions) wil or can be ſo much as morally conuinced, or in any ſort probably perſwaded by it, *That Proteſtants be the true viſible Church*; more then a man (in caſe of doubt) can be by the like argument, which a man may make to proue him-

D   ſelfe

felfe and his Brethren to be as wel fpoken of, as any in al the Parifh. Thus :

Thofe who are in heart true honeft men, are as wel fpoken of, as any in al the Parifh.

But I and my Brethren are in heart true honeft men. *Ergo*

As this proofe is not able to make any man not partially affected to beleeue thefe men to be wel fpoken of, or to be honeft men ; fo neyther can D. *Featlyes* proofe make any wife man beleeue Proteftants to be the true vifible Church, or to haue the true Faith.

Secondly, If the terme, *That Church*, be vnderftood onely of a particular Church (as for example, the Church of England) it is fo farre from a Logical Demonftration, as it hath not in it any Logical forme, according to any of the vfual Moods, *Barbara, Cælarent*, &c. But if it be vnderftood vniuerfally, *of euery Church*, that is, or may be ; then both *Maior* and *Minor* are falfe : and fo it cannot be a Demonftration, whofe propertie is to confift of moft certainely true propofitions. The *Maior* in this latter fenfe is falfe : for that there may be a Church, or Companie, who may haue inward Faith, eternal and vnchanged (as for example, a Church of Angels) who for want of vifible Profeffion are not fo vifible, as the Catholike Church ought to be. The *Minor* is falfe alfo: for the Proteftant Church hath not the true Primitiue Faith, neyther is that Faith they haue vnchanged , but fo often changed, and fo much fubiect to change, as one may fay (as a great Perfon in Germanie once faid of fome Proteftants) *What they hold this yeare, I doe in fome fort know; but what they wil hold next yeere, I doe not know.* Which is true, in regard they haue no certaine and infallible Rule, fufficient to preferue them from change. But if D. *Featly* fhal fay, That he neyther meant the

tearme,

tearme, *That Church*, in eyther of the aforefaid fenfes, but meant to fignifie by it, that one holy, Catholike, and Apoftolike Church, which the holy Scriptures doe fhew both to haue perpetual vnchanged Faith, and alfo to be perpetually vifible : Then indeed the *Maior* is true. But the *Minor* is moft falfe: and fo the argument is farre from being a Demonftration, efpecially when it endeuoreth to proue *Magis notum per ignotius*, *viz.* the Vifibilitie (which is eafily knowne) by the truth of Doctrine (which is more hard to be knowne) efpecially by onely Scripture of the fenfe : Whereof (according to Proteftants, who fay, The whole Church may erre) no particular man can be infallibly fure. For if the whole Church or Companie (to whom Chrift promifed the Spirit of Truth, to teach them al truth) may erre : Then much more may euery particular man erre ; and confequently, no particular man can be infallibly fure of the fenfe of Scripture.

Io.14. v.16. c.16. v.13.

Thirdly, This argument beggeth or fuppofeth that which is in queftion : For in asking, which is the true vifible Church, or Congregation of the true faithful ; we aske, at leaft virtually, which is the true Faith ; in regard, the true Church cannot be without this true Faith. Yea, therefore doe we aske which is the true Church; that of it, being firft knowne by other Markes, we may learne what is the true Faith in al points, in which we yet know not what is to be held for true Diuine Faith.

Fourthly, Although Faith be pre-required to be in fome or other members of the true Church ; yet inward Faith alone, without fome outward profeffion, by which it is made vifible, or fenfible, doth not fufficiently make a man to be a member of the vifible Church.

Let D. *Featly* therefore looke backe vpon his argu-

ment,

ment, and tel vs what Academical Learning taught him
to cal it a Demonſtration *a priori.*

But let vs heare how M. *Fiſher* did anſwer this argument,according to the Proteſtant Relator.

M. *Fiſher.* " I diſtinguiſh the *Maior.*

" That Church, whoſe Faith is perpetual, and vn-
" changed , ſo as the names of the Profeſſors may be
" ſhewed ; is ſo viſible , as the Catholike Church
" ought to be , and as M. *Fiſher* pretendeth the Ro-
" man Church to be : I grant it.

" That Church, whoſe Faith is perpetual, and vn-
" changed , yet ſo, as the names cannot be ſhewed in
" al ages ; is viſible, as the Catholike Church ought to
" be , and as M. *Fiſher* pretends the Roman Church
" to be : I denie it. To the *Minor* I apply the like
" diſtinction; and conſequently,to the *Concluſion* in the
" ſame manner.

D. *Featly.* " What ? anſwer you to the *Concluſion*
" alſo ? This is a ſtraine of new Logick.

This idle exception, M. *Fiſher* (attending to the matter) did not regard : but might haue told him,That it is
not vnuſual, after a diſtinction made both to *Maior* and
Minor, to apply the like to the *Concluſion.* For,although
it be true, That in a Syllogiſme,when *Maior* and *Minor*
are abſolutely granted, the *Concluſion* muſt not be denyed, nor diſtinguiſhed , but muſt be abſolutely granted;
yet when *Maior* and *Minor* alſo be diſtinguiſhed , the
Concluſion may be diſtinguiſhed. And I maruaile what
Rule of Logick D. *Featly* can bring againſt this ?

In like manner, if D. *Featly* did ſay any ſuch words
" as the Relator telleth : *viz.* A ſtrange diſtinction of
" the eternitie of Faith , by Profeſſors to be named,and
" not to be named : What are Profeſſors nominable, or
" innominable,to the eternitie of Faith?

If

If (I fay) D. *Featly* did fay thefe words ; it is like, M. *Fifher* did not regard them, as being impertinent : but might haue faid, That this diftinction had not relation to eternal Faith, but to a Church which hath eternal Faith : about which, it imports much to kr.ow, whether it hath Profeffors nominable, or innominable. For if it hath not, it is inuifible ; or, at leaft, not fo vifible as the true Catholike Church (of which, al forts in times paft haue learned, and in time to come muft learne the infallible Diuine Faith, neceffarie to Saluation) ought to be.

Therefore M. *Fifher* might wel (though I thinke he " did not) fay as the Relator telleth, *Tolle diftinctionem,* M. *Fifher*. " and conclude that which I denie : That the Faith of " the Proteftant Church is fo eternal, as the names of vi- " fible Proteftants in al ages may be fhewed.

To proue this, D. *Featly* made this argument, according to the Proteftant Relator.

D. *Featly.* " That Church, whofe Faith is the Catho- " like and Primitiue Faith , once giuen to the Saints, " without which no man can be faued, is fo perpetual, as " the names may be fhewed in al ages.

" But the Faith of the Proteftant Church is the Pri- " mitiue and Catholike Faith, once giuen to the Saints, " without which none can be faued.

Ergo, " The Faith of the Proteftant Church is fo " perpetual , as the names may be fhewed in al " ages.

Note here, That the Relator putteth in the Margent, ouer-againft the *Minor, Tollitur diftinctio.* But how falfe this Marginal Note is, appeareth to any who wil reflect vpon what the Diftinction was, and what I haue now faid of it : For this *Minor* fpeaking onely of Faith, doth not take away the diftinction applyed to the Church.

That

That which D. *Featly* thinketh to be a ſtraine of new
Logicke,to wit,to diſtinguiſh vpon a propoſition,with-
out applying the diſtinction to any particular tearme, is
not ſo ſtrange as he maketh it. As for example:When
one ſaith, *An Æthiopian is white*; neyther the tearme
Æthiopian alone, nor the tearme *White* alone in it ſelfe
needeth diſtinction,becauſe it is not *Æquiuocal*: but the
whole propoſition,being *Amphibological*, needeth; it being true, if it be meant, *The Æthiopian is white in the
Teeth :* and falſe,if it be meant, *He is white in his whole
Bodie.*

To the argument. M. *Fiſher* ſaid : *I denie the* Minor.
But marking, that hereupon D.*Featly* would haue transferred the Queſtion to endleſſe diſputes,about particular
Controuerſies,from the preſent general Queſtion,about
the perpetual viſible Church ; whoſe Profeſſors names
(as himſelfe ſaith) may be ſhewed in al ages. M. *Fiſher*
(I ſay) marking this, would not let D. *Featly* make his
proofe : but hauing ſaid, *I denie the* Minor ; he preſently
added,by way of explication,theſe enſuing words:

My firſt Queſtion was, Whether there muſt not be a
true viſible Church of Chriſt in al ages,of which al ſorts
muſt learne that infallible Faith, which is neceſſarie to
Saluation? and therefore, we muſt firſt finde ſuch a
Church, before men can know it to be ſuch,as they may
ſecurely learne of it,what is the infallible Faith,neceſſary
to Saluation.

While M. *Fiſher* was beginning to make this explication, D.*Featly* inſulted , as if M. *Fiſher* durſt not, for
Conſcience, denie the *Minor* abſolutely. To whom,
M. *Fiſher* ſaid : *I doe abſolutely denie it*. And then he
went forward with the aforeſaid explication. Which
ended, M. *Fiſher* ſaid : And hereupon I anſwer againe
to the ſaid *Minor* ; If this propoſition be taken ſimply
in

in it felfe, I abfolutely denie it : but if this propofition be confidered (as it muft be) as related to the firft Queftion, and the end thereof ; I further adde, That it is not pertinent to that end, for which the whole Difpute was intended : *viz.* To fhew to thofe who were not able by their owne abilities to finde out the infallible Faith, neceffarie to Saluation, without learning of the true vifible Church of Chrift : and confequently, Vifibilitie of the Church is firft to be fhewed, before the truth of Doctrine in particular fhal be fhewed.

To this (as the Relator faith) D. *Featly* replyed : *viz.*
" Firft, What fpeake you of thofe, who are not able by
" their owne abilities to finde out Faith ? Is any man
" able, by his owne abilitie, without the helpe of Diuine
" Grace ? Secondly, What helpeth the Vifibilitie, to
" confirme the Truth of the Church ? Vifibilitie in-
" deed proues a Church, but not the true Church.

Thefe words eyther were not fpoken, or M. *Fifher* did not regard them , being in the middeft of his anfwer : in which he went on, fhewing the neceffitie of a vifible Church, by a faying of D. *Fields* : viz. *Seeing the Controuerfies of Religion at this day are fo many in number, and fo intricate in nature, that few haue time and leyfure, fewer ftrength of wit and vnderftanding, to examine them : what remaineth for men, defirous of fatisfaction in things of fuch confequence , but diligently to feeke out which, among al the Societies of men in the World, is that Spoufe of Chrift, the Church of the liuing God, which is the Pillar of the Truth ; that fo they may embrace her Communion, follow her Direction, and reft in her Iudgement ?* D. Field in his Epiftle Dedicatorie.

M. *Fifher* therefore (I fay) being bufily fpeaking this, did not regard what D. *Featly* did then fay, but might eafily haue anfwered : Firft, That he neuer meant, that any were able of themfelues, without helpe of Gods
grace,

grace,to attaine the true Faith; which hindreth not, but
that some may haue that abilitie of Wit and Learning,
by which they can better examine Controuersies of
Faith, then those who want these abilities. Secondly,
Although Visibilitie alone doe not prooue the true
Church, yet it (supposing Gods Promises, That the true
Church shal be alwayes visible) much helpeth:and want
of Visibilitie,in any one age, proueth a Companie not to
be the true Church,

D. *Featly.* " The summe of your former answer was,
" That the *Minor* of my former Syllogisme was both
" false,and impertinent. It is neyther false,nor imperti-
" nent : *Ergo,* your answer is false, and impertinent.
" And first, it is not false.

M. *Fisher.* " I answer to the Antecedent , That it is
" both false,and impertinent : but I adde,That for the
" present it must be proued to be pertinent; or else it
" diuerteth vs from the chiefe end of our dispute:which
" was, as I said before,That infallible Truth may be
" learned of the true visible Church; and not the true
" visible Church,by first finding euery particular infalli-
" ble Truth : and by that,to conclude which is the true
" visible Church.

D. *Featly.* " I prooue that the *Minor* is pertinent :
" That *Minor* proposition , which together with the
" *Minor* doth necessarily and directly inferre the con-
" clusion of the *Minor* last denyed, is pertinent to the
" probation of that *Minor* denyed.

" But the *Minor* proposition of the third Syllogisme,
" doth necessarily and directly inferre the conclusion of
" the *Minor* last denyed.

" *Ergo,* the *Minor* of that Syllogisme is pertinent.

" M. *Fisher* did distinguish the *Maior.* That *Minor*
" proposition, which together with the *Maior* doth necessarily

" ceffarily inferre the *Conclufion*, fo as it may ferue for
" that purpofe to which the whole Difpute is ordained;
" I grant it to be pertinent.

" But if it doe inferre the *Conclufion*; yet not fo, as
" may ferue for that purpofe for which the whole Dif-
" pute was ordained : I denie the *Maior*.

Here (faith the Proteftant Relator) the Difputants
iarred, and fo the Writer ceafed.

What this Iarre was, is not fet downe, nor by me remembred,vnleffe it were about this fubfequent Syllogifme.

D. *Featly.* " That *Minor*, which together with the
" *Maior*, inferres the Propofition laft denyed,the whole
" proceffe hauing beene *per directa media* , is pertinent
" to that purpofe to which the Difpute is ordained.

" But the *Minor*, together with the *Maior*, directly
" and neceffarily inferres the Propofition laft denyed ;
" the whole *Proceffus* hauing beene made *per directa
" media.*

" *Ergo*, It is pertinent to that purpofe, to which the
" Difpute is ordained.

M. *Fifher.* " Your *Media* in your Syllogifmes were
" *directa*, but they tended not *ad directum finem.*

If M. *Fifher* did fay thefe words, his meaning may be
gathered out of his former explication : in which he
fhewed,how the direct end of the Difputation was (not
to treat of particular Controuerfies, but) to finde out
firft by other meanes the true vifible Church, whofe
Profeffors names may be fhewed in al ages out of good
Authors. Which being once found,men defirous of fatisfaction , might (as D. *Field* faid) reft in her Iudgement; who otherwife (as Lawyers without a Iudge)
might wrangle in euerie Controuerfie,without end.

Thofe *Media* therefore *directa* (as D. *Featly* tearmed
E   them)

them) might in some sort be so tearmed, as being di-
rected by D. *Featly* to his owne end, of transferring the
Question to particular Controuersies, but not *ad directum
finem*; that is, not ordayned to the direct end of the
whole Disputation : *viz.* To shew a visible Church of
Protestants in al ages, whose names may be shewed out
of good Authors. Which (supposing D. *Featly* would
haue proceeded sincerely) ought to haue beene his onely
end : as M. *Fisher* signified, by saying these words ;
*Responsum nullum dabunt prater vnum quod nunquam da-
bunt, ecce nomina.*

   D. *Featly* therefore had no iust cause to say, as the
" Protestant Relator maketh him say : It is a Bul,
" M. *Fisher*, *media*, *directa*, yet not *ad directum finem* ;
" that is, direct, and not direct : for *media* are said to be
" *directa* onely *ratione finis.*

   D. *Featly* (I say) had no iust cause to say this : and
M. *Sweet* might wel tel him of his fault, in seeking to
transferre the Question from the Church, to particular
points of Faith, as the Protestant Relator saith he did ;
saying :

   " Is not, *Transitio a genere in genus*, a fault in ar-
" guing? &c.

   But M. *Sweet* did not speake these formal words
which the Protestant Relator hath set downe : onely he
asked the Doctors, Whether it seemed strange to them,
that a Question should be transferred by a good Syllogisme : which he said, in regard D. *Featly* endeuored to
proue his argument to be pertinent, because his Syllo-
gismes were good.

   Here D. *Featly* (as the Protestant Relator telleth)
" said : I acknowledge, that *Transitio a genere in genus*,
" is a fault in disputing ; but I neuer heard, that the in-
" ference of the effect by the cause, was *Transitio a
       " ge-

" *genere in genus:* fuch was my argument. For Faith
" in a Beleeuer produceth profeffion and confeffion
" thereof, which makes a vifible member; and the like
" profeffion of many members, a vifible Church, Where
" the caufe is perpetual, the effect muft needes be per-
" petual : Therefore, where the Faith is perpetual, the
" profeffion thereof muft needes be ; and confequently,
" the vifibilitie of the Profeffors thereof, is this *Tran-*
" *fitio a genere in genus?*

But D. *Featly* did not fay al this : yet if he did, it
doth not make any thing againft M. *Sweet :* and for him
to fpeake of the caufe, being obfcure, when the Queftion
is onely about the effect, being more apparant and cleare
(as in our cafe) is a fault in honeft and fincere dealing.
Neyther is M. *Sweets* Logicke leffe to be efteemed, if
he had tearmed that fault, *Tranfitio a genere in genus:*
For a caufe as a caufe, and an effect as an effect doe not
onely differ *fpecie,* but alfo *genere:* and befide, a proofe
a priori and *a posteriori* are diuers kinds of proofes.

"Here (fayth the Proteftant Relator) thofe of
" M. *Fifhers* fide calling for Names, D. *White* faid :
" Where are your Names ?

" This is nothing but apparant tergiuerfation. You
" wil not anfwer any argument directly, nor fuffer vs to
" proceed in our arguments : and therefore I require
" you, M. *Fifher,* according to the order mentioned in
" the beginning, for each partie to haue an houre and a
" halfe for that you now oppofe, and fuffer me to
" anfwer.

" Proue by Chrift and his Apoftles, or by any of the
" Fathers for the firft fix hundred yeeres, thefe prefent
" Tenets of the Roman Church : and then he named
" (as the Proteftant Relator fayth) fixe particular
" Points.

E 2 But

But D. *White* did not fpeake thus, neyther did he in al the Conference make any fuch long difcourfe. Yet if he had fo faid, M.*Fifher* might wel haue anfwered,as the Proteftant Relator faith he did.

M *Fifher*. " When you D. *White*, or D. *Featiy*, haue
" proued your Church to be vifible in al ages, and na-
" med vifible Proteftants ; then wil I fatisfie your de-
" mands.

But before this was done, M. *Fifher* had no reafon to diuert to thofe particular matters,nor to produce Names of Catholikes in al ages ; in regard it was his aduerfaries fault to fpend fo long time in impertinent Syllogifmes, which fhould haue beene imployed in naming and pro-uing Proteftants in al ages:which by the prefcribed me-thod was firft to be done , before M. *Fifher* needed to proue any thing pertaining to the Roman Church.Wor-thily therefore might M. *Sweet* cal for Names of Prote-ftants, and wel might he fay : That if Proteftants had beene in al ages,their Names (at leaft fome) in euery age might be produced.

Vnto which, as the Proteftant Relator faith, D.*Featly*
" replyed, faying : That is a *Non fequitur*, &c. What
" fay you to a People of Africa,who(if we may beleeue
" *Plinie*) haue no Names at al?

" M.*Boulton*. Yet they haue defcriptions, and may
" be knowne by fome *Periphrafis*.

" D. *Featly*. What fay you then to the Heretikes,
" called *Acephali*, who are fo called, becaufe their Head
" and Author cannot be named, nor particularly defcri-
" bed ; yet the Author was a vifible man? Are al vifible
" mens Names vpon record ? Are al the Records that
" were in former times,now to be produced ?

" To this Obiection,M.*Boulton* anfwered:That thofe
" *Acephali* held fome particular Doctrine, which did

" amount

" amount to the nature of a Name, fufficient to diftin-
" guifh them from others; infinuating hereby,that thefe
" *Acephali* were not *Anonymi.*

Further, it may be anfwered, That it is not certaine,
whether they had any particular Author: for fome fay,
That they were a Companie, who in the Controuerfie
betwixt *Iohn* the Bifhop of Antioch, and *Ciril* of Alex-
andria, behaued themfelues like Neutrals , fubmitting
themfelues to neyther, as to their Head. Others thinke,
That they were certaine men, who being the fauorers of
Petrus Mogus the Heretike,did afterwards renounce him
from being their Head,becaufe he would not accurfe the
Councel of Calcedon. Others fay,That one *Seuerus*, Bifhop of Antioch,was their Author.

But howfoeuer this particular were, it doth not conclude,That there could be in al ages vifible Profeffors of
the Proteftants Faith, whereof no Storie nor other ancient Monument maketh mention of Names,or Opinions,
or Places of abode of any of them,or of thofe who op-
pofed them : as Stories make mention of fome of thefe
circumftances, both of the *Acephali,* and whatfoeuer o-
ther eminent Profeffors of euerie true or falfe Religion.

We doe not require, that al vifible mens names fhould
be vpon record, nor al Records produced. For although
to proue fuch a vifible Church as that of our Sauiour
Chrifts , defcribed in Scripture to be fpread ouer the
World, a fmal number of vifible Profeffors be not fuf-
ficient, as S. *Auguftine* prooueth againft the Donatifts ; *Aug.lib. de vni-*
yet to fhew how confident we are of our caufe, we for *tate Ecclefiæ.*
the prefent onely require , That three eminent Proteftants Names in al ages be produced out of good Authors. But they are fo farre from being able to produce
three,as they cannot name one in euerie age (as is clearely prooued in the Proteftants Apologie) neyther indeed

can

can they abide with any patience, when they be much preſſed in this Point : as appeareth by diuers who haue beene vrged ; and in particular, by D. *Featly*, in this Conference : who hauing beene called vpon ſeueral times to produce Names, as he had vndertaken ; at one time he burſt forth into theſe words, ſet downe by the Proteſtant Relator : *What ? wil nothing content you, but a Buttrie-Booke ? You ſhal haue a Buttrie-Booke, if you wil ſtay a while.*

Note (Reader) this Doctors want of grauitie and patience, and what a fit Title he giueth to a Catalogue of Names of Proteſtants, who (indeed) are more like to be found in a Buttrie-Booke, then in any good Record of Antiquitie : as hauing had their beginning of late in one *Martin Luther* ; who, after his Apoſtaſie, more reſpected the Buttrie, then any Eccleſiaſtical Storie.

But how vnwilling D. *Featly* was to bring out this his Buttrie-Booke, appeareth ; in that after the Auditorie had long ſtayed and often called for the Names of Proteſtants in al ages, which ſhould haue been giuen at firſt ; after not onely Catholikes, but alſo diuers of the Proteſtants (being wearie and not willing to heare any more of his dilatorie and impertinent Syllogiſmes) had entreated him to giue ouer his arguments, and to produce Names.

Firſt, he ſaid : If I ſhould giue ouer, M. *Fiſher* would ſay of me, as he ſaid of D. *White*, That I was at a *Non-plus* : and therefore I wil goe forward in arguing.

To which, M. *Fiſher* ſaid : Then wil I goe forward in anſwering.

But the Companie earneſtly calling for Names, D. *Featly* bad the Writer ſet downe in writing, That

he

he was willing to proceed ; but to satisfie the Companie, he would diuert vnto the Names.

Which M. *Fisher* seeing to be written, said : Vnlesse this be blotted out, it shal be set downe for Answer ; That *hitherto D.* Featly *hauing diuerted from the chiefe end of the Question, wil now speake to the purpose.*

M. *Sweet* also said : That it was a manifest wrong. Whereupon the former words were blotted out.

And it was written (as the Protestant Relator sayth)
" *That both the Disputants being willing to proceede,*
" *D.* Featly *was desired by the Companie, to produce the*
" *Names of such Protestants as were extant before Lu-*
" *ther, in al ages.*

This being written, and subscribed both by D. *Featly* and M. *Fisher*, D. *Featly* proceeded to his Induction. But before he would begin to name any, he first endeauoured to fore-stal his hearers with an il opinion against M. *Fisher*, saying :

There is no credit to be giuen to this man, who not onely slandered D. *White* in a former Conference, but also falsely writ what passed betwixt M. *Musket* and my selfe, in a certaine Disputation.

M. *Fisher* hearing this false slander, did rise vp , and for the honour of the Truth, and clearing of his Credit, did (before the Audience) solemnely protest, vpon his Conscience, That wittingly and willingly he did neuer wrong eyther D. *White*, or D. *Featly*, in report of any former Conference. And if any thing were false written, it was not willingly : but, as the Protestant Writer of this present Conference hath sometimes mistaken the words of the Disputants ; which, as he (being warned) did correct : so did I (said M. *Fisher.*)

To

To this,nothing was replyed : and therefore I ſuppoſe that the Audience was wel ſatisfied of M. *Fiſhers* ſincerritie in his Relation, and writing of the former Diſputations.

After this, D. *Featly* named for the firſt age, our Lord and Sauior Chriſt, and the Twelue Apoſtles, and S. *Paul,* and S. *Ignatius :* after which he ſtayed a while, as if he ſtudyed for more Names ; but not remembring any more, whom he would ſet downe for the firſt age, he ſaid : Theſe, not denying others, may ſerue for the firſt age.

Then turning to M. *Fiſher,* he ſaid : Let vs diſpute of theſe. No, ſaid M. *Fiſher* ; name firſt of al ages. What ? ſaid D. *Featly,* wil you not diſpute of Chriſt and his Apoſtles ? *Yes,* ſaid M. *Fiſher, in due place :* but firſt name the reſt in al ages, and then I wil anſwer you. What ? ſaid D. *Featly,* doe not Chriſt and his Apoſtles deſerue the firſt place ? M. *Fiſher :* I wil not anſwer, before you haue named the reſt.

Then, ſaid D. *Featly,* in a heat : Wel, you wil not diſpute of Chriſt and his Apoſtles ? Then you grant, Chriſt and his Apoſtles to be Proteſtants. And ſo inſtantly (without expecting M. *Fiſhers* anſwer) he turned himſelfe to the Audience, and ſaid : *He grants Chriſt and his Apoſtles to be Proteſtants.* Whereupon diuers of the Audience made ſuch a ſhowt (as if they had gotten a Victorie) with ſuch a noyſe, as M. *Fiſher* endeuouring to anſwer, for a time could not be heard. But he riſing vp, and with his Hand and Voyce crauing ſilence, made ſuch as would heare him, vnderſtand how falſely D. *Featly* had ſlandered him to his Face ; and eyther then, or vpon ſome like occaſion, he ſaid : *What may I expect behind my backe , when you thus miſ-report me to my Face ?*

                                                              And

And in this fort when many of the company were willing to depart, D. *Featly* (being called vpon as it feemed) by fome of his companions to goe away, did arife and offer to begone: yet in his ryfing he turned to *M. Fisher*, faying : *Will you difpute vpon Chrift and his Apo-ftles, or no?* To which *M. Fisher* fayd, *I will, if you will ftay,* And ftretching out his hand, he tooke D. *Featly* by his arme, offering to ftay him, yet he in that abrupt man-ner went away.

This is the true Relation of this laft paffage; by which the falfhood of that Relation which is made by the Proteftant Relator, may appeare: For to make the beft of D. *Featly* his Tergiuerfation, or rather plaine flight from proceeding in his Induction, and to caft fome colour ouer the matter, by which he may make Proteftants belieue, that D. *Featly* had reafon, and M. *Fisher* was to blame; Firft he maketh *M. Fisher* fay, *Tou shall not begin with Chrift and his Apoftles:* as if M. *Fisher* had prohibited him to begin with the names of Chrift and his Apoftles, which he did not : neyther did he fay thofe words at all, which the Relator reporteth. Se-condly he fuppreffeth in filéce *M. Fishers* expreffe yeal-ding to difpute about Chrift and his Apoftles, which M. *Fisher* did expreffe two feuerall tymes: once thus; *I will difpute of them in due place:* the fecond tyme when D. *Featly* would needs begon, and in going asked, will you difpute or no? thus, *I will, if you will ftay* . Thirdly he relateth a Syllogifme to be made in this laft paffage, which is not remembred; but if it were, it was very impertinent to an Induction, and may eafily be anf-wered out of that which was formerly fayd againft a like Syllogifme called by D. *Featly, A Demonftration à pri-ori,* but is proued not to be fo much worth as a proba-ble proofe *à pofteriori.* Fourthly he relateth a coniuring

F   charge

charge to haue byn made by D . *Featly* to M. *Fisher*, in this laft paffage , which was not made .

But to returne to the breaking vp of the Conferéce. So foone as D. *Featly* had in the abrupt manner afore-fayd , gone away, and left M. *Fisher* and M. *Sweete*, and diuers others of good ranke fitting at , or neere about the Table, amongft whome was the *Earle of Warwick*, who not liking (as it feemed) that the matter fhould end in that illfafhion , made a fpeach to M. *Fisher* , and tould him, that the Doctour fhould come againe , and giue the reft of the Names of Proteftant Profeffours af-ter fome dayes, it being requifite that the Doctour fhould haue tyme to ftudy for them. To which M. *Fisher* fayd, he was willing he fhould take tyme. Then the wryting of fuch things as had paffed in the Confe-rence (being fubfcribed vnder D. *Featly*, and M. *Fishers* hands) was wrapped vp in a paper, and fealed vp with three feales, one with my Lord of *Warwicks*, and the o-ther with two other feales, & left in *Syr Humfrey Lynde* hands, or fome other Proteftant , with promife that it fhould be kept vnopened till the next meeting , and that M *Fisher* afterwards fhould haue it , or a true cop-py of it : which promife hath not yet been performed, partly by reafon the next meeting was prohibited; but by whofe meanes this prohibition came, although I will not Cenfure (as the Proteftant Relator fayth, a Romanift hath confidently auerred) that the Prote-ftant party laboured to haue all future meetings, touch-ing this occafion, forbidden, becaufe they cannot make good that which they haue vndertaken about naming of Proteftant Profeffors in all ages ; yet I cãnot hinder men to haue fuch like fufpicion, becaufe I know it is impoffible for Proteftants to performe that vndertakẽ Taske.

                                        Now

Now whereas my felf haue heard that fome fufpe-
&ed, that the Catholike party had made meanes to get
the fecond meeting hindered, this idle fancy hath no
foundation of any probability. For all Catholikes are
confident, that Proteftants can neuer produce out of
good Authours, Names of the Profeffors of this their
new Reformation, no more then any other Sect of
Heretikes can produce the Names of men of their profeffion in all Ages fince Chrift : whereas Roman Catholikes in their printed Bookes ordinarily fet downe
the Names of their Profeffors, and chiefe Paftors in all
Ages : And foe the victory being fo certaine on their
fide, they had no reafon to hinder the meeting, wherby this queftion fhould be determined, efpecially in
fuch fort as is prefcribed in *M. Fishers* fecond paper (a-
boue rehearfed) written before the laft meeting. And
in particuler for *M Fisher* and *M. Sweet*, it is moft certaine, that they much defired the fecōd meeting, as may
appeare : Firft, in that the next day after the laft meeting, they went to *Syr Humfrey Lynds* houfe, offering to
giue vnto him a Catalogue of Names of fuch as they
would defend to haue been Profeffors of the Roman
Fayth in all Ages, that he might deliuer it to D . *Featly*
and D. *White* to confider of agaynft the next meeting,
vpon condition that they fhould alfo reciprocally deliuer vp to *M. Fisher*, & *M. Sweete*, a Catalogue of fuch
as they would defend to haue been Proteftants in all
Ages, to be confidered off againft the fayd next day of
meeting. The which offer feemed to another Proteftāt
(who was then in *Syr Humfrey Lynds* company) very
reafonable and equall. But *Syr Humfrey* fayd: *No, I know
the Doctors mynds, that they will not giue vp any Catalogue before the very meeting :* and he asked *M. Fisher*, why he did
fo much preffe the Doctors for names of men of their

profef-

profeſſion in all Ages? To whome M. *Fisher* anſwered
that the reaſon (to deale plainly) was, becauſe he was
fully perſwaded, that they could not giue vp any ſuch
Names. After this M. *Fisher* and M. *Sweete* reflecting v-
pon Syr *Humfreys* words, began to ſuſpect, that there
would be no more meeting, vnles the *Earle* of *Warwicke* (who had engaged himſelfe by his word to M. *Fisher* that it ſhould be) did preſſe the Doctours vnto it:
wherfore it ſeemed good that the *Earle* ſhould be moued heerunto by a letter writté by M. *Fisher* vnto him,
the copy wherof I haue thought good , to inſert heere
as followeth .

    Right Honourable Lord .

    I eſteeme it a ſpeciall prouidéce of God, that your
Lordſhip was preſent at a late Conference, wherin D.
White and D. *Featly* vndertooke to ſhew againſt me, &
my companion , that the Proteſtant Church had been
viſible in all Ages , and that their Profeſſors might be
named, eſpecially in all Ages, before *Luther* .   Your
Lordſhip may remember the ſubſtáce of all the proofe
to haue conſiſted in this, *That the true Church was alwayes
ſo viſible, as the Profeſſors therof in all Ages might be named: But
the Proteſtants was the true Church* ; we retuſed to diſpute
of the *Minor* , becauſe it transferred the queſtion , and
auoyded that plaine proofe of the viſible Church,
which was then propounded and expected. If, as they
conclude, they are able to name their Profeſſors in all
Ages , why did they refuſe to giue vs a Catalogue of
theirs, as we were ready to haue giuen them another
of ours ? Why went they about to proue they were a-
ble to name them, when with leſſe adoe they might
haue named them ? Where deeds are iuſtly expected,
words without deeds are worthily ſuſpected.

    Certainly heerby they are ſo farr from hauing diſ-
char-

charged themſelues, of the great enterpriſe they vndertooke, as they ſtand more engaged then before to the
performance of it: for hauing now profeſſed and acknowledged that the true Church, or (to vſe their owne
words) the Church which is ſo viſible as the true Catholike Church ought to be, (and the Church whoſe
fayth is *eternall* and *vnchanged*, muſt be) is able to name
her Profeſſors in all Ages, eyther for their owne honour, and for the ſatisfaction of the world, they muſt
ſet downe the Names of their Profeſſors in all Ages, or
els they ſhamefully diſcouer themſelues not to be that
true and viſible vnchanged Church which is able to
name them. Againe, at the length yealding as they did
to ſhew the continuall viſibility of their Church, by a
full induction of their viſible Proteſtants in all Ages
(which they ſeemed to vndertake with great confidence) why did they ſticke in the firſt Age alone, refu-
ſing to name their Profeſſors in the Ages following,
vntill the firſt were tryed? May not the Anſwerer
chooſe to deny which parte of the Argument he plea-
ſeth? And was it euer heard that he ſhould be inforced
to reply to one propoſition alone, before the whole
Argument, whether it were Syllogiſme or Induction,
were fully propounded? Very Nobly therfore, & prudently your Lordſhip in the end deſired another meeting, not doubting that your owne party within 3. or
4. dayes, would be content to giue vs the Names of
their Profeſſors in all Ages, as we were ready to giue
them the Names of ours, that therby both ſides might
be the better prepared for a ſecond Tryall, which whē
they haue performed, we ſhall not fayle to encounter
with them, eyther by way of ſpeach or wryting, as
your Lordſhip (all things conſidered) ſhall thinke fai-
reſt, or ſafeſt, or moſt conuenient for the diſcouery of
Truth.   F 3   But

But if your Lordſhip ſhall not be able to obtaine at their hands this your moſt iuſt and important Requeſt, the defect of proof on their part muſt needs be accounted a plaine flight; and no man hereafter can prudently relye his ſaluation vpon that Church, which (for want of perpetuall viſibility proued) they themſelues ſhall haue concluded to be falſe and faygned.

Thus expecting the yſſue heerof, and your Lordſhips further pleaſure from the mouth of this bearer, I remaine, this firſt of Iuly 1623.

Your Lordſhips ſeruant in Chriſt,
Iohn Fiſher.

By this Letter it may appeare how willing *M. Fiſher* and *M. Sweete* were, and yet are, of their part, to haue the matter ſoundly proſecuted, eyther by meeting or wryting. And I haue heard that the Earle to whome this letter was written, did ſend to *D. Featly,* ſo, as although there be a prohibition of meeting, yet it is expected that by way of writing *D. Featly* goe forward to performe his vndertaken Taske, and ſetting downe firſt the Names of ſuch as he iudgeth to haue been Proteſtant Profeſſors in euery Age ſince Chriſt : And then prouing out of good Authors, thoſe whome he nameth, to haue byn members of the Proteſtant Church, not condemning any one point wherin Proteſtants at this day do differ from the auncient and Roman Church, and eſpecially in any one of the 39. Articles which Engliſh Proteſtant Miniſters are ſworne vnto; and therfore ſo long as *D. Featly,* and *D. White* ſhall be ſilent, and not ſo much as by writing giue a Catalogue of Names of the Profeſſors of their Church, all ſorts of people may iuſtly take this their fayling for a flight, and for a ſilent graunting, that they haue not

had

had viſible Proteſtants in all Ages, whoſe Names may
be ſhewed out of good Authors, as the queſtion required. Wherupon followeth, that the Proteſtant Church
is not the true Church of Chriſt, nor the Preachers
therof lawfully ſent to teach, nor people ſecurely warranted to heare and learne of them, what is, and what
is not to be belieued, by Fayth neceſſary to ſaluation.

CHAP. III.
Of the yſſue of the Conference.

" THe Proteſtant Relator ſayth, that the iſſue of
" the Conference was, that the aforeſaid M. Bug-
" ges came to Syr Humfrey Lynd, & gaue him many thā-
" kes for the ſayd meeting, and aſſured him he was
" well reſolued now of his Religion; that he ſaw
" plainly that it was but the Ieſuits bragging without
" proofes: and wheras formerly by their Sophiſticall
" perſwaſions he was in ſome doubt of the Church, he
" is now ſo fully ſatisfied of the truth of our Religion,
" that he doth vtterly diſclaime the Popiſh Prieſts cō-
" pany, and their doctrine alſo.

I haue cauſe to doubt that this which the Relator
ſayth, is not true, for therby he maketh the old Gentleman to be but of a weake capacity, or of a very muta-
ble nature. For firſt I am ſure, there was no cauſe giuen
in the Conference of any ſuch effectuall reſolution to
be made by the old Gentleman. Secondly I cannot ſee
when this ſpeach ſhould be made by the Gentlemā to
Syr Humfrey. If immediatly after the Conference, it
would argue toto much want of capacity: for if he did
but rightly conceiue the true ſtate of the queſtion, in
which himſelfe had eſpecially deſired to be ſatisfied (as
I verily

I verily hope he did) he might eaſily haue marked the
inſufficiency of *D. Featly* his diuerting proofes, which
alſo were ſo anſwered, as the Audience for want of ſatisfaction in them, vrged him to leaue off, & to produce
Names of Proteſtáts in all Ages: the which producing
of Names being ſo often and earneſtly required to be
done in all Ages, and yet being only pretended (and
that moſt falſely) to be done for one Age, and the Cōference being ſo abruptly left of by *D . Featly* before he
would go forward to name men in other Ages, eſpecially in Ages before *Luther*, as the Queſtion required ;
any meane capacity might ſee, that the Queſtion in
which the old Gentleman deſired to be ſatisfied, was
not fully anſwered, nor conſequently he ſatisfied .

Moreouer the ſame Gentleman being preſent whē
the *Earle* of *Warwick* told *M. Fisher*, that *D. Featly* ſhould
at another tyme come againe to giue Names of Proteſtants in other Ages, he might eaſily, and doubtles did,
vnderſtand that as yet Names in all Ages were not giuen, nor conſequently the Queſtion ſatisfied, in which
he expected anſwere . Furthermore preſently after he
went away from the Conference, he told *M. Fisher*
himſelfe, that he was glad, that at the next meeting his
Queſtion ſhould be anſwered, which ſhewed that as
yet he did not conceiue it to be anſwered .

Laſtly, diuers dayes after all the trouble and ſtyrre
was paſt (which was made about the Conference)
the old Gentleman was not ſo reſolute a Proteſtant as
the Relator pretendeth : for meeting *M. Fisher* and *M.
Sweete*, he deſired them to giue him a Catalogue of
Names of Profeſſors of the Romā Church, ſaying, that
if after this the Doctors ſhould not giue him a Catalogue of Proteſtants, he ſhould diſlike their cauſe . Which
Catalogue M. *Fisher* and *M. Sweete* haue ready for him,
                                              but

but will not deliuer, till he get the Doctours to make theirs ready, that he may bring to them the Doctours Catalogue with one hand, and receiue theirs with the other to deliuer to the Doctours.

All that can be suspected is, that in the very tyme of the sayd styrre when the oldGentleman eyther was, or feared to be called in question, it may perhaps be, that he might say thofe words which the Relator mētioneth; but this (if it were) was only vpon frailty or humane feare of trouble, and not any firme and settled refolution grounded vpon the Conference; fith both before and after he shewed a contrary mynd, as hath byn fayd.

As for other idle and falfe reports of a great Lady(a), or any other Catholiks fayd to haue ben turned Proteftants vpon this Conference, I neglect them as being notorioufly falfe. It may be that fome Weaklings who not being prefent at the Conference, nor hauing commodity to heare what paffed, but from the lying lyps of fome Proteftants (*Who reported that Fisher was ouercome, and had yielded Christ and his Apostles to be Proteftants*) fome Weaklings I fay, might perhaps be ftaggered, vntill they heard the true report, that this was only an impudent flaunder, vttered by *D. Featly*, but in words and deeds contradicted by *M. Fisher*. But I make no queftion fo foone as thefe shall fee or heare what is heere related, they will be well fatisfied and confirmed in the Catholike truth; and that euen Proteftants themfelues, will be moued to harken more after the matter. And in cafe their Doctours doe not giue them a better Catalogue of Names of Proteftants in all Ages, then they did in this Conference, they will doubt, as they haue caufe, that the Proteftant Church hath not byn fo vifible in all Ages, as (euen

(a) This great Lady did exprefly fay: that the conferēce did make a-gainft Proteftants, euen as it was related by you Proteftant relator.

And another Lady, who was prefent at the conferēce did proteft(to one that afked her, how it moued her) that she was by it confirmed in Catholique religion,

by gion,

by D. *Featly* his argument is proued) the true **Catholike** Church ought to be; and consequently that it is not the true Catholike Church, which in their Creede they professe to belieue, and out of which (as euen *Caluin* confesseth) they cannot hope for remission of their sinnes, nor saluation of their soules.

CHAP. IIII.

Contayning a Reuiew, and Reflection vpon the Premisses.

NOw hauing made an end of this Relation, I am to intreate the Gentle Reader, to reuiew it, or reflect vpon it, and to call to mind and marke. 1. The occasion, and consequently the end of the disputation. 2. The Question and true meaning of it. 3. What Methode was most fit to haue been obserued in treating of this question. 4. What course was taken by the Protestant Disputant, & what by the Catholike Respondent. All which being duely considered, thou wilt better see what is to be iudged of the whole Conference, and wilt make to thy selfe more benefit of the matter treated in it, then perhaps hitherto thou hast done.

§. 1. *About the Occasion, and end of the Conference.*

1. The occasion of this Dispute was, as thou hast heard in the Relation, that a certaine old Protestant Gentleman was told (as the truth is) that there is no saluation out of the true Catholike Church, and that to belieue the Catholike Church, is one of the Articles of the Creed, which euery Christian is bound to belieue and know: and that this Church was no other besides

besides the most auncient and vniuersally spread ouer the world, the knowne Catholike Roman Church, which hath had, and can yet shew visible Pastours & other Professors in all Ages: and that the Protestant Church (wherof for the present, he was a member) sprung vp of late, and could not be the true Church of Christ, as not hauing had (as Chrifts true Church ought to haue) Pastours and Doctours, and lawfully fent Preachers fo visible, as the Names of them may be shewed in all Ages out of good Authors. And this was the occasion of the difpute ; for heerupon the old Gentleman was fo much moued in confcience to doubt of the Proteftants Religion, that he could not be quiet till he had made meanes to get this matter difcuffed in a Conference betwixt Catholike and Protestant Deuines, in fuch fort as in the Relation hath byn told. And therfore, the end of this Conference was to giue this old Gentleman and others that should heare it, fatisfaction in this most important & neceffary point. I call this point, *most important and neceffary*, in regard the certainty of euery other point belieued by infallible diuine Fayth, neceffary to faluation, dependeth vpon it. For although euery point belieued by diuine Faith be in it felfe moft true, and by reafon of the Diuine reuelation (made knowne to the world by Chrift & his Apoftles) moft certaine and infallible ; yet this truth & infallible certainty therof is not made knowne to vs (according to the ordinary courfe of Gods prouidence) but only by the meanes which God hath appointed, to wit, by Paftors, Doctors, and Preachers of the true visible Church of Chrift.

Eph. 4. v. 11 &c.
Rom. 10. v. 14. &c.

§. 2. *About*

§. 2. *About the Question and meaning of it.*

The Queſtion propounded to be treated in the
Conference vpon the occaſion, and for the end afore-
ſayd, was.

Whether the Proteſtant Church was viſible in all Ages,
" *eſpecially in the Ages before* Luther : *and whether*
" *the Names of ſuch viſible Proteſtants may be ſhewed*
" *in all Ages, out of good Authors?*

The reaſon why this queſtion was propoſed rather
then any other, was, for that the old Gentleman was
already perſwaded that there muſt be in all Ages a viſible Church of Chriſt, hauing in it viſible Paſtors &
Doctors, and lawfully ſent Preachers who are by Almighty God appointed and authorized to teach, and
of whom all ſorts of people are commaunded & warranted to learne infallible Fayth neceſſary to ſaluatio.
And further, that this Church, and theſe her Paſtors &
Preachers, haue byn in all Ages paſt, not only viſible,
but ſo viſible as the Names at leaſt of ſome Paſtours
teaching, and ſome people learning the true Fayth in
all Ages, might be produced out of good Authors. And
therfore, as he had heard, the Roman Catholiks made
no difficulty to produce out of good Authors the Names of their Paſtors & people in all Ages : ſo he much
deſired to heare, whether the Names of Proteſtant Paſtors and Preachers in all Ages could not alſo be produced out of good Authors : for if they could, he meant
to remaine a Proteſtant as he had been all his life time :
but if they could not, he thought it neceſſary to leaue
the Proteſtants, and to adhere to the Roman Church,
to learne of it Faith neceſſary to ſaluation.

By

By this appeareth that the fenfe and meaning of the Queftion could be no other then that which M *Fisher* explicated in the Conference : viz. *Whether the Prote-stant Church was in all Ages fo vifible, especially in the Ages before* Luther, *as the Names of Proteftant Paftors and Preachers in all Ages may be shewed out of good Authors.* And further that in cafe the Proteftant Difputant ſhould vndertake (as he did tooto boldly vndertake) the affirmatiue part, faying, and offering to proue in generall, that the Names of fuch Paftors and Preachers of Proteftāt Religion may be ſhewed in all Ages out of good Authors ; it ſhould further be required (as *M.Fisher* required of him) that he ſhould actually name in particular in euery feuerall Age fuch Paftors and Preachers as he thought he could proue and defend to be Proteftants. For if the Queftion had not been thus vnderftood, it ſhould not haue been anfwerable to the occafion and end aboue fayd . Neyther could the Proteftant Difputant fufficiently fatisfie the doubt of the old Gentlemā, being chiefly caufed in that he had heard, that no Proteftant could name Paftors and Preachers of his profeffion in all Ages out of good Authors ; So as (to fatisfy this doubt)it was not fufficient only to fay, nor only in generall to proue by fuch Syllogifmes as D. *Featly* made, (which were fuch as the old Gentleman (I dare fay)did not vnderftand)that the Names of Pro-teftants in all Ages may be ſhewed, but as M.*Fisher* had ſhewed him a printed booke, in which Roman Ca-tholike Paftours and people were in particuler named in all Ages : fo he expected Proteftant Paftours, and people of all Ages to be named in particuler, and after proued and defended to be Proteftants, as *M. Fisher* was ready to proue and defend whom he would in particuler name, to be Roman Catholikes.

Further-

Furthermore although it may seeme to some not
much materiall, whether the Proteſtant Diſputant
hath begun to name firſt thoſe of the firſt Age, & next
of the ſecond, and ſo downward vntill *Luther*, or cō-
trarywiſe to beginne with *Luther* and ſo vpward till
the Apoſtles and Chriſt ; yet both the words of the
Queſtion, & the doubt of the old Gentleman had byn
far better ſatisfied, and the Tergiuerſation which D.
Featly vſed in the firſt age auoyded, if M. *Fisher* had vrged him, as he might, firſt to beginne with the Age
immediatly before *Luther* (a confeſſed Proteſtant) and
ſo go vpward vntill Chriſt , the confeſſed Fountayne
of infallible perpetuall vnchanged Truth : for then it
would haue been cleerly ſeene , euen by the Confeſſiō
of learned Proteſtants, particularly *Luther* himſelfe and
others; that thoſe who eyther are named, or can yet
be named by *D.Featly*, after he hath ſought (as I am
told he went to ſeeke) Records in the great Library in
Oxford, were not viſible Proteſtants, but of a different
Profeſſion, Fayth, and Religion, and ſo different, as
that they cannot be iuſtly deemed members of one and
the ſame Proteſtant Church with *Luther*, after his Apoſtacy from his Religious Order, and reuolt from the
Roman Catholike Fayth. For proofe wherof, I for
breuityes ſake do refer euery one who deſireth full ſatisfaction in this point, to what is largely related and
proued in the Proteſtants Apology, in diuers places ,

(1) Luth. ep. but particularly *tract. 2. cap. 2. sect. 11. subdiuision 3.* And
ad Argentin. will only content my ſelfe to cyte theſe few teſtimo-
anno 1525. nyes for their ſakes, who haue not commodity to ſee
(2) Conradus that booke.
Schuſhelb. in
Theol. Calu.   Firſt therefore (1) *Luther* himſelfe ſayth : *We dare*
lib.2. fol. 130. *boaſt that Chriſt was firſt publiſhed by vs.* Wherefore the
B.verſus finē, Lutheran (2) *Conradus Schushelburg* ſayth : *It is impuden-*
                                                              cy

cy to ſay that many learned men in Germany (and the like is of other Countreys) *before Luther did hould the doctrine of the Lutheran Ghoſpell*. And another (3) of them not only ſayth in effect thus much, but proueth it by this argument : *If there had beene right beleeuers that went before* Luther *in his office, there had beene no need of a Lutheran reformation* . Another ſayth : *It* (4) *is ridiculous to thinke that in the tyme before* Luther *any had the purity of doctrine, and that* Luther *ſhould receaue it from them, & not they from* Luther: *conſidering* (ſayth he) *it is manifeſt to the whole world, that before* Luthers *tyme, all Churches were ouerwhelmed with more then* Cymerian *darkenes, and that* Luther *was diuinely rayſed vp to diſcouer the ſame, & to reſtore the light of true doctrine*. And leaſt this may be thought to haue beene only the conceipt of *Luther* and *Lutherans* (who yet could better tell then D. *Featly*, D. *White*, and ſuch other new Maiſters) I will add heereunto what is ſayd, firſt by (5) *Caluin*, who doth acknowledge, *That in this Lutheran reformation, there was made a diſceſſion or departure from all the world* . Secondly by (6) *Bucer*, who calleth *Luther; the firſt Apoſtle of the reformed doctrine*. Thirdly, by *Beza* (7) a principall Caluiniſt, who teacheth that at this tyme, ordinary vocation of the Church-men was no where extant, and conſequently teacheth, that ther was at that tyme no viſible Church; and ſo if any Church at all, it was only inuiſible, as is affirmed euē by our owne Engliſh Proteſtant Deuines , namely M. (8) *Iewel*, who ſayth, *The truth was vnknown and vnheard of* when Martin Luther *and* Vldericke Zuinglius *firſt came to the knowledge and preaching of the Ghoſpel*. And M. *Perkins* (9) who ſayth : *We ſay, that before the dayes of* Luther, *for the ſpace of many hundred yeares an vniuerſall Apoſtacy ouerſpread the whole face of the earth, and that our* (Proteſtant) *Church was not viſible to the World.*

I might

(3) Geo. Mylli. in Auguſtanæ Confeſſionis explic. art. 7ᵒ de Eccl. pag.
137 .
(4) Benedict Morgeſt . trac. de Eccl, pag. 145.

(5) Calu. in l. epiſt. ep. 141.
(6) Bucer. ep. ad Epiſ. Hereford.
(7) Beza in Theol. ep. epi. 5.
(8) Iewell in his Apolog. of the Church. 4 c. diuiſ. 2 & in his defence 42 .
(9) Perkins in expoſit. of the Creed .

I might adde many more (✝) teftimonyes of o-
thers, who eyther in expreffe teaimes, or in effect affirme the Proteftant Church to haue beene in many
Ages before *Luther* latent, and altogeather inuifible:
which indeed was the common opinion of Proteftãts
at their firft vpryfing; who on the one fide thought
they could with fhiftes, bettter anfwere places of fcripture, which made often and honourable mention of
the Church, then they could anfwere the euidence of
Hiftories, and of their owne experience fhewing that
no vifible Proteftants were extant before themfelues :
But now of late, diuers plaine places of Scripture and
Fathers hauing beene produced, and fuch euident reafons deduced out of them, prouing ineuitably that the
true Church of Chrift, of which all forts muft learne
infallible fayth neceffary to faluation, muft needes be
vifible in all Ages, as, to omitt others, are thefe : *My*

Ifa. 59. v. 21.   *fpirit which is in thee, and my wordes which I haue put in thy
mouth, shall not depart out of thy mouth, nor out of the mouth of
thy feede, nor out of the mouth of thy feedes feede from hence-*

Ifa. 61, 9,   *forth for euer*. Againe: *Their feed shall be knowne in Nations, and their branches among people : all that fee them, shall
know them, that thefe are the feed which our Lord hath bleffed.*

Ifa. 60, 11,   Againe: *Thy gates shalbe opened continually day and night,
they shall not be shut, that the ftrength of the Nations and their*

Matth. 5, 14,   *kinges may enter into thee : for the nation and kingdome which
shall not ferue thee, shall perish. You are the light of the world :
a Citty built vpon a hill cannot be hid . Tell the Church &c .*

Matth. 18, 17, *He that will not heare the Church, let him be vnto thee as an*
Matth. 28, 19, *heathen and Publican. Going, teach all Nations, baptizing them*
&c.   *&c. Behould I am with you* (to wit, your felues, and fucceffors teaching and baptizing) *all dayes vntill the end of
the world*. Conformable to which Scriptures, are alfo
innumerable plaine places of ancient Fathers, which
                                                        may be

may bee feene in *Coccius* : and among others S. Augu- Coccius in
ftine who faith: *that the Church being built vppon a mou-* thefauro Cō-
tayne cannot be hid . trouerfiarum,
    Out of thefe, and other plaine places of tomo 1.lib. 8.
of Scriptures & Fathers, euident Reafons allo may be art. 1.
Aug. in pfal.
deduced , fhewing that the Church muft needs bee 47.lib.de vnit.
vifibie in all ages. As for example , that otherwife it Ecclef. cap.16.
cannot bee fuch a Church as Chrift did inftitute: nor & 25.
could it pertorme thofe offices which Chrift appointed
it to pertorme: nor could thofe which were in it be
inftructed by it: nor thofe which were out of it be cō-
uerted to it: nor Heretiques (pretending to be the
Church) cōvinced not to be it. Wherfore our later Pro-
teitants being not able to fayle any longer againft
this ineuitable *Scylla,* without apparent daunger to
fplit their boate, would needes (rather then turne
back to the fafe hauen of the vifible Catholique Roman Church) aduenture vpon the *Charybdis* of con-
temning all Monuments of ancient hiftories , and the
plaine experience of their primitiue Proteftant Patri-
arches, hoping to efcape by landing vpon the imagi-
nary Iland of inuifible recordes, fuppofed to haue byn
written, and after fuppreffed in the pretended Popes
perfecution of the vifible Members of their inuifible
Church, in the Ages before *Luther,* (a fhift very vnfafe
and fuch, as if it were good, might ferue any other
Sect of ancient, or prefent Heretiques, (as well as our
moderne Proteftants) if they would pretend to haue
had a continuall vifible Church of their profeffion .)
But alas, who feeth not, that thefe be meere imagina-
ry *Chymæra's* , or dreames ? For if any fuch people had
beene (practizing efpecially rites of their religion ,
though neuer fo fecretly) they could not euen with a
Giges ring haue paffed vnfeene, but eyther with their
       H   pofitiue

positiue profeſſion of their owne doctrine, which in
ſome caſes obligeth all true beleeuers, or at leaſt with
negatiue profeſſion of fayth, by which all faychfull
men, and at all tymes are obliged neuer to make ſhew
and profeſſion of a contrary religion; they, or ſome of
them could not chooſe but to haue beene noted. And
if for that cauſe any perſecution were in that age, as
is ſuppoſed, infallibly they would haue beene taken
(as others of other Religions, in like caſes ordinarily
are taken) and impriſoned, or otherwiſe ſo puniſhed,
as the world could not haue beene ignorant of their
perſons, nor Hiſtoryes ſet out by friendes or enemies
ſilent, in ſetting downe (as vſually is done) their
names, conditions, opinions, puniſhments, and perſecutions, in ſuch tyme, ſuch place &c. And if ſuch recordes of ſuch conſpicuous things had been ſet down
in hiſtoryes, it is not poſſible that the memory of ſuch
notorious matters could be razed both out of bookes,
and out of the mindes of men, who without booke do
continually deliuer in words to their ſucceſſors what
they ſaw with their eyes, or heard with their eares of
their predeceſſors, or read in books to haue byn don to
ſuch perſons as profeſſed ſuch a Religion, or to haue
beene done to ſuch bookes, in which mention was
made of ſuch perſecution, made againſt profeſſors of
that Religion.

    To ſay therefore that ſuch perſons were, and yet
no record in any booke or other memory of them, or
that once ſuch Recordes were, but after were by the
Pope razed, or burned, and yet no mention made in
any booke, or other monument that ſuch razing or
burning of bookes was by ſuch a Pope, at ſuch a tyme
&c. (as we can yet out of good Recordes tell the
bookes bnrned by Diocleſian the Grande Perſecutor
                                                        of

of Chriſtians:) To ſay (I ſay) this, is ſenſeleſſe, and plainely ſheweth, that theſe men who ſought to a-noyd the *Scylla* of an inuiſible Church, by this ſhift fal into the *Charybdis* of ſpeaking againſt ſenſe and expe-rience, and indeed runne backe vpon the *Scylla* of the ſame inuiſible Church ; for auoyding whereof they deuiſed this ſandy ſhift of inuiſible Perſecutours, in-niſible Perſecutions, inuiſible Recordes of nameles (ſuppoſed to be viſibly perſecuted) members of the Proteſtant Church in all Ages before *Luther.* O miſe-ry! O madnes of our poore deceaued Proteſtants! What? Is it poſſible, that *Luther* and *Lutherans*, *Caluin* and *Caluiniſts*, yea our owne Countrey-men prime Proteſtants, conuinced with the cleere euidency of things in their own dayes, and with plaine Recordes of all ancient Monuments for former ages, doe con-feſſe (as you heare euen now) that *Luther* was the firſt that announced, or publiſhed Chriſt; that he was the firſt Apoſtle of the Reformed doctrine ; and this ſo certainely, that they do account it impudency and ri-diculous to ſay, That there were other viſible Prote-ſtants in *Germany* before *Luther*;that they proue by ar-gument this to be impoſſible ; that they acknowledge themſelues in this Lutheran Reformation to haue de-parted from all the world;that at *Luthers* and *Caluins* comming no ordinary vocatiō of Church-men(with-out which the viſible Church cannot be) was extant in any place ; that the Church both then, and for ma-ny hundred yeares before was wholly latent and in-uiſible ? Is it poſſible, I ſay, that all this ſhould be cō-feſſed by the primitiue Parents, and prime Doctours of Proteſtancy, and that now their profeſſed children & ſchollers, and in reſpect of them, Punyes in Prote-ſtant diuinity, dare be ſo bold (as D . *Featly* was in

the

the late conference) to controlle and contradict thofe
his grand Maifters, in not only affirming, but offering to proue by a *Syllogifme,* and by a *Lemonftration à
priori*, that the Proteftant Church hath beene in all
Ages vifible; and (O wonder !) fo vifible, as the names of the particular men may be fhewed in all ages
out of good Authors: and further offering to fecond
this *Syllogifme,* by a full *Induction,* in which he vndertooke actually to fet downe their particuler names in
euery feuerall age ? *Surely* the aforefayd Proteftants,
if they had beene prefent, would haue wondered to
fee fuch boldnes, and would haue cenfured this attépt
to be ridiculous impudency.

By this may appeare how notorioufly the old
Gentleman, and the reft of the Proteftant Audience
were abufed by D . *Featly,* vndertaking fo boldly to
proue both by *fyllogifme* and *Induction,* the affirmatiue
part of the aforefayd queftion, which was propofed to
be treated in the conference, the Negatiue whereof
is fo plainely confefsed by fo many Prime Proteftants,
as now we haue heard .

§. 3. *About the Method.*

Concerning the Method, which had beene fir-
teft to haue beene obferued in treating the aforefayd
Queftion; it is to be noted , that there be two feuerall methodes of finding out infallible diuine truth
in all points neceffary to faluation, the finding wherof was the chiefe end, for which the aforefayd Queftion about the perpetual vifibility of the Church, was
propofed to be treated of.

The firft methode or way is, that euery man
eyther by his owne wit, or by hearing another difcourse

courſe do examine throughly ech particuler point of diuine Fayth, about which Controueſſy, or Queſtion is, or may be made, what is, and what is not to be beleeued vnder payne of damnation; the which requireth , 1. Ability and ſtrength of naturall wit, and skill in Latin, Greeke, Hebrew, and other languages, and ſome art by which he may vnderſtand the tearmes and ſtate of the Queſtion, and all that is written of it . 2. That he reade, or heare , and vnderſtand all that is written of that Queſtion in holy Scriptures, Councells, Fathers, and moderne Writers, and in the originall Languages and Copyes; and what els may be ſayd of it, *pro* and *contra,* by learned Diſputants. 3. That he doe maturely weigh and ponder al that is ſayd, both for the affirmatiue and negatiue part of the Queſtion . 4 . That by prayer and good life he obtaine the aſſiſtance of Gods ſpirit to illuminate his vnderſtanding, in matters which exceed the capacity of his naturall wit . 5 . That all this premiſed , he of himſelfe (without relying vpon the Iudgement of any Church) frame a firme and infallible Iudgement, what is, and what is not to be held, for truth neceſſary to ſaluation ; and this being knowne, by it, as by a rule , to iudge which company of men are , or are not the true viſible Church of Chriſt in al Ages. Now who ſeeth not that this methode, or way of attayning found reſolution in all particuler points of Fayth, & by that to iudge what company of men are, or are not the true viſible Church in all ages , cannot be fit and conuenient to be preſcribed to all , or indeed to any ſort of men, and eſpecially to ſuch, as neither haue extraordinary ability of naturall wit, or skill in languages, nor art requiſite to vnderſtand the tearmes, and ſtate of all Queſtions, nor leaſure to

read

read, or heare, nor ftrength of iudgment to weigh and
ponder all that is, or may be fayd of them, nor fuch
extraordinary guiftes of prayer and other vertues, as
they may prefume to haue gotten particuler afliftance
of Gods fpirit, more then other men, whereby they
may aſſure themſelues, that they in particuler (without relying vpon any Churches iudgement) can firmely and infallibly iudge in euery Queſtion about
points of Fayth, what is, and what is not to beleeued,
as a truth neceſſary to faluation.

   The 2.methode, or way, which indeed is both
moſt eafy, and may giue full fatisfaction to all fortes,
confifteth in thefe 3. points. 1. To beleeue and acknowledge, as euery Chriftian is bound by the articles of his Creed, that there is, and hath beene in all
Ages a vifible Catholique Church of Chrift, which is
the Pillar of truth, and in it a vifible company of Paftours and Doctours, and lawfully fent Preachers, affifted by the fpirit of God (who haue
learned of their predeceſſours, and they of theyrs,
ftill vpwardes vntill Chrift his Apoftles, who learned of Chrift, and Chrift of God his Father,
the infallible Truth in all pointes of fayth) of
whome by Gods appointment all forts haue in all A-
ges paft (as appeareth by Hiftoryes) learned, and muft
in tymes prefent, and to come, learne the infallible
truth in all matters of Chriftian fayth neceſſary to faluation. The 2. is, to difcerne which company of
Chriftians are this vifible Church of Chrift, and who
be thefe Paftours, Doctours, and lawfully fent Preachers, of whome all forts of men may fecurely learne
what is, and what is not to be held for infallible truth
in all matters of fayth neceſſary to faluation. The 3.
is, to heare and belieue, and obey whatfoeuer this
           Company

Iſa. 59.v.21.
60.v.11.61.v.
9.
1.Tim.3.v.15.
Ephef. 4.v.4.
11.11.13.14.
Tertul. lib. de
præfcript.

Company of Chriſtians haue in all Ages taught, and what the preſent ordinary Paſtours, Doctours, and Preachers thereof do teach to be diuine and infallible truth, neceſſary to ſaluation : which to do, will not be hard to thoſe, who do truely feare and loue God, and be meeke, and humble in hart, and who can, and will for the loue and ſeruice of Chriſt captiuate their vnderſtanding, and ſubmit it to the obedience of faith, which muſt be done by mortifying and denying their owne priuate opinion, that they may follow the ſenſe and iudgment of Chriſt, ſpeaking in, and by his Ca-tholike Church, *VVhich whoſoeuer heareth, beleeueth, & obeyeth, doth heare, beleeue, and obey Chriſt.* And, *VVho-ſoeuer contemneth, or will not heare, beleeue, and obey the Church, he contemneth Chriſt, and by Chriſts owne cenſure is to be accounted, as an Heathen or Publican.*

Luc. 10.v. 16. Matth. 18.v. 17

Now, concerning the firſt and third of theſe points, as no doubt or difficulty was moued either by the old Gentleman, or Syr *Humfrey Lynde*, or the Doctours, or any other of the Company preſet at the Conference, ſo there is no reaſon why any difficulty ſhould be made therof at all. And as for the 2. point it ſeemeth to me there ſhould be no great difficulty, in regard it is already agreed of all ſides, that there muſt be one or other ſuch Company of Chriſtians, and a-mong them Paſtors & preachers ſo viſible, as is ſaid ; and none beſides the Catholique Romaine hitherto hath ſhewed a ſufficient Catalogue of names of men in al Ages, who can with any colour be proued or de-fended, to haue beene profeſſors of the true, diuine, infallible, Catholike, primitiue, vnchanged faith, firſt deliuered by Chriſt, and his Apoſtles, &. after continued in an orderly ſucceſſion of viſible Pa-ſtors & Doctours appoynted by God to be allwayes

in the Church of purpose, to preserue people of all a-
ges from wauering in doubt of any point of faith, or
being carried about with the wind of any vpstart Errour. Neither indeed can any such Catalogue be giuen, but it may be manifestly shewed to be insufficiet,
as either wanting names of men in some ages, or containing names of such as may certainly be proued
to be no Protestants, but to differ in doctrine of fayth
one from another, and to condemne one or other of
the 39. Articles, vnto which English Protestant Ministers are sworne. Neuertheles if any one be not yet
satisfyed in this point, but will haue the Question
made, whether the Protestant Church hath beene so
visible in all Ages, as the names of their Pastours and
Doctours may be shewed out of good Authors, I doe
not see what better methode can be prescribed for an
easy, speedy, & certaine resolution of the question, &
sound satisfaction of all sorts of men, that shall desire
to be resolued in this most necessary and important
question, then that which M. *Fisher* prescribed in his
second paper written before the Coference, in which
he required his Aduersaryes, 1. To set downe names
in all ages of mē which they thought to be Protestats.
2. To proue out of good Authors by some doctrine of
theirs different from the Roman, that they were Protestants. 3. To defend thē to be Protestants, shewing
that they did not differ in faith one from another, nor
condemned any of the 39. Articles, vnto with all
English Protestant Ministers are sworne, in regard
otherwise they cannot be al of one Protestāt Church:
I doe not (I say) see, what fitter methode can be prescribed for cleering the afore said Question of such visibility as is required, and presupofed to be in the true
Catholique Church, then by actuall naming, prouing

uing and defending, as is aboue ſaid. For only to ſay
there were, or to offer by arguments, exceeding the
capacity of the comon ſort of auditors, to proue, that
there were men in all ages profeſſing Proteſtancy,
ſo viſible, as that their names may be ſhewed out of
good Authors, is no ſufficient ſatisfaction; when eſpecially one being vrged actually to ſhew theſe names, he will not ſhew actually any names, but of one
or two ages, and ſuch names as the Roman Catholiks,
his aduerſaries, by better right may & will name: and
being ſtill preſſed to name more, he will not name
more, but deſireth firſt to diſpute of theſe; which not
being permitted till all be named, he moſt falſely then
affirmeth that his Aduerſary doth grant theſe to be
Proteſtants, and ſo runneth away: To doe thus
(I ſay) (as D. *Featly* did) is no fit way to giue ſatisfaction to all ſorts, expecting reſolution of the aforeſaid
moſt important Queſtion. As it were a very inſufficiét
way to giue ſatisfaction in a debt of twenty peeces
of gold to another his creditor, if inſteed of actual pay-
ment required, he ſhould ſay, and offer to proue by a
Syllogiſme, yea by a Demonſtration *à priori,* that he
can pay him the ſaid twenty peeces : and being vrged
to lay downe the particular peeces of gold, he ſaith,
that by an Induction he will lay downe thoſe peeces
of gold one after another ; and being further preſſed
to do ſo, he not hauing one peece of gold of his owne
taketh out of his Creditors purſe one, or two, or more
peeces, and laying downe one or two of them, ſayth,
loe heere is one or two towardes the twenty ; and
being neuer ſo much vrged, he will not lay downe
any more vntill his Creditour firſt diſpute with him,
whether theſe two or three peeces layd downe, be
his owne or no : and being heereupon ſeriouſly told

by his Creditor, that vnles he layd downe al the peeces of gold, he did not satisfy the debt, but lost his
credit, and forfaited his band, he then falleth into paf-
fion, and fayth: What, will you haue me eate my
dinner at a bit? I cannot lay downe all at once: Will
you difpute with me about thefe or no? Which his
Creditor refufing to do, vntill all the twenty peeces
be actually layd downe, he laftly fayth: Well, you
will not difpute about thefe? You graunt thefe to be
myne: and fo without expecting anfwere, he turneth
to the company, faying; he granteth thefe to be myne,
and taketh vp his cloake and runneth away, not re-
garding that his Creditor fo foone as he can open his
mouth, biddeth him ftay, and denyeth any fuch grant
to haue beene made by him: yea offereth to difpute
with him of that point, if he will ftay: I fuppofe no
man will thinke this kind of dealing to be an honeft
and good fatisfaction in a debt of money: and therefore much leffe fhould it be accounted good in matters
of farre more importance and value, and fpecially in
fatisfying this (by D . *Featly* vndertaken) debt of
fhewing names of vifible Proteftants in all ages, out
of good Authors .

§ . 4. *About the manner of proceeding of the Difputant.*

By this which hath beene now fayd, and that
which was heard and feene by thofe who were prefent at the Conference, may appeare how vnfittly D.
Featly proceeded in his Syllogifme, and his Induction:
for in the one, to wit, his Syllogifme, he endeauoured
to auoid that plaine methode prefcribed by M. *Fisher*
before the meeting, of naming men in all Ages, and
prouing and defending thofe he named to be Proteftants

stants, and sought to draw the disputation into particuler Controuersies, which the capacity of those (for whose satisfaction the disputation was ordained) and of diuers others who were present, could not sufficiently comprehend. Now concerning the other, to wit his Induction ; first, it was long before he could be drawne to it : secondly hauing vndertaken to make it full (and as the Question required) in all Ages, he (hauing only made it (and that most falsely) for the first Age) would not proceed further, vnles his Aduersary would first dispute with him (in particular Controuersyes) about those whome he named in the first age : which particular disputation (being of meer Tergiuersation and delay) becaufe his Aduersary would not presently permit, but told him, that he must first make his full Induction, and then he would answere him as much as need should be in all particulers ; he either hauing no patience to expect, or rather intending to take any such lyke occasion to break off the Conference, before he should be further pressed to giue this full Induction (which with credit he can neuer giue) made such an abrupt end, as in this my Relation is declared.

Now, for the manner which both D . *VVhite*, & he obferued in the processe of the conference, it was noted, that it had not that *decorum*, which the circumstance of their persons and places should promise. For it no way suited with the gray haires and grauity of a Doctor, and a Deane, to haue laughed and fleered so much as D . *VVhite* did, vpon no caufe. And for D. *Featly*, both his lookes, speaches, iests, and gestures were such, as did not become him, but might better haue beseemed a Stage-player then a Doctour and an Archbishops Chapline, and discouered a mind not so

tempered, as had beene requifite in one who pretended to be a Teacher of true Diuinity. Finally his
whole carriage in this bufines fhewed, that he rather
fought to pleafe his Audience, and to gaine applaufe
to himfelfe, then foundly to fatisfy that moft important Queftion, of the vifibility of the Proteftant
Church.

On the other fide, M. *Fisher*, and M. *Sweet* behaued themfelues moderatly, not only in the eye and
iudgement of Catholiques, but alfo of others: fo as e-
uen their greateft Aduerfaryes could not take exception againft them. And one of the principall Proteftants prefent hath fince (in refpect of temper & mo-
defty) giuen fpeciall commendations of them, & far
preferred them before his owne Church-men. And as
the methode which M. *Fisher* prefcribed before the
meeting, is already fhewed to be the fitteft that could
be, for giuing good fatisfaction to the old Gentleman
and all others, fo in my opinion both he and M. *Sweet*
did very well to ftand (as they did) conftantly to it,
prudently forfeeing, when the Aduerfary would haue
diuerted them from it, and warily fo anfwering his
his arguments, as that for all he could fay, they would
not fuffer themfelues to be tranfported from the propofed Queftion, and the prefcribed Methode; but ftil
kept the Aduerfary to the point, & would not permit
him to diuert, either to difpute about Chrift or his A-
poftles, or any other point, vntill names were giuen in
all Ages, which was the point demanded and vndertaken. The which courfe they tooke vpon iuft and
good reafon, and not for any diftruft or diffidence (as
fome Proteftants did inconfideratly imagine) that
they could not defend Chrift and his Apoftles not to
haue beene Proteftants, or any particular point of
those

those which D. *Featly*, or D. *VVhite* vnfeafonably propofed, or any other held (in fuch fenfe, as it is held as
a point of fayth) by the Catholike Roman Church ;
which they could, and would haue defended, & proued if need had beene, or if the meeting had beene intended and appointed for that purpofe. The reafon
therefore why M. *Fisher* might well refufe to enter into fuch particuler difputes, before full Induction of
Names were ended, was , for that this had beene to
follow two Hares at once, and fo to catch neither ,
and to leaue that which was moft pertinent to the
prefent Queftion, and which moft imported to be decided in the firft place, as being the oly thing in which
the old Gentleman, and many other of the Audience
did particulerly expect, and defire to be fatisfyed, and
being a moft eafy and affured meanes to help them
to be fatisfyed in all other matters in Controuerfy ; &
without which , it is moft hard, or rather impoffible
euer to attaine certaine and infallible Refolution in
all particular, euen moft neceffary , points of fayth , as
M . *Fisher* exprefely fhewed, and proued by a fentence aboue cyted out of D . *Field* .

    A fecond reafon might be ; for that all difputatio
about particulers (before the true Church were by
her perpetuall vifibility , or fome fuch euident marks
found out, and acknowledged, as a fufficient meanes
appointed by God to inftruct all forts, in matters of
fayth, and to preferue vnity, and determine Contro-
uerfyes of fayth) would haue beene fruitleffe & endleffe . Which was the reafon why M . *Fisher* , in another former conference had with a certaine Minifter
would not enter into any particulers , vntill he had
asked thefe generall Queftions : 1. *VVhat grounds the
Minister would stand vpon* ? The Minifter anfwered,
                                     Scripture.

Scripture: which M. *Fisher* accepting wrote downe, and then asked. 2. *VVhether he would belieue nothing but expreſſe wordes of Scripture?* The Miniſter anſwered *Yes, he would alſo beleeue a good Conſequence out of Scripture.* This alſo M. *Fisher* accepted, and wrote downe, and further asked. 3. *If it should happen, that the conſequence which the Minister should bring, should not be thoght good by him: and è* contra*, the Conſequence brought by him should not be thought good by the Minister, who should iudge and end that fruitleſſe, and otherwiſe endleſſe contention and Controuerſy?* The Miniſter ſayd: *The Church.* M. *Fisher* very willingly accepted and wrote it down; & 4. asked: *VVhether after the Church shall haue iudged and decyded ſuch a Controuerſy, it should be lawfull for any priuate man to oppoſe his iudgement against that, which the Church had ſo determined?* As for example, when *Catholikes* and *Arrians* hauing alleadged Scriptures, and *pro* and *contra* brought conſequences out of thē, about the Diuinity of Chriſt our Lord; The Church in a generall Councell iudged the conſequences of *Arrians* to be naught, and thoſe of the Catholikes good. The Miniſter ſayd: *No, it was not lawfull for any priuate man to oppoſe his iudgement against ſuch a Iudgement of the Church.*

   Theſe Queſtions being asked, M. *Fisher* ioyned iſſue vpon a queſtion, bidding the Miniſter chooſe what he thought moſt materiall againſt Roman Catholikes, and let it be tryed, whether the Church did iudge for Catholikes, or Proteſtants. The Miniſter did chooſe the Queſtion about *Merits*, and tooke for his *tenet*, *That there was not any Merit of man before God.* And when the day of tryall came, the caſe was ſo cleere againſt the Miniſter, in the ancient Fathers (whome the Miniſter granted to be the Church) euen

by

by confeffion of the *Magdeburgians*, that the Minifter had no fhift, but to diuert the difputation
from the fubftance of the propofed Queftion,
to a circumftance of *Commutatiue Iuftice*, and that
equality betwixt the *VVorke* and the *Reward*, which is
written of by *Bellarmine*. About which circumftance
M. Fisher was content to difpute after he had plainely
fhewed the fubftance of *Merit* out of the ancient Fathers. Comming therefore to difpute about the aforefayd circumftance of *Merit*, *M. Fisher* found, that there
would be no end, nor fruit of the argument, in regard
the ancient Fathers had not fpoken of it in expreffe
tearmes, as they had done of the fubftance of *Merit*, &
no other vifible Church of this prefent age was agreed on, to whofe iudgement this matter fhould be finally referred. By which experience, *M. Fisher* hath
learned, how endleffe and fruitleffe it is, to wafte
wordes about particulers, vntill both partyes be agreed which is the true Church, not only in ancient tymes, but alfo of this age. So as after ech party hath
fayd what he can, the finall refolution of the Queftion may be referred to that prefent Church, which
(hauing without interruption of Paftours and Doctors, and without change of doctrine fucceffiuely def-
cended from the true vifible Church of anciet tymes)
is by this, and other Markes proued to be the pre-
prefent true Church, whofe Iudgment no priuate man
muft oppofe. This Queftion therefore of the continual
fucceffiue vifible Church, being fo neceffary to end al
Controuerfies, and being now propofed to be treated
of betwixt *M. Fisher* and *D. Featly*, *M. Fisher* had great
reafon not to permit fpeach of any other particular
Queftion, vntill by his prefcribed Methode, he had
gotten it clearly feen, that the Proteftant Church was
not

not, and the Catholique Roman Church was the only true Church, to whome it pertayneth to giue Iudgment of, and determine Controuerfies, and to inftruct
all forts of men in the true Faith, and not to permit
men by their priuate interpretations of Scripture to
wander in errors, or wauer in incertainties , or fpend
their tyme in fruitles, and endles difputations about
controuerfies of faith: It being moft certaine, that thefe
can neuer be with fruite, and fully ended, but by the
cenfure of the true vifible (not only ancient but alfo
prefent) Church, which muft when doubt is (as moft
often is) made, tell vs, what particuler books be true
bookes of Scripture and Fathers, which be true tranf-
lations, and which be right interpretations : for both
about Scriptures & Fathers fuch Queftions may arife,
and cannot be well decided whout the Iudgement of
the true prefent vifible Church, in regard Scriptures
and Fathers do not alwaies fufficiently expreffe what
is to be held in the aforefaid Queftions ; neither will
one priuate man, in fuch cafes, follow anothers opinion, when ech man will be eafily inclined to thinke
that he hath as good Scriptures, or Fathers, or Reafons, or all thefe togeather, to plead for the truth of
his opinion, as another hath for his .

    This reafon may be confirmed out of *Tertullian*
who in his golden booke of *Prefcriptions*, giueth diuers
reafons why Heretikes (who reiect the authority of
the Church) fhould not be admitted to difpute out of
Scriptures . Firft, *for that (by their difputations) they*
weary thofe that be firme, they ouercome thofe which be
weake , and thofe which be in a middle difpofition , they dif-
miffe with fcruple or doubt. Another reafon *Tertullian* giueth, becaufe, *this Herefy doth not receaue fome Scriptures,*
or if it receaue , it peruerteth them to their owne purpofe,

Terrull . de
prÆfcrip.c.15.

Cap. 17 .

                                                              with

with additions and detractions; and if it receaue fome, yet not whole, or if whole in fome fort, yet by falfe expofitions it turneth them (from the right) *to a peruerfe fenfe . And a peruerfe, or corrupt fenfe* (fayth he) *is as contrary to truth, as is a peruerted or corrupted Text.* Cap. 19:

Tertullian therefore for thefe reafons iudged beft not to make the combat in Scriptures, but that this gappe fhould be ftopt, and that Heretikes fhould not be admitted to any difputation of Scriptures ; and he telleth how this may be done, faying : *It muft be exa-* Cap. 20. 21. 22 *mined to whome the poffeffion of Scripture doth belong, to the* & fequent. *intent that he who hath no right vnto them, may not be admitted vnto them.* And further he fheweth, *That the right order of thinges requireth, that firft it only be difputed, to whom the Fayth belongeth?* (As if he fhould fay, which is the true vifible Church?) *VVhofe are the Scriptures? From whome, by whome, when, and to whome was deliuered that difcipline, by which they are made Chriftians? for where there shall appeare the truth of Chriftian fayth and difcipline to be* (as doubtles it is in the true vifible Church of Chrift) *there shalbe truth of Scriptures, and expofitions, and al Chriftian Traditions.* And hauing fhewed how Chrift did promulgate his doctrine by the Apoftles, he further prefcribeth : *That, what Chrift, and his Apoftles did preach, muft be learned no otherwife then by the Churches which they founded: fo as euery doctrine agreeing with thofe Apoftolicall & Mother-Churches, that is to be deemed true ; and what doth not agree, to be iudged falfe.* And therefore to make it apparent, that the Heretikes opinions (although pretended by themfelues to be cóformable to Scriptures, and fuch as may be proued out of Scriptures) are not Apoftolicall, nor true, he vrgeth them (as M. *Fisher* vrged D. *Featly* to shew the beginning of their Churches, and to vnfould the order of their Cap. 1.

K   *Bishops*

Bishops, so from the beginning running downe by succession, *as that their first Bishop had some of the Apostles , or some A-* *postolicall man, who perseuered with the Apostles, for his Au-* *thor and Predecessour ;* and hauing giuen examples of the Catholike Churches, who can thus vnfould the order of their Paſtours, and namely *Rome* for one , he ſayth afterwardes : *Confingant tale quid Haeretici* : Let Heretiques euen feigne ſome ſuch like thing.

Thus we ſee what *Tertullian* did ſay to Here- tikes of his tyme, by which we may learne what we may ſay to the Nouelliſts of our tyme, whome (offe- ring to diſpute with vs about Scriptures) we may al- togeather debarre from Scripture, and may examine them , as *Tertullian* did thoſe of his tyme, ſaying : *VVho* *are you ? VVhen, and whence came you ? VVhat haue you to* *do in my ground, you that are not myne ? By what right doſt* *thou,* O *Marcion* (we may ſay, O *Martin Luther*) *cut down* *my woods ? By what licence doſt thou ,* O *Valentine* (O Caluin) *diuert, or turne aſide my fountaynes ? By what po-* *wer doſt thou,* O *Apelles* (O Anabaptiſt) *remoue my limits?* *VVhy do you,* O *the reſt of Heretikes, ſow and feed according* *to your owne will vpon my Land and paſture ? It is my poſſeſ-* *ſion, I am the ancient poſſeſſour, I haue the firme Originalls* *from the Authors themſelues, to whome the propriety did firſt* *belong : I am the heyre of the Apoſtles; as they did ordaine in* *their Teſtament and laſt will, as they did commit it to my* *faythfull Truſt , as they did adiure me, ſo I hold it . But you* *they haue diſinherited and caſt out, as ſtrangers and ene-* *myes &c.* So as by this preſcription of *Tertullian* , vntill D. *Featly*, or ſome other can by other markes then by alleadging wordes of Scripture (as by perpetuall vi- ſibility, and interrupted ſucceſſion of Biſhops &c.) proue Proteſtants not to be Heretikes, but the true Church of Chriſt, and the right heyre of the Apoſtles,

to whome cōsequently belongeth the moſt ancient &
firſt poſſeſſion ot Scriptures, M. *Fisher* had good reaſon and right to deſerie diſputing with him (out of
Scripture) of Chriſt and his Apoſtles, vntill he had
made his full Inducłion of Names of Proteſtant
Church-men, and vnſoulded the orders of their Pro-
ſtant Biſhops, ſo running downe from the beginning
by ſucceſſion, as that their firſt Proteſtant Biſhop had
ſome of the Apoſtles, or ſome Apoſtolicall man, who
perſeuered with the Apoſtles, for his Author & Pre-
deceſſour. The which I accompt to be ſo impoſſible
for him to doe, as I dare, and do challenge him, ſaying with *Tertullian*: Confingant tale quid Hæretici:
Let D. Featly (or any of his fellow Proteſtants) *at leaſt
feigne* (becauſe I am ſure they cannot find) *Names of
Proteſtant Bishops, and Paſtors, whome they do imagine* (for
proue they cannot out of good Authors) *to haue beene
in all ages.* Which whiles they do not, al ſorts of people
haue iuſt cauſe to thinke, that neither D. *Featly*, nor
D. *VVhite* can performe that taske, which they did tooto boldly vndertake of naming, prouing, and defending viſible Proteſtants in al ages: & therupon al men
may, as I do, conclude, *That the Proteſtant Church hath
not beene ſo viſible in all ages, as the Catholike Church ought
to be* : and conſequently, *the Proteſtant Church is not the
true Catholique Church which we profeſſe to beleeue in our
Creed* ; Neither conſequently, *are their Paſtours, and
Doctours and Preachers lawfully ſent, or ſufficiently au thorized, to teach and expound Gods word* ; nor conſequently,
*are people ſecurely warranted to learne of them, what is,
and what is not to be beleeued by infallible diuine fayth
neceſſary to ſaluation* ; nor indeed ought they to beleeue
or heare them at all, but ought to vnite themſelues to
that *One, Holy, Catholike, Apoſtolike, perpetually viſible Ro-*

man

man Church, hearing, beleeuing & obeying the Paſtors thereof; whereby they may haue infallible iuſtruction in all matters of fayth, ſecure direction for all matters concerning good life, in ſuch ſort as they may attaine remiſſion of their ſinnes, and ſaluation of their ſoules; the grace of God in this life, and endles heauenly happines in the next. Vnto which I beſeech ſweet Ieſus to bring vs all.   Amen.

FINIS.

AN

APPENDIX

CONTAINING

An Answere to some Vntruthes, obiected by D. White, *and* D. Featly, *against* M. Fishers *Relations, or* VVritings.

LTHOVGH M. *Fishers* confcience be to him a thoufand witneffes, and thofe which well know him, will giue, to fuch as doubt, fuffi-cient affurance, that he did not in any of his Relations or Writings, wittingly and willingly vtter any vntruth ; but according to his beft memory , or by re-lying vpon the memory of others whom he deemed worthy of credit , related, and writ euery thing con-formable to that he iudged to be true: Neuerthelefle, fith D. *White* , and D. *Featly* haue accufed him, as if he were a fhamelefle lyar ; I haue thought it conue-nient (for the good of thofe, who being ouer credu-

L   lous

lous of thefe Doctours reports, fhall haue conceiued
amiffe of *M. Fishers* fincerity, and fo hindred themfelues from taking benefit of his Relations or Writings) to make Anfwere to their cheife accufations,
omitting diuers others of leffe moment, although
no leffe vntruely obiected againft him .

The firft is *D. Whites* verball Accufation; who (to a
certaine Gentleman of the Innes of Court, cõming to
him to be fatisfyed about fomthing foũd in a Copie of
M. Fishers Relatiõ of the firft Conference)vttered thefe
words(as the Gentleman told his friend,)& offered to
iuftify it if it were denyed;) What hard hap had I to
deal with that lying fellow, that paltry lying fellow?
he is Superior of the Iefuits, but for his ill carriage of
that bufineffe he had like to lofe his place ; Heerby infinuating, that the Relation was falfe, and that the bufines had not ben well carried.

But this to be a falfe Accufation may appeare, firft,
in that *M. Fisher* did before this, come to *D. Whites*
Camber, and read vnto him his Relation ; which *D.*
White could not then (in more frefh memory) accufe of any fallhood, but only faid, that he did not remember fome one or two of the paffages, which is no
fufficient argument to conuince the Relation of falfhood, efpecially when not only *M. Fisher*, but fome
others who were prefent at the Conference can affure
that fuch paffages were truely fet downe, and *M Fisher*
did at that tyme in Doctor Whytes fight adde fo much
more to his Relation, as *D. White* could reduce into his
memory, which fheweth he had no will to relate
falfe, or omit any pertinent Truth .

Secondly, when *M. Fisher* came againe to *D. White*
his houfe, to aske the caufe why he had called him a
lyar? The Doctour could not produce any one parti-
cules

Euler in which M. *Fisher* had related falſe.

Thirdly; For the carriage of that buſines, M. *Fisher* appealeth to the cenſure of thoſe who were preſent, who haue teſtifyed both then and after, that the carriage of that buſines was good on M. *Fishers* part, and the euent, to wit the confirmation of the Lady (for whom the Conference was) in the Catholique Fayth, ſheweth that M. *Fisher* did not carry himſelfe ill, eyther in the firſt, or any other later Conference.

Fourthly; It is a meere fiction, that M. *Fisher* either was then ſuperiour of the Ieſuits, or that he had like to haue loſt his place, or ſuſtained any other diſgrace among his brethren, for any of his Conferences.

Another accuaſtion is made by D. *White* in the very beginning of his Reply to Ieſuite Fisher, in theſe words: *Mirum eſt.* &c. It is ſtrange, ſaith S. Auguſtine, that there ſhould be ſuch a great diſtance betweene the front of a man and his mouth, that the ſhame of his forehead ſhould not repreſſe the impudencie of his tongue. It is vntrue, that his Royall Maieſty gaue you any applauſe, or the leaſt occaſion to coniecture that he was taken with any paſſage of your diſputation: for you propounded nothing to demonſtrate your owne *Tenet*, or confute ours, worthy of that great preſence; and ſomtymes you were driuen to diſſemble your owne *Tenet*, otherwhile by wyer-drawne diſtinctions and euaſions, to elude the weight of his Maieſties arguments. As for thoſe words of his Royall Maieſty, *I like you the better*, they were vttered vpon this occaſion: When the Ieſuit being preſſed about the point of Temporall Authority &c. did at the firſt ſeeke euaſions, in the end kneeling downe, he ſayd, I will deale plainely with your Maieſty: Vpon this, the King ſaid, I like you the better. Wherin he was ſo

far

,, far from gracing the whole diſputation, that not long
,, after his Maieſty tould him, he neuer heard a verier
,, &c. Thus farre the Doctour.

Before I anſwere this accuſation, I might meruayle
that ſuch a ſeeming-graue Doctour, intending to
blame another, could haue ſo ſmall care of being free
from fault, eſpecially that fault, for which he blameth
the other, although the other had been more blame-
worthy, then the Ieſuite was in this matter. For as
Cato ſayth: *Turpe eſt Doctori, cùm culpa redarguit ipſum :* It
is a ſhame for a Doctour, or Teacher, to be guilty of
that fault which he reprehendeth in another: & much
more ſhame, that he ſhould commit that fault in the
very act of reprouing another who is not guilty of it.
The fault with which he taxeth the Ieſuit, is Vntruth.
Let vs therefore examine, whether the Ieſuite, or the
Doctour haue vttered vntruth. All that the Ieſuite
,, ſayd, was this: Although your Maieſties firſt ſaluta-
,, tion carried a ſhew of ſeuerity, yet your diſmiſſing me
,, was benigne and gracious, not only pardoning my
,, earneſtnes in defending the part of the Catholique
,, Church, but alſo ſaying: *I like thee the better.*
,,   The true cauſe of which ſpeech of the Ieſuite, was
not (as the Doctour ſiniſterly and vntruely interpreteth) that he thought, or would haue others belieue,
that his Maieſty did applaud, or was taken with any
paſſage of his diſputation ; but to tell his Maieſty, that
as a good Angell firſt terrifieth, and after doth leaue
one in comfort ; ſo his Maieſty did firſt terrifye him
with ſeuerity of his firſt ſpeech, but in the end com-
forted him by pardoning his earneſtnes, and ſaying : I
like thee the better. The true occaſion of which words
of his Maieſty was not (as *D. White* vntruely relateth)
that the Ieſuite did at firſt ſeek euaſions, and in the end
said

said he would deale plainly;but that the Iefuit remembring how in the difcourfe of the difputation he had
diuers tymes (vpon earneftneffe to anfwer for the Catholique caufe) interrupted his Maieftyes fpeech, and
fearing that this his earneftneffe had been offenfiue,
he kneeled downe faying: *I befeech your Maiefty pardon
my earneftneße*; vnto which his Maiefty faid, *I like thee
the better*(to wit , as the Iefuite did interpret, for being
earneft in difputation:) after which words , his Maiefty prefently departed, without fpeaking any more to
the Iefuit,and therefore did not (as the Doctour relateth) tell the Iefuite,he neuer heard a verier &c.

To anfwere therefore the accufation, I fay firft, It is
vntrue, that the Iefuite vttered any vntruth in this
paffage,for he did not fay,that his maiefty did applaud
or was taken with his difputation , but that he pardo-
ned his earneftnes , and faid; he liked him the better:
which was true .

Secodly, whereas the Doctour fayth, that the Iefuit
did diffemble his *Tenet*, & that he fought euafiōs(about
the point of Temporall power) and that in the end he
kneeling downe fayd, I will deale plainly with your
maiefty: All this is vntrue,for the Iefuit did at firft tell
his maiefty,that thofe of his Order held the moft mode
rate opiniō about the Popes tēporall power,for which
he cited Bellarmine, neither did he euer after fay cōtrary to this,or deny this,or fay,I will deale plainely &c.

Thirdly, whereas the Doctour faith, that the Iefuit
propounded nothing worthy that great prefence, to
demonftrate his owne *Tenet &c*.This is but the cenfure of an Aduerfarie : for although it was not expected, that the Iefuit fhould demonftrate, or confute,
but onely anfwere, for which it was fufficient that he
kept him in his trenches,and by good diftinctions anf-

wered.

weered Arguments;yet D. *White* might remember, if it pleaſe him, that the Ieſuit (as occaſion' was offered, & he permitted to ſpeake)obiected (though very briefly) ſomching, which D. *White* endeauoring to anſwer, his Maieſty did not like D. *Whites* anſwer,and ſhewed his diſlike, ſaying to the Doctour; *Go not that way &c.* and I meruaile why the Doctour doth now relate the Cóferences, if indeed he do thinke a true Relation were any aduantage againſt the Ieſuite .

Fourthly;whereas the D. affirmeth in his Preface, that *the Ieſuite vaniſhed away from the diſputation with foyle and diſgrace;*and here he ſaith, that *his Maieſty tould the Ieſuit he neuer heard a verier &c.* All this is vntrue, for no ſuch words were ſaid to the Ieſuit in his hearing; neyther can it be truely ſayd , that the Ieſuit had the ſoyle;for neither would his Maieſty haue ſet downe (as he did)points in writing for the Ieſuit to anſwer,if either the victory had ben already gotten, or that he had accounted the Ieſuite ſuch a contemptible and foyled Aduerſary, as the D. would make men belieue: Neither would the Lady (for whoſe ſake the Conference was made) haue continued ſo conſtant as ſhe did,and doth; in her perſwaſion both of the goodnes of the Catholique cauſe, and the learning of the Ieſuite, if ſhe had not obſerued, that he being all alone, had reaſonably well performed his part againſt ſo eminent Oppoſers.

Thus much may ſerue to cleere M. *Fiſher* from theſe vntrue accuſations, and may ſufficiently warne men from being too credulous of whatſoeuer other like haue ben, or ſhalbe by D.*White* framed againſt him.

D. Featly maketh many Accuſations of M. *Fiſhers* vntruths pag. 17. 18. 19. 20. &c. Vnto all which I anſwere in generall, That not one of theſe were for-
ma ll

mall vntruths, but either D. *Featly* miſtakes or miſre-
ports. For M. *Fisher* did according to this beſt memory,
or building vpon the memory of others whom he
had cauſe to truſt, ſpeak and write euery thing truely,
or at leaſt not wittingly vntruly.

And for a taſt of D *Featly* his miſtaking or miſrepor-
ting, let it be noted, that the firſt vntruth with which
he chargeth M. *Fisher*, is the Title of the booke, *An*
anſwere written by A.C. which can be no vntruth, but at
moſt the concealing of one truth by another truth, although it be granted that M. *Fisher* made that Anſwer:
for M. *Fisher* is A. C. *id eſt*, A Catholique; which
was the true meaning of the Author, when he ſet
thoſe letters to conceale his Name.

The ſecond Vntruth alſo, with which he chargeth
M. *Fisher*, is more groſly, if not willfully and wittingly
miſtaken and miſreported. For pag. 2. the Authour of
the Anſwere doth not ſay (as D. *Featly* heere reporteth abſolutly) *That D. Featly hath confeſſed &c.* but, *I am*
told, that D. Featly hath confeſſed. &c. which I am ſure
is true. So as, if D. *Featly* (fuſpecting as it ſeemeth
worthily his owne credit) had not confirmed ſome
of his accuſations with the authority of other Atteſtatours, I would let them all paſſe without any other
anſwere, then this: D. *Featly* affirmeth this, and that to
be vntruthes; M. *Fisher* denieth any thing to be ſaid
or written by him (in that right ſenſe in which it was
meant, and according to his owne, and others beſt
memory) to be vntruth; *vtri credendum?* And I doubt
not, but all who are not partially affected, & do know
both parties, eſpecially *intus, & in cute*, and will conſider the matters, will ſay they will belieue M. *Fisher*
rather then D. *Featly.* But becauſe D. *Featly* hath alleadged others, and gotten them (as it ſeemeth) to
ſubſcribe

subscribe to an Attestation of some particulers; I think
it needfull to make a more speciall answer to the Attestation it self in generall, and to some of the chiefe
things in particuler.

First, for the Attestation in generall, I cannot belieue, that it was subscribed by the common consent
of all the Attestatours, out of their seuerall, certaine, or
speciall memory of ech particuler ; but do rather
iudge, that D. *Featly* himself hauing framed it, did get
the attestatours to subscribe; which they did (supposing
they did, of which I haue cause do doubt) trusting his
memory rather then their owne, or following that
preconceipt, which the Protestant Relation had first
imprinted in their memory. So as the Attestation is
not to be weighed, as if it had the authority of all the
parties subscribing, but as reduced to the priuate authority either of D. *Featly*, who in likelihood framed
it, or to the Authour of the Protestant Relatiõ, whose
authority is not to be credited further, then the matter
it self doth require.

The reason which moueth mee to thinke, that the
Attestation was not framed by the common consent
of all the Attestatours, out of their seuerall, certayne
knowledge, and speciall memory of ech particuler, is;
First, for that it is not credible, that euery one of the
Attestatours (especially old M. *Buggs*) had so good
memories, as to remember (independantly one of
another) so many particulers, so punctually, so many
moneths after the Conference.

Secondly, for that some particulers of the Attestation are certainly knowne to be false; and therefore
sith it is not lyke that so many, & so worthy persons
would wrong themselues so much, as to affirme apparent falshood, as if they knew it true vpon their
owne

owne knowledge or ſpeciall memory; it is to be thought, that ſome one partially affected party did fancie to himſelf, what he thought fitteſt for the credit of the Proteſtant, and diſgrace of the Catholique Diſputant, and that the reſt belieued what he affirmed : Or, without euer examining particulers, did ſuppoſe in generall, that all was true that was written in the Atteſtation, and ſo ſet their hands to it; As I haue heard in another like caſe, that one being taxed for ſetting his hand to a certaine falſe writing, anſwered, that he neuer looked into it, but truſted thoſe who deſired him to ſet his hand to it.

It being therefore to be preſumed that the Atteſtation, as alſo the Additions, are D. *Featlyes* owne, or ſome others of no greater credit then himſelf ; it may ſuffice for anſwer, to oppoſe the credit of M. *Fiſher*, and M. *Sweet*, and diuers other Catholiques of knowne ſincerity, who being preſent at the Conference, did diligently attend, and do well remember, that at leaſt ſome points of the ſayd Addition and Atteſtation are falſe, and eſpecially ſuch as are eſteemed of moſt moment, namely, *That M. Fiſher ſayd the word, Tranſeat,* which moſt certainly he ſayd not ; and that he *did not take* D. Featly *by the arme ſaying, I wil if you will ſtay,* which moſt certainly he did ; And that, D. *Featly did make his Adiuration onely in the end of the diſputation, and this with a loud, and earneſt voice,* when as it is perfectly remembred that he made his Adiuration about the beginning of the diſputation, and not in the end, at leaſt with ſo loud and audible voice, as M. *Fiſher*, and other Catholiques did heare it.

Theſe three (being the points principally ſtood vpon to be falſly related in the Addition and Atteſtation) are perfecly remembred, and wilbe confirmed if

M. need

need be, by oath ; And therefore neither the Addition
nor the Atteſtation is to be accounted to haue been
framed out of the ſpeciall memory of ſo many, and ſo
worthy perſons, whoſe names are in the printed Copy
ſubſcribed ; neyther doth either the one, or the other,
being found thus falſe , deſerue to be credited in any
other point, ſo far forth at leaſt as they are cōtradicted
by the Catholique Relation , which was ſet out by
one, who will not wittingly lye to gaine a world.

Thus much may ſerue for anſwer to *D. Featlyes* accuſations of *M. Fisher* for vntruths, contained in the
Addition or Atteſtation: yet becauſe I perceiue the Atteſtatours do ſpecially inſiſt vpon that paſſage ſet
downe in the Atteſtation (which they ſay is of moſt
moment) in which the Cath. Relation ſaith, that *D.
Featly* did in his riſing, and offering to goe away, turne
to *M. Fisher* ſaying, *Will you diſpute about Chriſt and his
Apoſtles, or no?* To which *M. Fisher* ſaid , *I will if you will
ſtay*, and ſtretching out his hand tooke *D. Featly* by the
arme offering to ſtay him &c. about which paſſage
the Atteſtatours ſay: We(that were preſent, and diuers
" of vs next the Opponent) auow , that the Ieſuite vſed
" no ſuch word at all, nor geſture of that kind, as in truth
" he could not, being not ſo neere in place to *D. Featly*
" as that he could take him by the arme , they being pla-
" ced at the oppoſite ends and corners of the Table; ney-
" ther did *M. Fisher* ariſe out of his place to take *D. Featly*
" by the arme, nor if he had, could he then come to reach
" *D. Featly*, there being many that ſate, or ſtood cloſe
" crowding about the table, and betwixt thoſe two. Becauſe, I ſay, the Atteſtatours do ſo ſpecially and peremptorily ſtand vpon this laſt paſſage , I will heere ſet
downe what *M. Fisher* (who can beſt tell) doth affirme, and will(if need be) vpon his oath confirme , to
wit,

wit, That he is most certaine he did speak those words,
and vse that gesture which the Catholique Relation
specifieth: and therefore he meruaileth at the exceeding boldnes of D. *Featly*, who maketh so many, and so
qualified persons wrōg themselues so much by saying,
Wee anow, that the Iesuite vsed no such word, or gesture &c.
For the Iesuit is most sure he did , and therefore could
vse such words and gesture, and some of the Catholique Auditory do well remember, that he did. If the
Attestatours had only said, We do not remember any
such word, nor do know how any such gesture could
be (in respect of distance) vsed by the Iesuit, I could
haue allowed their saying, and could haue shewed
how it might be true , albeit the word & gesture were,
as certainely it was, vsed by the Iesuit. For at that tyme
vpon D. *Featly* his slaunderous speach, in which(with
extreme and dasperate boldnes) he tould the auditory
before M. *Fishers* owne face, that M. *Fisher* granted
Christ and his Apostles to be Protestants (which all
that sate nigh M. *Fisher*, and attended , knew to be
false) many of the Protestant Auditory did not
only take distast , but thereupon made so great noyse,
as M. *Fisher* disclayming from that slaunderous speach,
could not for a while be heard , and thereupon also
many did rise vp, and offred to go away , and so some
euen of those who were between D. *Featly* and M. Fisher did remoue , and left space sufficient for D. *Featly*
to come so nigh at his vprising & offering to go away,
that M. *Fisher* might easily, by rising and reaching his
arme ouer the table , take him by the arme, as the Catholique Relation reporteth, and as indeed he did; and
yet it might well be , that in this generall noyse and
going away of some , and remouing of some of the
next to D. *Featly* , the Attestators might not heare, or

obserue

obſerue the Ieſuits word or geſture;and ſo might truely
ſay,we do not remember any ſuch word, nor did obſerue the remouing of ſome, nor D. *Featlyes* comming
neere, nor M. *Fiſhers* riſing &c. But to auow abſolutly,that M. *Fiſher* did not ſay, nor did nor could do,
as he is moſt aſſured he could and did, deſerueth iuſt
blame of exceeding great boldnes in the principall de-
uiſer of the Atteſtation, and ouer much credulity in
the Subſcribers; both which faults may iuſtly take
away authority from the whole Atteſtation, or at leaſt
giue iuſt cauſe to ſuſpect it, ſo far forth as it is contradictory to the Cath. Relation. Neither can the credit
of it be defended by that obiection, which the Atteſtatours, or D. *Featly* for them, make out of the reflexion of the Catholique Relatour; for that ſpeach in
which M. *Fiſhers*, and M. *Sweets* conſtancy is commended in keeping their Aduerſary to the point, was
meant onely of the reſt of the time of the diſputation; But this yeelding to diſpute if D. *Fealy* would
ſtay,was when M. *Fiſher* ſaw him to be going away,
and the words were ſaid to get D. *Featly* ſtay the due
tyme fit for that diſpute about Chriſt, which was after
D. *Featly* ſhould haue named Proteſtants in all ages.
So as there is no contradiction in theſe two ſayings,
nor indeed in any other which D. *Featly* hath put in
his Table of contradictions, as will eaſily appeare
to any who with a more impartiall affection and
ſharper ſight, then it ſeemeth D. *Featly* had, will reade
the Catholique Relation, and obſerue, that there is
not in the ſeeming contrary ſentences rightly vnderſtood, an affirmation and negation of altogether one
and the ſame thing, which is requiſite in a Contradiction; but ſome or other obſeruable difference, either in the matter, manner, or tyme &c. ſo as both
                                        may

may be, and are true.

Laftly, Whereas D. *Featly* maketh the Atteftators, in refpect of D. *Goads* Reply, call in queftion the truth of *M. Fishers* proteftation, in which he affured that he did not wittingly and willingly wrong either *D. White*, or *D. Featly* in his Relations or writings; *M. Fisher* faith, that he did not then heare, or mark that Reply of *D. Goade*, but now anfwereth; firft, that whether the errour were aduantagious or no, he is fure it was not wittingly and willingly committed, neither did he intend to take any aduantage by it; neither is it a good fequele, if the errour had bene more aduantagious then it was, that therefore there is iuft caufe to fufpect it to be wittingly and willingly committed. For although comonly no mā doth wittingly & willingly erre but for his owne aduantage, yet it doth not follow that euery errour wihich is aduantagious is wittingly and willingly, committed, efpecially when the party protefteth as *M. Fisher* did, that it was not wittingly and willingly committed.

Secondly; *M. Fisher* hauing now lately looked into that very paper which then he wrote, findeth (in that place againft which D. *Featly* tooke exception) that there is not any errour, at which (confidering *antecedentia & confequentia*) *M. Fisher* could take aduantage, as he will be ready to fhew to D. *Goade* whenfoeuer it fhalbe reafonably, and with his fecurity required; for the place is yet markeably extant in the paper to be feene, where that which was (vpon D. *Featly* his exception) added, is rather neceffary for more explication, then for any aduantage which could be taken.

I forbeare purpofely to make any anfwer to any of thofe groffe Imputations, which *M. Gee*, hath fet

M 3   out

out in print againſt *M. Fisher,* and other **Catholique**
Prieſts;for being as they are groſſely falſe, no wiſe man
will belieue them : neither do they deſerue any other
Anſwere .

F I N I S.

A
REPLY
TO D. VVHITE
AND D. FEATLY:

Who haue vndertaken to shew a Visible Protestant Church
in all Ages, by naming, prouing, and defending Visible
Protestants in all Ages, out of good Authors.

THE FIRST PART.

In which is shewed, that neither they, nor any other, haue performed
this vndertaken Taske, in such methode and manner as M. Fishers
Questiō (proposed to the sayd Doctours in a Conferēce) required: And
much lesse haue they, or can they, or any other, shew such a Visible
Protestant Church in all Ages, and Nations, as Christs true Church is
(in the Prophesies and promises of holy Scripture) described. Whence
it followeth, that the Protestant Church, is not the true Church of
Christ.

Their seed shalbe knowne in Nations, and their offeringes in the mid-
dest of the people : All that shall see them, shall know them,
because these are the seed which our Lord hath
Blessed. *Isa. 61: Vers. 9.*

Permissu Superiorum, M. DC. XXV.

IN this first Part (besides D. White and D. Featly) diuers other Protestant VVriters, to wit, M. Bernard; M. Rogers; the Authour of the Booke called, The perpetuall Visibility; the Authour of the Booke called, Luthers Predecessours; & D. Vshers Sermon, all treating this Question, are examined, and refuted.

THE PREFACE

TO THE READER.

ENTLE READER.

I suppose thou mayst haue heard of a Conference betweene *D.VVhite* and *D. Featly* Protestant-Ministers on the one side, and *M. Fisher*, and *M. Sweet* Iesuits on the other syde; in which (both partyes being agreed, that the true Church of Christ (of which men are to learne true, diuine infallible Fayth necessary to saluation) hath bene and must be visible in all ages) the Question proposed by *M. Fisher* (at the intreaty of an old Gentleman, who desired satisfaction,)

was

was. *VVhether the Proteſtant Church had, bene alwayes viſible? And whether the names of Viſible Proteſtants in all ages, could be produced out of good Authors ?*

    The which Queſtion being explicated, and a methode preſcribed by *M.*

See the Anſwere to a Pamphlet called, Fiſher catched in his owne Net. *Fiſher* ; in a paper ſent to the Doctours before the meeting (as is declared in the Catholique Relation of that Conference) the Doctours did vndertake to ſhew a viſible proteſtant Church in all ages, both by a Syllogiſme, and by an Induction of Names of Viſible men, whom the ſaid Doctours ſhould out of good Authors proue, & defend to haue bene Proteſtãts, & conſequétly (according to the methode preſcribed) they ought to haue named men in all pages, differing in Fayth from Roman Catholiques, and agreing in the ſame Proteſtant Fayth, and Religion which is contayned in the 39. Articles (vnto which all English--Proteſtant--Miniſters are

                                       bound

bound to fubfcribe) without contradicting, and condemning any of them.

It therfore, hath bene expected,
that the Doctours, who did make this
bold offer (feconded with a promife of Ibid.
performance, made by the right Honorable Earle of Warwicke in their be-
halfe) would not haue failed in their
printed Books to fet downe a complete
Catalogue of the Names of Proteftants
in all ages, with proofes and defences
fufficient to shew a Vifible Proteftant
Church in all ages, and to confront
thofe Catalogues of Catholique Romane profeflors, which are fet downe by
Gualterus in his *Tabula Chronographica*,
by *M. Fisher* in his Reply to *M. VVotton*
and *M. VVhite*, by S. N. in his *Appendixe
to the Antidote* (lately defended by L. D.)
and others. But hauing perufed the late
printed Bookes which thefe two Doctours haue fet out againft *M. Fisher*,
and alfo the bookes of diuers other Proteftant

teftant Minifters, who (perceauing this
Queftion to touch deeply the credit &
life of their Proteftant Church, which
either muft be shewed alwayes vifible,
and of an vnchanged Fayth, or muft be
denied not to be Chrifts Church) haue
endeauored to make Anfwere, and in
the beft fort they could, to shew a Vifible Proteftant Church; yet I cannot
find, that any one of them hath giuen a
good anfwere to *M. Fishers* Queftion:
neither is there hope (as will appeare
by the enfuing examination of euery
one of their feuerall Anfwers, and by
the Replyes made vnto them) that
either they, or any other can giue good
anfwer to this Queftion. And therfore
I hope, that euery one (who is not
wilfully blynde, or carelefly negligent
in a matter which fo much importeth,
and neerly concerneth his faluation)
will confider of the cafe, and finding (as
by this enfuing difcourfe he will finde)

that no fort of Proteſtants, or any other
ſect of ancient or moderne Heretikes
can (as the Roman Catholique can)
ſhew their Church to haue bene alwayes viſible, and neuer to haue changed the firſt receiued Fayth; he will (as I
wiſh) reſolue, that no fort of Chriſtians,
differing in doctrine of Fayth from the
Romane Church, are, or can be Chriſts
true Church ; and therupon will determine to renounce all vpſtart Nouelty
of whatſoeuer Hereticall Congregation, and imbrace the moſt ancient, and
neuer changed Fayth of the Roman
Catholique Church.

A TA:

8

A TABLE
OF THE CHAPTERS
of this first Part.

THE

THE I. CHAPTER.

About the Vtility of M. Fishers *Question (requiring Names of Visible Protestants in all Ages, out of good Authors) for finding out the true Church, and, by it, the true Fayth.*

EFORE I begin to examine and reply vpon the Answers of such as haue vndertaken to answer M. *Fishers* question, I think it will not be amisse to make a brief recapitulatiō of some part of that which M. *Fisher* hath set downe more at large, in a booke called *The Treatise of Fayth*, and in his Reply to M. *Antony Wotton*, and M. *Iohn white* Ministers, who wrote against that Booke. For although, I could wish that euery one (who is desirous of satisfaction about the whole foundation and frame of that one, true, diuine, infallible, entire Fayth, which is necessary to saluation) would get, and read those bookes themselues, in which he may find prooued at large that which heere I intend briefly to intimate; yet in regard

B that

that euery one cannot get thofe Bookes, nor haue lea-
See the
Treatife of
Fayth. And
the Reply
to *M. VVot-
ton* and *M.
VVhite* in
defence of it.
Eph. 4. 5.
Hebr. 11. 6.
Rom. 10. 14.
15.
fure to read them, I defire the Reader at leaſt to obſerue
& beare in mynd, efpecially thefe moſt profitable , neceffary, and important truthes. Firſt, that there is one infallible, entire Fayth, without which it is vnpoffible to
pleafe God and to attayne faluation. Secondly, that the
only ordinary infallible meanes to attayne this Fayth,
is neither Scripture alone, nor the naturall wit of any
man, nor priuate fpirit, but the teaching of the true,
continually Viſible Church of Chriſt. Thirdly, that
the eaſieſt and readyeſt way , to difcerne this true viſible Church of Chriſt, from all Hereticall Conuen-
ticles, who may pretend to teach the pure doctrine of
Chriſt, is by help of hiſtories , to finde which of all viſible forts of Chriſtians , that be now in the world,
can ſhew a viſible, well proued , vninterrupted Catalogue, and as it were pedegree of Paſtours teaching, &
people belieuing the firſt receiued Fayth of Chriſt in
all ages, without any change. As to difcerne the prefent lawfull heyre of an vnſtayned ancient Family,
from all baſtardly brood of fuch, as may pretend (as
euery one may pretend to be lawfull heyre of that family, by faying they haue the vnſtayned bloud in their
bodyes of the firſt Aunceſtor) the eaſieſt and readyeſt
way, were by help of hiſtoryes to finde which of the
Pretendours can ſhew a viſible, well proued, vninterrupted pedegree of his vnſtayned predeceſſours, vpward vnto, or downward frō the faid firſt Anceſtour.

For like as, after fuch a pedegree being ſhewed by
one, the like wherof could not be ſhewed by any
other, euery one would prefently iudge , and fay certainly, *This man is lawfull heyre.* Neither would they regard the other Pretendours Plea of hauing in their bodyes the firſt anceſtours pure bloud , as knowing that
                                                          this

this is, or may be a common Plea of all Pretendours, and that about this Plea endleſſe arguments may be made, to and fro, without hope that this Queſtion ſhould euer be decided, vntil this dilatory Plea ſet aſide, Hiſtoryes be pretended, and out of them Names of men be ſhewed, who were knowne, or comonly held to be the lawfull heyres in euery ſeuerall Age of that firſt Anceſtor, and who conſequently had his true bloud in their body: Euen ſo, after one ſort of Chriſtians, to wit Roman Catholiques, haue (as already they haue) *See Gualte-* ſhewed ſuch a viſible, well proued, vninterrupted Ca- *rus his Ta-* talogue, and as it were pedegree of the Names of Pa- *bula Chrono-* ſtours in all ages teaching, and people belieuing the *graphica, &* firſt receiued Fayth of Chriſt, without change, the like *others.* wherof no other ſort of Chriſtians can ſhew; euery one may, and ought preſently to iudge, that according as was prophecyed by Iſay, *Iſti ſunt ſemen cui benedixit Do-* *minus;* Theſe are the ſeed which our Lord hath Bleſſed, to wit, with his promiſed ſpirit, and Word of Truth, as the ſame prophet teſtifyeth , *My ſpirit which is in thee,* *Iſa. 61. 9.* *and my words with I haue put in thy mouth , ſhall not depart* *Iſa. 59. 20.* *out of thy mouth, nor out of the mouth of thy ſeed , nor out of* *Pſal. 2. 8.* *the mouth of thy ſeeds ſeed, from henceforth for euer;* eſpe- cially when the conſent of Hiſtoryes do teſtify, that theſe haue ſucceſſiuely had, and yet haue, viſible Poſ- ſeſſion of the houſe, goods and lands of Chriſt ; to wit, the viſible Church (in which is all truth of heauēly do- ctrine, and all grace of holy Sacraments) vnto which belonge all Nations , which by the gift of his eternall Father was made Chriſts inheritance , and therfore theſe are moſt certainly Chriſt his true heyres, and haue true Authority to teach true doctrine, and miniſter Sa- craments; & doubtleſſe do teach his true doctrine, and rightly adminiſter his true Sacraments . Whatſoeuer

therfore

therfore other forts of chriftians, different from thefe
fhall plead, and fay, We haue Chrifts true fpirit, we
teach pure doctrine, we rightly adminifter his Sacraments; this their Plea muft not be regarded, in regard
this is the common Plea of all Pretendours; about
which, endleffe Arguments may be, and are made to
and fro, without hope to decide the Queftion, vntill this plea fet afide, Hiftoryes be produced, and out of
them Names of men be fhewed, who were in euery
feuerall age knowne to be lawfull heyres of chrift, and
to haue had by fucceffion vifible poffeffion of Chrifts
houfe, his church, and his goods, the true doctrine and
Sacraments, and his lands, to wit, his Inheritance of all
Nations.

Now this being obferued and borne in mynde, I
hope the difcreete Reader will make good benefit of
this enfuing difcourfe, and will fee, that M. Fishers queftion was, and is very profitable, neceffary, and important, both for confirmation of Roman Catholikes in
their Fayth, and refolution to continue in vnity of the
Roman church; and to make Proteftants fee, that they
are not the true church of chrift, and confequently,
that it is impoffible for them to pleafe God, or to attayne faluation (according to the ordinary courfe of
gods Prouidence) vnleffe they (forfaking their new-
found no-Fayth, and no-church) repent, and returne
to that One, Holy, Catholique, Apoftolique, alwayes
Vifible, Vnchanged and Infallible Roman Fayth, and
church, which can, and already hath, in diuers printed
Books fhewed a vifible (well proued, and eafy to be
defended) catalogue of the Names of Paftours teaching, and people belieuing in all ages, the vnchanged
Fayth of Chrift; the like whereof no Proteftant, or
whatfoeuer other fort of chriftans, euer did, or can
                                                    fhew

shew for confirmation of their Fayth and church, as now I am to declare by examining and replying vpon such as haue of late endeauoured to answer M. *Fishers* Question aforesaid.

THE II. CHAPTER.

In which, M. Fishers Question is explicated, and D. Whites, and D. Featlyes Answere giuen in the Conference, is shewed to haue byn very deficient.

THOSE that haue read, or shall read a Booke lately set out, called: *An answere to a Pamphlet, intituled: Fisher catched in his owne net*; will easily see by the occasion and end of the Conference related in that booke, *Cd.* 4. §. 1. & 2. that the true meaning of M. *Fishers* Question, was as followeth.

Whether the Protestant Church was visible, and so visible in all ages, as the Names of the Professours of their Fayth, may be found in good Authours? And in case any say, (as D. *Featly* said) that such men be found in good Authors, M. *Fishers* question required, 1. That such mens Names be actually set downe in all ages. 2. That good proofes be brought out of good Authors, that ech man named was a Protestant, that is to say, differed in Fayth from the present Romane Church, and agreed in Fayth with the present English Protestant Church, which requireth

requireth euery Minifter to fubfcribe to all their 39.
Articles, and excommunicateth all that deny any part
of the faid Articles. 3. That he which fetteth downe
the Names, do defend againft M. *Fisher* and M. *Sweet*,
that none of the men named, did differ in Fayth from
the Proteftant Englifh Church, nor condemne any
one of the 39. Articles ; The which, when it fhalbe
performed, M. *Fisher* did, and doth yet, vndertake in a
like proportionable fenfe, 1. To fet downe Names of
Roman Catholiques in all ages. 2. To bring proofes
out of good Authours, that euery one by him named,
was a Rom. Catholique, that is to fay, differed in Fayth
from the prefent Proteftant Church, and agreed in
Fayth with the prefent Rom. Church. 3. To defend
againft D. *White* and D. *Featly*, that none of the men
whom they fhall name, did cōdemne any one point of
doctrine of Rom. Fayth, defined in the Councell of
Trent.

Alfo in the faid Anfwer to the Pamphlet aforefaid,
it may be feene, how D. *Featly* and D. *White*, infteed
of performing what M. *Fisher* had required, did endeauour what they could, to fpend the tyme otherwife in
Impertinencies, without euer offering to fet downe
(which fhould haue ben firft done) Names of particuler Proteftants, vntill they were by the often vrging of
M. *Fisher* and M. *Sweet*, and at laft euen by Proteftant
Auditors, forced to name fome ; and then alfo they did
not, as the Queftion required, name men in al ages, but
only in the firft or fecond age; neither did they Name
any one confeffed Proteftant, nor any fuch as they
could proue, or defend to be Proteftants, in manner
aforefaid; for although D. *Featly* offered to difpute about
thofe few he named, yet this was only done either to
take occafion to break off the Conference, or that he
                                                     might

might in a cunning manner, change the state of the
Queſtion, and ſo diuert the Audience from obſeruing
his want of ability to performe his vndertaken taske of
naming Proteſtants in all ages, which by the Order
preſcribed in the explication of *M. Fiſhers* queſtion,
ſhould haue been firſt, and fully done before any proof
were brought.

The proofes which he intended to bring (as *M.
Fisher* had reaſon to coniecture by the reſt of the whole
courſe of his ſpeach in the Conference) were not
ſuch as the Queſtion required, to wit, producing good
authors, who did plainly ſhew thoſe he named to be
Proteſtants, but by alleadging of particuler texts of
ſcripturs, or ſentences of Fathers, about the ſenſe whereof he knew he could ſo wrangle with his Aduerſary
without end, that the Audience ſhoud neuer cleerly
vnderſtand of what Religion thoſe were which he
named, whiles he would wreſt the words to one ſenſe
which his aduerſary vnderſtood in another; which
courſe or Method of prouing had ben to no purpoſe,
but to ſpend the tyme without fruite, or euer coming
to an agreement in the maine queſtion, in which the
Audience expected and deſired to be reſolued. In
which ſort euery other wrangling Heretique of whatſoeuer ſect, although moſt abſurd and moſt newly in-
uented, may vndertake againſt *D. Featly* to name,
proue, and defend men of his Profeſſion to haue ben
in all ages; whom if *D. Featly* permit to diſpute about
Chriſt and his Apoſtles, before he vrge him to name
me of ſucceding Ages, that Heretique will, I doubt not,
wrangle about theſe only (out of textes of Scriptures
and ſentences of Fathers) whole dayes, and yeares without end, and will neuer yield that Chriſt and his
Apoſtles were of any other opinion, then ſuch as is
ſutable

sutable to his sect, especially in any matter fundamentall or substantiall, supposing libertie be graunted to him (which Protestants take to themselues)to account no book of Scripture to be Canonicall, no translation true, no Interpretation right, no consequence good, no matter fundamentall or substantiall, but which it shall pleafe him, or thofe of his sect, or his, or their priuate spirit, to allow for such.

Now, if D. *Featly* would not (as doubtles he would not) thinke, such a wrangler to haue sufficiently named some men of his profession in all ages by only naming Chrift and his Apostles, and some others in the firft, second, or third Age, nor sufficiently to haue proued or defended the to be of his sect or opinion, by only alleadging and disputing about texts of such Bookes and Translations as himself liketh, and with such Interpretations onely which himself alloweth, and about such matters only which himself will account fundamentall and substantiall: If I say, D. *Featly* would not account such a wrangling Heretique (an Arrian or Anabaptift for example) to haue by this manner of proceeding, performed his vndertaken taske of naming, prouing, and defending out of Good Authors men of his profession (Arrians or Anabaptifts) to haue ben visible in all ages since Chrift; then ought not D. *Featly* himself, and much lesse any other wife man thinke, that D. *Featly* & his assistant D. *White* haue performed what they vndertooke in the Conference, by their like manner of proceeding.

THE

THE III. CHAPTER.

In which is shewed, how many Ministers after the Conference aforesayd, haue endeuoured to make Answere: and that none haue sufficiently answered M. Fishers Question.

N the precedent Chapter I haue made it plaine, that *D. White* and *D. Featly* did not (during the time of Conferéce) sufficiently answer the propofed Queftion, nor confequently fatisfie the Iudicious & vnpartiall Auditours of the aforefaid Conference: Now it refteth to be examined, whether they, or any for them, haue (according to promife made in their behalf) yet fatisfied their obligation, either by a fecond meeting (which may perhaps be excufed vpon iuft reafon) or in writing, which *M. Fisher* in his letter to the Right Honourable Earle of *Warwicke* required, and might haue ben without offence performed by the Doctours. And I find that the aforfaid Doctours haue ben fo long filent fince that tyme, that diuers other Proteftant writers, being (as it may be prefumed forry and afhamed, that their Doctours did giue no better fatisfactió) haue thought fit to fet out ech one his feuerall Pamphlet; as if forfooth, they could & would giue a more full and fatisfying anfwer.

The firft is one *M. Bernard*, who wrote the Pamphlet called, *Looke beyond Luther*.

The fecond *M. Rogers*, who writeth an Anfwere to

C   *M. Fishers*

M. Fishers fiue propofitions.

The third masketh himfelf vnder the letters. *W. C.* who in a Dialogue promifeth to anfwere the Queftiõ, and to difcouer *Fishers* Folly.

The fourth is, the Author of a Booke intituled: *The perpetuall Vifibility of the true Church.*

The fifth, is a booke intituled : *Luthers Predeceffors,* or an Anfwer to the Queftion, *Where was your Church, before Luther?*

And now lately, D. *White* hath fet out a large Volume called : *A Replye to Iefuite Fisher &c.* in which he doth a litle touch this Queftion.

And more lately D. *Featly* hath fet out, *His Romish Fisher catched, and kept in his net.*

After this againe D. *Vsher* hath fet out a Seimon, in which he toucheth this fame matter.

And laft of all, is crept out another forry Pamphlet, called *The Proteftant Kalendar.*

All which I haue examined in fuch order as they haue come forth;but I cannot find in all, or any one of them a good Anfwere to *M. Fishers Queftion* : which not being found, Proteftantes may well doubt, or rather certainely know, that neither their Doctours, nor any other can make fufficient Anfwer to that queftion, vn-leffe they wilbe fo honeft, as to confeffe, that there were only two famoufly knowne Proteftants, called *Nullus* and *Nemo*; that is in Englifh, *None,* & *Not any one,* who were vifible in all ages before Luther.

THE

THE IV. CHAPTER.

About M. Bernards, *Looke beyond Luther*.

IN M. *Bernards* Booke I obserue, 1. That the man had a good will to make simple people belieue, that there were Protestáts in such plenty in all the first Ages, as that he needed not name the in particuler, but only in generall, by saying first (as euery Heretique will say for his owne Sect) *Protestant Religion is found in Scriptures*. The which he proueth only by saying, that in the Protestant Bookes (as other Heretiques may say of their Bookes) Textes of Scriptures are quoted for what they affirme; which Reason if it be well pondered, may as well proue, that not onely all other Heretiques, but also the Diuell himselfe, are of the Protestant Religion, in regard not only all Heretiques (as *Vincentius Lirynensis* noteth) can, and do plentifully quote places of Scriptures, but also the Diuel himself wanteth not his alleadging (euen to Christ himself) the very words of the scripture: Therefore if onely quoting places, or citing words of Scripture can make Protestant Religion, there is no doubt but it was before *Luther* in the *Arrians*, *Pelagians*, and other damned Heretiques, and in the Deuill himself; which is more then I suppose *M. Bernard* would haue to be proued by his said reason.

Vincentius Lyr. contra Hær.

It is therefore no good reason, for, as *Vincentius Lyrinensis* noteth, besides words of scripture we must ad-

Vbi supra.

ioine

C 2

ioine Ecclefiafticall (Catholique fenfe) which M. *Ber-*
nard cannot proue to be in Proteftant Catechifmes or
Homilyes,fo far forth as they teach doctrine contrary
to the Rom. Church. Neither can M. *Bernard* fufficiently fatisfie by onely faying, that Proteftants haue
the true fenfe from the fpirit of God, for fo alfo will
euery Heretique fay and thinke, in regard the Prince
of darknes hauing once by pride and felfe conceipts
blinded their vnderftanding, can eafily transfigure
himfelf fo,as to feeme to them to be an Angell of light,
and worke fuch feeming holy motions,and heauenly
2.Cor. 11. 14. Confolations in their hearts,feconded with the found
of the words of the Scripture, as maketh them (poore
foules) belieue that they haue in their brefts the Holy
Ghoft himfelfe teaching them all Truth,fo as they can
better interpret fcripture,then all the ancient and prefent Doctours of the Church. Thefe be ftrong delu-
fions of Sathan which cannot better be difcouered &
auoyded then by humbly fubmitting ones Iudgment
and fpirit to the vnanimous confent of the ancient, &
prefent Paftours and Doctours of the Cath. Church;
holding all which they hold, and reiecting all which
they reiect, and accounting that to be Gods true fpirit
which agreeth with them, and that not to be of God
which in any matter of Fayth and religion difcordeth
from them,according to that Rule of difcerning fpirits
which is giuen by S. *Iohn* in thefe wordes: *Nos ex Deo*
1. Ioan. 4. 6. *fumus &c.* We, fayth S. *Iohn*, (and with him all ancient & prefent lawfull vifible Paftours of the Church
agreeing in one) are of God, he that heareth vs, is
of God,he that is not of God,doth not heare vs; in this
we know the fpirit of Truth,and the fpirit of Errour.
     2. I obferue in M.*Bernards* booke,that hauing in gene-
rall without naming particulers challenged the Ancient
                                          Fathers,

Fathers, Martyrs, & ſome of the preſent Romā Religiō to haue ben profeſſors of the Proteſtant Fayth, he doth not proue this (as *M. Fisher* required to be proued) by alleading ſome good Authours who plainly ſhew theſe to haue ben Proteſtants, or to haue differed in Fayth from the preſent Rom. Church in ſome point, held by Proteſtants, and not to haue condemned any one point of the Proteſtant Fayth contained in the 39. Articles aforeſaid Neither is *M. Bernard* able to defend againſt *M. Fisher*, that all thoſe ancient Doctours and Martyrs, or preſent Roman catholiques (which he will by hooke and crook draw to be ſauourers of Proteſtant Religion) did hold nothing contrary to the 39. Articles; which is a needfull condition to make them to be members of the preſent Engliſh Proteſtant church, in regard it doth excommunicate *ipſo facto*, euery one that ſhall hould any thing contrary to any of the ſaid Articles; for thus ſayth the firſt Canon of the Engliſh Proteſtant Church: *Whoſoeuer shall hereafter affirme, that any of the 39. Articles agreed vpon by the Archbishop &c. are in any part ſuperſtitious, or erroneous &c. Let him be excommunicated, ipſo facto.* Now either all, or at leaſt many of the Ancient Fathers did, and yet in their writings do, affirme ſome or other part of the doctrine contained in the ſaid 39. Articles to be erroneous: *Ergo*, they are no members, but excommunicated out of the preſent Engliſh Proteſtant Church. I meruail therefore, that *M. Bernard* durſt be ſo bould, as to account the auncient Fathers members of his Church; But who ſo bold as blind Bayard, and who more blinde then *M. Bernard*, who (as he confeſſed to one in London) neither hath the Fathers writings, nor euer read them, but truſted, as he ſaid, honeſt men; when indeed he truſted only ſome other Prote-

See the Booke of Canons, Can. 5.

ſtants,

C 3

ftants, whofe fincerity and skill he had great caufe to fufpeᴄt, in regard Proteftants are fo ordinarily taxed for falfifying the fenfe, and fometymes the very words of the Fathers, as that before one giue credit to any one of their Note-bookes, or printed bookes, he had need carefully to examine what they alleadge, comparing it with the Fathers owne writings, and not to contét himfelf only to fee the words truly alleadged, but to fee *Antecedentia* and *Confequentia*, and the whole connexion of the matter, that fo he may difcerne whether they alledge them in the right fenfe or no. But this *M. Bernard*, by his owne confeffion, hath not done, therefore no man ought to credit his bold and blind affertions, affirming that the Ancient Fathers & Martyrs &c. were Proteftants; nor can they confequently accounr, that he hath fufficiently anfwered *M. Fishers* Queftion.

THE V. CHAPTER.

Concerning M. Rogers *his Anfwere to* M. Fishers *fiue Propofitions.*

BY this which hath ben faid againft *M. Bernard* his *Looke beyond Luther*, it may be eafily feene, that *M. Rogers* hath not fufficiently anfwered *M. Fishers* Queftion aforefaid; for with a bold Audacitie he nameth for Proteftants, famoufly knowne Roman Catholiques, to wit, the chief writers of of the firft 700. Yeares, and among others euen *S. Bede*, whofe writings and profeffion of life (being a profeffed Roman Catholique Monke) fhew him to be no Proteftant. The like may be faid of diuers others, but at this tyme it may fuffice to giue this one example to fhew, that *M. Rogers* naming all thofe he named, fpake without booke, or without hauing at hand, or looking into his books, and that he might afwell haue named the Pope, and Cardinals, and Bifhops, Priefts, Monkes, and all other Religious perfons of the prefent Roman Church to be Proteftants, as he nameth the faid ancient Fathers.

And I meruayle why, hauing gone halfe the way (as he fayth) he maketh a flop there, and doth not with the like audacity goe on, in naming other famous Rom. Catholiques in euery of the other Ages, namely, fuch as *Gualterus* in Latin, and the Author of the *Appendix to the Antidote* in Englifh, haue fet downe for members of the Rom. Church. Neither can I fee any reafon why he did not, but that (as it feemeth) he was not refolued whether it were better to put in his Catalogue the Names of damned Heretiques which difagree in diuers points of Fayth from all ancient and prefent Paftours and Doctours of the Church, and euen from the Proteftants themfelues; or els to put in Names of Popes, Cardinals, Bifhops, Priefts, Monkes, and other Religions men, whofe writings and profeffion of life palpably fhew, that they held the prefent Roman doctrine, and communicated with the Rom. Church, and (as ancient Fathers haue done before them) condemned fome or other Proteftants doctrine, euen of thofe 39. Articles of the Englifh Proteftant Church, although they be more craftily compofed, then the Articles of other Proteftant C hurches.

I might

I might therefore without more adoe, conclude, that *M. Rogers* hath not ſufficiently anſwered *M. Fiſhers* queſtion, in regard he hath neither named Proteſtants in all ages, neither hath he ſufficiently proued them he named to be Proteſtants, neither laſtly can he defend thoſe he named to be Proteſtants, but by ſuch falſe ſuppoſitions, and bad definitions, and ſuch other ſhifts, as any *Arrian*, or Anabaptiſt, or whatſoeuer other abſurd Sectary may by the like defend the ſame perſons to haue ben of their Religion or ſect. Neuertheleſſe becauſe the method or manner of proceeding vſed by *M. Rogers*, in anſwere of *M. Fiſhers* fiue Propoſitions, hath gotten him the Name and credit of a Worthy Oxford-Deuine, I haue thought good to examine more particulerly his ſaid Anſwere to *M. Fiſhers* fiue Propoſitions, the which are theſe enſuing:

A true Copie of M. Fishers fiue Propoſitions.

Eph. 4.5.
Heb. 11. 6.
Rom. 10. 14.
15.
Eph. 4. 11.

1. It is certaine, there is one, and but one, true infallible Fayth, without which none can pleaſe God.
2. This one Infallible Fayth, cannot be had according to the ordinary courſe of Gods prouidence, but by hearing Preachers, and Paſtours of the true, viſible Church, who only are lawfully ſent, and authorized to teach the true Word of God.
3. As therefore this one Infallible Fayth hath ben, and muſt be in all ages, ſo there muſt needs be in all ages Preachers, and Paſtours of the true, viſible Church, of whom all ſorts of people haue in tyme paſt (as appeareth by hiſtoryes) learned, and muſt learne in all future tymes, the ſaid Infallible Fayth.
4. Hence it followeth, That if Proteſtants be the true viſible Church of Chriſt, all ſorts of men who in euery age, haue had the aforeſaid Infallible Fayth, haue learned it by Proteſtant preachers, whoſe Names may

may be found (*in* ✳ *Hiftories, as the Names of thofe are found*) who in feuerall Ages did teach, and conuert ✳ Thefe people of feuerall Nations vnto the Fayth of Chrift. words are

5. Hence further followeth, that if there cannot left out in *M.* (as there cannot) be found in Hiftories Names of Pro- *Rogers*Copy, teftant preachers who in all ages did teach all forts of Faythfull people, and who conuerted feuerall Nations vnto the Chriftian Fayth ; Hence followeth, I fay, that Proteftants are not the true Vifible Church of Chrift, neither are their Preachers lawfully fent, or fuf- ficiently authorized to teach;nor people fecurely war- ranted to learne of them that one Infallible Fayth, without which none can poffibly pleafe God, nor (if they fo liue and dye)be faued.

If any Proteftant will anfwere, let him fet downe Names of Proteftant Preachers in all ages who taught people Proteftant doctrine, in euery feuerall age; or confeffe there was no fuch before Luther, or at leaft not in all ages, to be found in Hiftories. Thus far the Copy of *M. Fishers* Propofitions.

An Examination of M. Rogers Anfwere to the Fiue Propofitions aforefaid.

I find firft, that he granteth the firft three without any exception, which I defire may be diligently noted and well pondered. For out of thefe three grounds (to wit, 1. that there is one, and but one Fayth neceffary to faluation : and 2. that this Fayth (according to the ordinary courfe of Gods prouidence ,)cannot be had otherwife then by hearing the preaching or teaching of lawfully-fent paftours : and 3. that this Fayth hath ben in all ages paft (as appeareth by Hiftories) taught by Paftours of the true vifible Church who only are lawfully fent : Out of thefe three grounds, I fay, eui- dently followeth that, which is *M. Fishers* fourth Propofition, to wit : *If Proteftant Fayth be the true Fayth,*

D *and*

and their Church the true Church (or as M. *Rogers* had rather say, a true Church) *of Christ, then their Protestant
Fayth, differing from the Roman Fayth, hath ben taught in all
ages by Lawfully-sent visible Protestant Pastours, whose Names
may be found in Historyes, as Names of others are found, who
did teach the true Fayth of Christ in all ages.*

This to follow out of the aforesaid three grounds,
is, as I said, most euident; neither doth M. *Rogers* make
any bones to grant, saue only that it may be, he will
make a bogge at the word, *Histories*, as not finding it
in his copy, nor thinking it perhaps necessary, that the
names of Protestant Pastours, who taught the Protestant Fayth in all ages past, be found in Hystories; but
vnderstanding the word, *Hystories*, as M. *Fisher* vnderstood it, to wit, for some or other kinde of Records
or monuments, as *D. White* also vnderstood it, when
he said; *Things past cannot be shewed but by hystories*; I do
not see why M. *Rogers* may not absolutly grant the
fourth proposition, euen as it was set downe by M.
Fisher himself; for if any visible Protestant Pastours
were in all ages, teaching especially any such Protestant doctrines, as now are taught, they would haue
ben named, and spoken of, and written of, as well
as others are, who haue in all ages past taught all
sorts of true and false doctrines, in regard there cannot be assigned any reason either of the part of Gods
prouidence, or humane diligence, why the names of
others, euen false Teachers, in all ages, should be set
downe, and preserued in histories yet extant, rather
then the names of such as Protestants deeme to be
the only true Teachers of pure doctrine; for doubt-
lesse both God, who is zealous of his honour, and
carefull to honour and preserue the memory of them
that would honour him, would for his honours sake
haue

In his Way
to the church
pag. 358.

Gloria meam
alteri non
dabo. Isa. 42.
8.

haue procured honorable memory ot ſuch as did by
teaching truth honour him; and men carefull of their
ſoules health(which they cannot attayn (according to
the ordinary courſe)but by hearing ſuch Paſtours only,
who haue had lawfull Succeſſion from Chriſts Apoſtles) haue more reaſon diligently to looke, that memory be preſerued of ſuch Paſtours, and of pure diuine
Truth taught by them, then of others who taught any
other falſe,and not pure doctrine.

Certaine therfore it is, that the names(or ſome thing
equiualent to Names) and the doctrines of true Paſtours, who did in all ages paſt, teach true diuine doctrine,may be found in Hiſtories,as well as the Names
and doctrines of others are found who did teach any
other doctrine. And therefore if Proteſtants haue had
any Paſtours, teaching true doctrines in all Ages,
doubtleſſe their names would be extant in Hiſtories
yet extant : which being preſuppoſed and granted, as
M. Rogers ſeemeth to grant, by granting *M. Fiſhers*
fourth propoſition , I do not ſee how *M. Rogers* can
deny *M. Fiſhers* fifth propoſition ; for, it being ſuppoſed
that if Proteſtant preachers were, their names would
be found in Hiſtoryes (as *M. Fiſhers* fourth propoſition
granted by *M. Rogers* ſuppoſeth); it may be well inferred, that if no ſuch mens names be found in Hiſtories, then no ſuch men were in all ages, nor conſequently are Proteſtants the true Church of Chriſt, for
it hath had ſuch in all ages: I do not therefore ſee, I
ſay, how *M. Rogers* can deny *M. Fiſhers* fifth propoſition,ſuppoſing he graunt,as he graunteth,his fourth
Propoſition; for although abſolutly ſpeaking , an Argument drawne from negatiue authority be (as *M. Rogers* auerreth) of it ſelf of no force ; and ſo Proteſtants
arguments which are vſually made againſt vs,out of

negatiue

Quicunquē gloʳificaue-rit me, glo-rificabo eum: & qui me contemnunt ignobiles erunt. 1. Reg. 2. 30. In memoria æterna erit iuſtus. Pſal. 111. 7.

negatiue Authority ; as for example, the scripture sayth
nothing of this or that ; or the Fathers of the first 300.
yeares make not expresse mention of this or that, *Ergo*
no such thing is, or is of no force: Yet when the negatiue Argument is grounded in an already granted affirmatiue proposition, as it is in this our case, the negatiue argument is of great and vndeniable force.

As for example, if we did grant this proposition;
If such, or such a thing were, holy Scripture would
haue spoken of it, or the Fathers of the first 300. yeares
would haue made expresse mention of it; If I say, we
granted this, we could not deny the aforesaid negatiue Argument vsually made by Protestants, to be of
force against vs. But we deny, and Protestants cannot
proue the said Affirmatiue, and so the negatiue Argument hath no force against vs. Now *M. Rogers* doth
not, nor in reason cannot deny *M. Fishers* fourth proposition, which is an Affirmatiue, whereupon his fifth
negatiue proposition is grounded; And therefore *M. Rogers* ought not to deny, but must needs graunt *M. Fishers*
fifth, and so all his fiue propositions ; which being
graunted, if he will make a good Answer as he pretendeth, he must first set downe Names of Protestant Pastours in all ages, and not content himselfe with naming some whome he thinketh to be Protestants, and
with saying, he hath gone halfe the way.

Secondly : If he will satisfie *M. Fishers* other
Paper, as he pretendeth to do, he must proue and defend them to be Protestants, as *M. Fishers* paper requireth, and must bring out some or other good Authors,
who do cleerely shew them to hold all, or some principall points of Protestant Fayth, differing from Catholique Roman Fayth, and not to condemne any of
the 39. Protestant Articles, and must not content himself

felf with making fuch arguments as he maketh, which
are moft infufficient, either to conuince, or probably to
perfwade either his Aduerfary, or any indifferent iudicious Reader; for thefe be his Arguments .

Firſt, A Caufis; *thus*:
The Fayth contained in the Scriptures, hath had
vifible Profeffors in all ages:
But the Proteftant Fayth is contained in the Scriptures: *Ergo.*

2. A Signis ; *thus*:
The Fayth which hath teftimonies of Antiquity,
Vniuerfality, and Confent of Fathers, and other wri-
ters in all ages, had vifible Profeffeurs in all ages:
But the Fayth of Proteftants hath thefe Tefti-
monies : *Ergo.*

3. Ab Exemplis : *thus*:
Names of fuch as profeffed the Proteftants Fayth
in all ages.

100. Chrift and his Apoftles.
200. S. Iohn : Ignatius: Polycarpus: Iuftinus Martyr:
Irenæus.
300. Tertullian : Clemens Alex: Origen: Cyprian:
Lactantius.
400. Athanafius: Cyrill Hierofol: Ambrofius : Nyf-
fenus : Hieronymus.
500. Ruffinus: Chryfoftomus: Auguftinus : Cyril-
lus Alex: Theodoretus : Socrates: Zozomenus.
600. Fulgentius: Enagrius: Gregorius Primus.
700. Beda : Damafcenus : Alcuinus.

Thus hauing gone halfe way, I conclude with this
Argument,
The Proteftant Fayth being that which is contained
in Scriptures, was receiued and taught by all the Orthodoxe Fathers :

But

But the Fathers aboue named be al Orthodox: *Ergo.*

Now, who doth not fee, that thefe arguments be moft infufficient, and that they may be moft eafily anfwered, by denying the Proteftant Fayth to be contained in fcriptures, or to haue teftimony of Antiquity, Vniuerfality, and Confent, or to haue ben profeffed by thofe Fathers which *M. Rogers* named? Who doth not alfo fee, that the fame Arguments may be more ftrongly retorted againft Proteftants, by onely altering the word, *Proteftant*, into *Catholique*? in regard our Cath. doctrine may be, and is ordinarily proued by playne Teftimonies of fcriptures and Fathers, euen by Côfeffion of diuers learned Proteftants themfelues. I meruayle therefore that *M. Rogers*, being accounted a worthy Oxford-Deuine, would affirme, & offer to proue, and defend Proteftants to haue bene in all ages, vpon fo fleight groundes: which if they be admitted for good, euery fect of heretiques may affirme, and proue, and defend men of their fect to haue ben Vifible in all ages. For Triall wherof, I wifh it may be imagined, that there were an Anabaptift (for example) who held all the Proteftant Fayth, fauing onely fome few Negatiues, and namely, that it is not lawfull to baptize Infants; And that this Anabaptift had framed to himfelf fuch falfe rules, as *M. Rogers* hath fet downe to himfelf, to wit:

1. *That Fayth is affirmation and not negation*; by which rule it feemeth he would not haue any negatiue propofitions, although found in fcripture, to pertaine to Fayth. 2. *That they that are in the affirmatiue, muft proue, & not thofe who are in the negatiue;* By which feemeth to follow, that a man who had tyme out of minde quietly poffeffed his land or religion, were bound to proue his right, before his vpftart aduerfary who denieth him

him

him to haue right, haue giuen a good reason of his deniall. 3. *That what was not a poynt of Fayth in the primi-*
tiue ages, cannot after be a point of Fayth ; As if there were
not some points which were at first not held necessary
to be belieued, euen by Orthodox Fathers, which af-
terward by examination and definition of the Church
in generall Councels, were made so necessary to be
belieued, as that whosoeuer did not belieue them, were
accounted not Orthodoxe, but Heretikes. And 4. *That*
the Anabaptist Fayth is that which is contained in Scripture and
the Antient Creeds ; *and the Anabaptists Church is a Society*
of men, which professeth the Fayth contained in scripture , and
the Ancient Creeds ; as (if an Anabaptist may be Iudge)it
will be held so to be.

And 5. *That hauing distinguished Fayth* (as M. Rogers doth) *into doctrines fundamentall and necessary , and*
doctrines not fundamentall, but accessorie , or not necessary,
he may be yet further allowed to reiect all Church
authority , and not to be satisfied with what is taught
by any Church, ours or his owne , (as M. Rogers confesseth he is vnsatisfied)and consequently being left to
his owne liberty , may apply this distinction as he
shall please, accounting onely that to be necessary
which he listeth so to accou͡t. I wish, I say, that such an
Anabaptist were imagined, and that M. Rogers were to
be his Opponent , that it might be seene whether this
Anabaptist could not as well by these aforesaid rules,
definitions, and distinctions affirme, proue, and defend
his Fayth and Church to haue ben alwayes Visible
against M. Rogers, as M. Rogers doth, or can by his
rules, definitions and distinctions affirme, proue, and
defend the Protestant Church to haue ben alwaies
Visible, against Catholiques ; or whether M. Rogers
could better conuince such an Anabaptist, not to haue
the

the auncient Fayth, or not to be a member of the continuall Viſible Church, then a Catholique can conuince *M. Rogers*.

For prooſe wherof let it be ſuppoſed, that *M. Rogers*
could (as he cannot) produce out of Scriptures, and
Fathers, and other writers in all ages, as manie, and as
plaine and pregnant affirmatiue ſentences againſt the
Negatiue doctrine of Anabaptiſts, as Catholiques ordinarily do againſt Proteſtants Negatiues ; And then
I aſke *M. Rogers*, whether this Anabaptiſt may not (as
vſually Proteſtants do) take one or other exception,
either of argument, or booke out of which the ſentence.
is cited, as if it were not vndoubtedly Canonicall, or
authenticall, or againſt the Tranſlation or Tranſcript,
or printed Copie, as not certainly knowne to be conforme to the firſt Autographon or Originall, or againſt
the Interpretation and ſenſe of the Wordes, or the
Conſequence gathered out of them, as if ſome other
ſenſe were intended by the Authour; Or if none of
theſe exceptions can be made, whether he may not
at leaſt ſay, that it is not the Fayth or conſent of all Antiquity, which doth hold ſuch an affirmatiue, contrary
to his negatiue doctrine, but onely the opinion of ſome
one or few, while others hold the contrary, or ſeeme
doubtfull; Or if it be ſhewed to be the generall doctrine of all who had occaſion to write of that matter,
without any one teaching contrary, whether he may
not deny the point to be fundamentall, and ſay, that
they differ not from him in doctrine neceſſary, but
only in doctrine acceſſary, & that notwithſtanding
this difference they may, & are poſſeſſours of his Fayth,
and members of his Anabaptiſt Church.

All this, doubtles, he may ſay, and ſo defend ancient
Fathers to be of his Fayth and Chuch, as well as *M. Ro-*
ers

gers can defend them to be of his Fayth and Church.
Neither can the *M. Rogers* difprcue what the Anabaptift auerreth, but with the fame breath he difproueth
his owne book, and maketh it appeare to euery iudicious Reader, that he neither can truely name, foundly
proue, nor in any good fort defend, either the ancient
Fathers, or any other Orthodoxe whom he nameth, or
any lawfull Paftours, or others, Catholiques or Heretiques, before Luther, or indeed *Luther* himfelf, to haue
held the entiere Proteftant Fayth; For if all Proteftant
doctrines which be differēt from the Fayth of the Rom.
Church, may be called doctrines of Proteftant Fayth, it
may be euidently fhewed that none of the aforefaid did
al in points of Fayth agree with the Englifh Proteftant
Church, whofe Minifters are bound to fubfcribe to
the 39. Articles aboue mentioned.

But if all Proteftant doctrines which be different
from the Roman Church her Fayth, be not doctrines
of Proteftant Fayth, I require *M. Rogers* to fhew me
which (in particuler)be, and which be not doctrines of
Proteftant Fayth, that it may be difcerned who did, and
who did not hould the Proteftant Fayth: and that
withall he giue me a fubftantiall ground, well proued out of fcripture, Why thofe particuler points which
he fhall affigne, are points of Proteftant Fayth, rather
then others contained in the 39. Articles. If he fay (as
he hath already feemed to fay) that none of their
negatiue doctrines pertaine to their Fayth, and that
all which is affirmed by Proteftants, is affirmed by Roman Catholiques, and that this affirmatiue doctrine
onely doth pertaine to Fayth; it will follow that Proteftants haue no Fayth different from Roman Catholiques; out of which it will further follow, that thofe
Englifh Proteftants who fhall hold fome of the 39.

Articles and deny the reft, may be fayd to haue no Fayth different from thofe which fubfcribe to all the 39. Articles; which laft Confequence if *M. Rogers* grant, I aske why the booke of the Canons doth excommunicate *Ipfo facto*, fuch halfe Proteftants? Why do their Bifhops imprifon them as Heretiques, and not account them members of their Church? And why may not Rom. Catholiques by as good, or better right account Proteftants (who deny fo many points defined in both ancient and recent generall Councells) to be Heretiques, excommunicated, and no members of the ancient, and prefent Catholique Church?

    2. I aske, what Scripture, or Reafon affureth, that no Negatiue doctrine pertaines to Fayth? for Scripture hauing in it fo many negatiue fentences, which are to be belieued, affureth the contrarie: neither is there any reafon which can affure a man that he is freed from belieuing (for example) this negatiue, *Deus non mentitur,* God doth not lye, rather then from belieuing this affirmatiue, *eft Deus verax,* God is a true fpeaker ; for both being faid by one and the fame God our Lord, Truth it felf, and both being propounded by one and the fame Catholique Church his fpoufe, affifted by his fpirit, the fpirit of truth, as fpoken by god in holy fcripture, both are equally to be belieued ; neyther can any without danger of eternall damnation, deny or doubt of either thofe, or any other, euen the leaft point of Catholique Fayth, as we may learne out of *S. Athanafius* in his Creed faying that: *Whofoeuer wilbe faued, it is needfull that he hold the Catholique Fayth,* which vnleffe ech one hold entire, (that is, in all points) and inuiolate, (that is, in the true vncorrupted fenfe of the Cath. Church) without doubt he fhall perifh euerlaftingly. So as, whether the doctrine be negatiue or affirmatiue, whe-
ther

Athanaf. in Symbolo.

ther fundamentall or acceſſory, ſuppoſing it be a
doctrine propounded by the Cath. Church, as reuealed by God, it muſt be belieued *explicitè* or *implicitè*, and
may not raſhly, or (which is worſe) aduiſedly be denyed or doubted of, & much leſſe may the contrary be
obſtinately maintained againſt the knowne Iudgmēt
of a lawfull generall Councell, or the vnanime cōſent
of the Paſtours of the Church; in regard our Sauiour
hath expreſly auerred, *That he who deſpiſeth them, deſpiſeth*
himſelf, and him that ſent him, to wit, God his Father. And
againe: *He that will not heare the Church, let him be to thee as*
an Heathen and Publican. All which ſheweth, that ſuch as
do obſtinately deny, or doubtingly diſpute againſt any
the leaſt poynt knowne by Church-Propoſition to be
a point of Cath. Fayth, is worthily accounted an
Heretike, a deſpiſer of God, an excommunicated perſon, and noe member of the true Catholique Church,
and one who if he ſo liue and dye without repentance
cannot be ſaued, but (as *S. Athanaſius* without any want
of Charity pronounceth) *he ſhall without doubt periſh*
euerlaſtingly .

Luc. 10. 16.
Matt. 18.17.

    Whereas therefore it is certaine, that Proteſtants
hould diuers Negatiue doctrines, not only not found
in, but contrary vnto Scriptures, Councells, and Fathers, and other Orthodoxe Authors in all ages; It euidently followeth, that *M. Rogers* hath not yet named,
nor can name, nor hath proued, nor can proue, or defend any of thoſe he nameth, or vndertaketh to name,
to haue ben viſible Proteſtants in all ages before *Lu-*
ther, and conſequently he cannot be ſaid to haue made
any good Anſwer eyther to *M. Fiſhers* queſtion, or to
his fiue propoſitions, or to his other Paper written to
explicate the ſenſe of his ſaid queſtion .

THE

THE VI. CHAPTER.

Concerning VV. C. his Dialogue.

LTHOVGH this which hath ben already said, may suffice to shew the wisdome of W. C. not to haue ben so great, as to be able to giue a good Answere to M. *Fishers* Question, and much lesse to discouer (as he predenteth) any Folly in *M. Fisher*, for proposing the said Question, being so profitable, necessary, and important as it is, for discerning which is the true Church, of which all sorts are to learne true, diuine, infallible Fayth, necessary to saluation; Neuerthelesse sith it hath pleased either the Authour, or the Printer of this Dialogue to combine it with M. *Rogers* his booke, as if it did say something more to the purpose then M. *Rogers* hath said; I haue thought it not amisse briefly to examine the substance of it.

First therefore I find, that whereas M. *Fishers* Question required, 1. That Names of visible Protestants be set downe in all Ages. 2. That proofes out of good Authours be brought, to shew the partyes named, to haue ben Protestants, not Roman Catholiques. 3. That they be defended to be such against all such Arguments which may be brought by M. *Fisher*, or any other Roman Catholique; W. C. hauing proposed this blind question, *Where the Protestants Church was before Luther?*) maketh a more blind Answere, saying; *It was where the Protestants doctrine was*; for it is more vncertayne

certayne what is Proteſtant doctrine, then where the Proteſtant Church is, in regard it will be graunted by all, that the Proteſtant Church is at this day in *England*; but what is the pure Proteſtants doctrine, whether *Lutheriſme, Caluiniſme,* or *Parlamentariſme*, or who be the men that profeſſed pure Proteſtant doctrine in all Ages, is not ſo eaſily diſcerned.

Wherefore W. C. conſidering (as it ſeemeth) that he had not well anſwered, maketh his Antilogiſt to aske, Who theſe were? What Countrey people? Who taught thoſe doctrines which Engliſh Proteſtants teach? To which queſtion W. C. maketh an Anſwere as blind as the former; for he only ſaith, *That if we looke vpon the Churches of Aſia, Africa, and Æthiopia, and conſider them before the myſterie of Iniquity came to the height, we ſhall ſee that they held the ſame doctrine, and forme of a Church that Engliſh Proteſtants haue* (not in all, but) *in all ſubſtantiall things pertayning to religion.* If you aske W. C. what men? In what citty? At what tyme, in particuler, he meaneth? He is as mute as a fiſh. And being further demaunded, whether all theſe men taught, in al things, as *Luther* did? He ſaith, *That this is a peece of Sophiſtry.* If you aske, wherin the Sophiſtry doth conſiſt? He leaueth you to gheſſe; only he ſayth, *They ſhould haue agreed in all things with Luther, and thankes be to god they do alſo, in all ſubſtantiall points, which be Articles of Proteſtant Fayth*; and that they diſagreed from *Luther* and *Caluin* only in opinions about matters not pertayning to Fayth, as the Ancient Fathers diſagreed one from another in ſome opinions, and yet were all of one Fayth and Church, both among themſelues, and with *Luther* and *Caluin*, in regard all agreed in ſubſtantiall points of Fayth. If you aske him, how he knoweth that all the Fathers, and his *Aſian, African,* and *Æthiopian* Churches did agree with

E 3 *Luther*

Luther and *Caluin* in all substantiall things, and onely differed in matters of opiniō not pertayning to Fayth? you must take his *Ipsedixit*, his bare word; And if that will not serue, you must trust the bare word of his Maister D. *Whitaker*, who sayth to Papists: *Patres sunt in maximis nostri, in multis varij, in minimis vestri:* The Fathers are ours in the greatest things, in many things various, and yours in the smallest things; which to me seemeth a Ridle, and needeth an *Oedipus* to expound it vnto vs.

For I aske 1. What be those great matters in which the Fathers are Protestants? If he assigne any affirmatiue points of Protestant Fayth, M. *Rogers* hath already told vs, That all which Protestants affirme, Roman Catholiques affirme; so as the Fathers, and those *Asian*, *African*, and *Æthiopian* Churches cannot in holding these be protestants, more then they are Rom. Catholiques. If he assigne any of the Protestāts negatiue poynts as deniall of the Reall Presence, deniall of merits, Inuocation of Saintes &c. he can neuer find any such negatiues in the Fathers; and if he could, M. *Rogers* would tell him, that negatiues do not pertaine to Fayth, but are onely a trauersing, and condemning of the contrary affirmatiues.

Secondly I aske, what be those *Multa*, many things in which, *Patres sunt varij*, the Fathers are various? If they be matters which were not defined by vnanime Consent of Doctours, or by generall Councells, in these Fathers tymes; this proueth well that these notwithstanding, vnity of Fayth and Church mightbe among the Fathers, but it proueth not that like vnity of Fayth and Church is betweene them and *Luther* and *Caluin*, for these our new Maisters held errours contrary to the knowne Consent of Fathers and Generall

Coun-

Contra rat. Camp.

Councells, in which fort no ancient Orthodoxe Father euer did hold errour .

Thirdly I aske, what be thofe *Minima* leaft things, in which the Fathers are confeffed by *D. Whitaker* to be Roman Catholiques? Let *M. Crashaw* call them *Minima*, or *Maxima*, as he fhall pleafe: The truth is, that the Fathers do agree with vs in all , and do either exprefly or implicitely, hold all as we do , and do not condemne any one of the leaft points of Catholique Roman Fayth. And although the matter, or materiall obiect of one point of Fayth may be faid to be greater, or more fubftantiall then another, and may be more needfull to be exprefly knowne and belieued by all forts, then fome other; Yet if we haue refpect to the formall obiect, to wit diuine Reuelation, and the manner of belieuing them infallibly, *explicitè* or *implicitè*, and the obligation of not denying, or not doubting of the leaft of them being duely propounded by the Catholique Church, all of them are alike fubftantiall, and fo connected one with another , as he that belieueth any one (*virtually* at leaft) belieueth all ; and he that doth deliberatly, and efpecially obftinatly, deny or doubt of any one (at leaft *virtually*) doth deny Infallible Certaintie of all, and doth affent to thofe points which he lifteth to belieue, onely by wilfull fallible opinion , or onely by humane (falfly imagined to be diuine) Fayth, as I proue by this Argument .

An Argument prouing, that he that denyeth the authority of the Church in any one point, taketh away Infallible Certainty.

{ The firft } Whofoeuer deliberately denyeth, or
{ Maior. } doubteth of any point, deliuered as a diuine infallible truth, by the full authority of the Church, doth not, nor

can for that tyme , giue infallible credit to any other point , deliuered as a
diuine infallible truth, by full authority of the fame Church.

{ The firſt }   But he that giueth not, nor cā giue in-
{ Minor. }   fallible credit to any point deliuered,
as a diuine infallible truth , by full au-
thori y of the Church , excludeth from
himſelfe, or deſtroyeth in himſelf al diuine infallible Fayth .

Ergo , he that deliberatly denieth, or doubteth of
any one point deliuered as a diuine truth by full
authority of the Church, excludeth from himſelf,
or deſtroyeth in himſelf all diuine infallible Fayth.

The firſt *Maior* I proue : For whoſoeuer doth not
giue infallible credit to the full authority of the Church
in any one point , neyther doth, nor can at that tyme
giue infallible credit to it in any other, for it being one
and the ſame in all points, deſerueth one and the ſame
credit in all : and therefore if it deſerue not infallible
credit in any one, it deſerueth not infallible credit in
any other.

Secondly, we can not in reaſon giue infallible credit to the authority of the Church in one point more
then in another, vnleſſe there be ſome Infallible reaſon
mouing vs to belicue the authority of the Church in
one point,more then another.

But there is not any Infallible reaſon , mouing a
man to giue infallible credit to the authority of the
Church, more in one point deliuered by it, then in
another .

Ergo , whoſoeuer deliberatly denieth , or doubteth
of any one point deliuered, as a diuine Infallible truth
by the full authority of the Church, neyther doth, nor
can

can in reaſon at that tyme giue infallible credit to any
point deliuered, as a diuine infallible truth, by the full
authority of the ſame Church.

This laſt *Minor* I proue ; for the onely chiefe reaſon
which moueth vs to giue infallible credit to any point
deliuered by full authority of the Church , is not the
greatnes or litlenes of the matter, nor the more, or leſſe
euidence of the truth (which in the chiefeſt matters of
Fayth is moſt obſcure to vs) but the promiſe of Chriſt
which aſſureth vs that himſelf, and his holy Spirit will
alwayes be with the Church to teach it all truth ; ſo as
wheſoeuer the Church doth teach by her full authority,
it is not ſhe , conſidered onely as conſiſting of a Company of men who may erre , but God himſelf, (who
cannot erre , and who ſayth , *He that heareth you, heareth
me,*) vnto whom we may, & muſt giue infallible credit
in all matters great and little, euident and not euident
or moſt obſcure.

But this reaſon moueth not to belieue the Church
in any one point of Fayth more then in any other,
but eyther to moue a man infallibly to belieue all, or
nothing propoſed as diuine truth, by full authority of
the Church .

Ergo, There is no found reaſon to moue a man infallibly to belieue the Church in any one point of Fayth,
more then in another.

If it be anſwered that the reaſon of difference is,
for that ſome points are more clerely expreſſed in the
Scripture then other, & that the truthes themſelues are
of greater importance in ſome points then in another , and therefore do more oblige vs to belieue the
Church propoſing ſome truths then other: I reply that
the Infallibility of the credit giuen to any one Article
propoſed as a diuine truth by the Church, doth wholly

F   depend

depend vpon the inlallibl· authority of God, ſpeaking in, and by the Church, which is as grea· in his affirming things ſmall, and not cleerly expreſſed in ſcripture, or not expreſſed in ſcripture at all, as in things moſt great, & moſt cleerly expreſſed in ſcripture; otherwiſe Gods infallible authority were not (as it is, and ought to be) abſolutly Infinite, nor ſo great as may be imagined: for that infallible authority which can breed infallible credit in all things ſmall and great, obſcure & cleere, expreſſed and not expreſſed in Scripture , is far greater, then that which doth onely breed infallible credit in great and cleere matters, expreſſed in Scripture. And although the more importance of the matter, or the more cleerneſſe of the truth, eſpecially expreſſed in Scripture, may more oblige vs to take expreſſe notice of it, and conſequently actually and particulerly to belieue it more then other leſſe important or leſſe cleere truthes; yet ſuppoſing we once haue notice that theſe other leſſe important and leſſe cleere truthes were deliuered by the ſame authority of God ſpeaking in, and by his Church, by which we are to take notice both of the moſt important and moſt cleere truthes, & of that ſcripture by which we learne them to be important and cleere, we are bound with equall infallible credit to belieue the ſmalleſt and moſt obſcure things, as the greateſt and cleereſt: neither can we after ſuch notice, without great iniurie to Gods infinite infallible authority , deny or doubt of the truth of the leaſt, or moſt obſcure point propoſed by God ſpeaking to vs eyther by himſelfe immediatly, or by meanes of the authority of the Church.

If W. C. will for all this, make a diſtinction in points of Fayth , accounting ſome ſubſtantiall , in which all the aunçient Fathers and his *Aſian, African,* &
Æthio-

Æthiopian Churches were of one and the ſame Fayth
with Luther and Caluin ; and others not ſubſtantiall,
in which ech of theſe might diſ-agree, without being
of a different Fayth or Church ; I muſt intreate him to
define, or deſcribe, or giue vs a Catalogue of all ſubſtantiall points of Fayth, or to ſet downe a Rule well
proued out of Scripture, by which all may certainly
know what is, and what is not a ſubſtantiall point of
Fayth and Religion, that it may be examined whether the *Italian* Churches be more ſtrangers from ſauing Fayth, as W. C. would perſwade vs, then his
Aſian, African, or *AEthiopian* Churches.

   I muſt alſo intreate him to tell vs, when the Roman
Church, in which once ſauing truth (as *S. Paul* telleth *Rom. 1, 8.*
vs) was no ſtranger ; when, I ſay, did the Roman
Church caſt the ſauing truth out of *Italie,* and all Eu-
rope, into the onely *Aſian, African,* and *AEthiopian*
Churches? In what Age? Vnder what Pope? Vpon
what occaſion? for theſe, and the like Circumſtances
(not imagined, but well proued out of good Records)
I muſt intreate W. C. to ſet downe, and to ſee that the
Records which he citeth be not feigned to haue been
once written, and after burned, but eyther yet extant,
or of which once to haue ben extant and after burned
ſome mention is made in one, or other good Record
yet extant.

   When W. C. ſhall haue ſatisfied theſe my moſt rea-
ſonable requeſts, then I ſhalbe content to anſwer his
queſtion about the Viſibility of the Church in Antichriſts time, which he imagineth, but doth not, nor can
proue to be already paſt. In the meane time I may tell
him, that the Rhemiſts anſwer doth nothing help him
towards the anſwere of *M. Fiſhers* queſtion ; for according to the *Rhemiſts,* in Antichriſts time the Church

ſhall haue true Paſtours, and thoſe knowne both to the Faythfull, and alſo to the Perſecutors, who could not perſecute men who were altogether vnknowne. As therefore in the firſt perſecutions of Chriſtians, the Names of Paſtours and people were knowne to the world, and may be found in Records yet extant, ſo it is required in *M. Fiſhers* Queſtion, that in this pretended paſt tyme of Antichriſts perſecution, the Names of perſecuted Proteſtant Paſtours be produced in all ages, at leaſt two or three in ech age: which while W. C. doth not, neyther his bold ſaying, that he can in all ages point forth men preaching Proteſtant doctrine, nor his citing of *Raynerus*, nor his foure Bookes which he ſo highly commendeth, (to wit, *Illyricus* his *Catalogus Teſtium veritatis*, D. *Iohn whites Way*, D. *Reynolds Theſis*, *Amandus Polonus*) do, nor can ſatisfy *M. Fiſhers* Queſtion.

Firſt I ſay, that W. C. hath not anſwered *M. Fiſhers* Queſtion, by his bold ſaying, that there is not one Age ſince the dayes of Chriſt, wherin he cannot point forth men preaching and profeſſing as Proteſtants do; for this bold aſſertion he doth not otherwiſe proue, then by falſly preſuppoſing, without all proofe or probability, that all the tyme in which Proteſtants affirme Papiſtrie to haue raigned (which ſome ſay hath byn twelue or thirteene hundred yeares) was the tyme of Antichriſt, in which the Church was chaſed into the wildernes, and ſo oppreſſed, that it had not any publique ſtate or regiment, nor free exerciſe of holy functions, yet it was not vnknowne to the Faythfull that followed it, nor to the Enemies that perſecuted it: All which if it were true (as it is moſt falſe) doth not poynt forth men preaching as Proteſtants do, in any one age, and much leſſe in all ages before Luther: for it onely would proue that ſome Chriſtians were, but

whether

whether they were Proteſtants, or of ſome other profeſſion, reſteth ſtill to be particulerly proued.

Secondly I ſay, that W. C. hath not anſwered M.
Fiſhers queſtion by his citing of *Raynerus* a Popiſh in-
quiſitour, who writeth (as W. C. ſayth) that the *Wal-*
denſes were more pernicious to the Church *of Rome*
then all the other Sects, for three cauſe: The firſt cauſe
is, for that they were of longer continuance, for ſome
ſay this Sect hath byn ſince the tyme of the Apoſtles.
The 2. cauſe is, becauſe it is more generall, for there is
almoſt no land in which this Sect doth not creepe.
The 3. cauſe, for that all other Sectes do bring an hor-
ror with the haynouſnes of their blaſphemies againſt
God; but this Sect hath a great ſhew of godlines, becauſe they liue iuſtly before men, and belieue all things
well concerning God, and all the Articles which are
contained in the Creed, onely they hate, and blaſ-
pheme the Church of *Rome.*

This ſaying of *Raynerus* W. C. thinketh may ſerue
to ſtop the mouthes of Papiſts from euer more asking
where the Proteſtant Church was before Luther? But if W.
C. would conſider what was granted by D. *White* and
D. *Featly* in the Conference with M. *Sweet* and M. *Fi-*
ſher, to wit, that the true Church is ſo viſible, as the
Names of the Profeſſors in all ages may be ſhewed
out of good Authors, he will finde that this ſaying of
Raynerus (ſuppoſing it be rightly cited) can neyther ſtop the mouthes of Papiſts, nor ſatisfie the Conſcience of Proteſtants; for firſt, this which *Raynerus*
ſayth, doth not proue *Waldenſes* to haue ben in all ages,
nor to haue ben Proteſtants. For he only ſaith, that
ſome ſaid, they were from the tyme of Pope *Silueſter,*
and ſome that they were from the Apoſtles; but what
ſome were theſe trow yee? I find recorded in good Au-

F 3   thors,

46   *W. C. his blind Questions and Answeres.*

See Coeffeteau against Plesfis. thors, that thefe fome, were fome of the *Waldenfes* themfelues, who although knowne to haue their beginning of one *Waldo Anno Domini,* 1160.(as *Illyricus,* one of W. C. his owne chiefe Authors, confeffeth) bragged as Proteftants (knowne to haue had their beginning from *Luther Anno Domini,* 1517.) do brag that they haue their beginning from the Primitiue Church, of the firft 300. yeares, yea from the Apoftles.

Secondly, the *Waldenfes* (as alfo Proteftants) may be faid to haue ben fo Ancient, either in refpect of that doctrine which they hold Common with vs, or in refpect of hauing patched vp the reft of their doctrine, with receiuing fome or other part of the doctrine of Heretiques of former ages; in which fenfe I do not enuy their Antiquity, neither haue they any caufe to brag of it, for moft Heretiques hold fome Ancient doctrine in common with vs, and in fome one thing or other agree with the moft ancient Heretiques, for (as *Raynerus* in the fame place noteth) all Heretiques although damning one anothers doctrine, yet agree in oppugning the Roman Church, which doth not proue all thefe to haue been of one, and the fame Fayth and Church, one with another, or with the Orthodoxe in all ages, more then the tying together of *Sampfons* foxes by the tayles proueth, that they were all one foxe, or that ech of thefe foxes had his head turned towards the fame way, vnto which ech of the reft (while they looked ech one his feuerall way) did turne himfelf.

Thirdly, Admit that *Waldenfes* had been in all ages, it little auayleth W. C. his caufe, vnles he firft proue *Waldenfes* to haue ben Proteftants; which he neyther doth, nor cã do better then is done by M. *Fox,* who is in this point largely refuted by the Authour of the *Three Conuerfions,* in *his Examen of Foxes Kalendar*, and others.

If

If W. C. do thinke to proue *Waldenfes* to haue been Proteſtants, for that *Raynerus* fayth, they belieued right concerning God, and all the Articles of the Creed, and did liue iuſtly before men; I Anſwer, that this doth not proue that they were Proteſtants, nor members of the true viſible Church; for firſt, if this were not (as the former ſpeach was) ſome of the *Waldenfes* owne brags, *Raynerus* may meane, that this ſhew of piety and right belief, was onely in the ſight of men; for he affirmeth their errors to be in theſelues blaſphemous & wicked.

Laſtly, although their beliefe had extended it ſelf to all the Articles of the Creed, yet this is not inough to cleere them from being Heretiques; for one may in ſome ſort & ſenſe belieue all Articles of the Creed, and yet be an Heretique, or not a Catholique Chriſtian, & conſequently no member of the true viſible Church; as wee may learne out of S. Auſten, who in his booke *de Hæreſibus* recounteth many Hereſies, ſome of which are of points not directly and expreſly oppoſite to any of the 12. Articles of the Creed, nor ſeeming to be a- *Aug. l. de hæref.* bout any matter of great moment; yet he pronounceth that whoſoeuer doth hold (eſpecially obſtinatly) againſt the knowne Fayth of the Church, any one of theſe, or any other hereſy, is no Catholique Chriſtian; neyther indeed can any one who holdeth ſuch an obſtinate er- rour or hereſie, haue in him true diuine infallible Fayth of any other Article or point contained in the Creed, as is already proued: neither is that Argument good, which W. C. and others ſeeme to make their chief ground of challenging the Fathers, and others to be members of the Proteſtant Church. The doctrine of the Fathers & others, is all one in ſubſtance with the doctrine of Pro- teſtants in this age: Ergo, the Fathers and others are all of one Fayth and Church with Proteſtants of this age.

This

This Argument, I fay, is not good.

Firlt, becaufe that the Antecedent is falfe, and cannot be proued but by fuch fhifts, as I haue already refuted. Secondly, The Confequence is naught; for, to haue vnity of Fayth is required, that the parties do not onely belieue fome principall points of Fayth, but they mult belieue *explicitè* or *implicitè* all; in regard we read, that for one word or fyllable of true Fayth denied, diuers haue ben caſt out of the Church; yea *S. Greg. Nazianzen* fayth: *Nihil periculofius hijs Hæreticis effe poteſt:* there can be nothing more perillous then thofe Hereoques, who running vprightly in the reſt, with one fyllable as with a drop of poyfon, do infect our Lords fincere Fayth. Thirdly, It is not inough to belieue euen all the things which other Chriſtians belieue, vnleffe one do belieue them for the fame infallible formall reafon of Gods reuelation fufficiently applyed and made knowne to vs by infallible authority of the Church, for if they belieue the fame points not for this, but for fome other formall reafon, or for this formall reafon not fufficiently applyed to our vnderſtanding, it is not the fame, but a different kind of Fayth; for diuers kindes of formall reafons muſt needes make different kinds of habits and acts of Fayth: *Habitus enim & actus fpecificantur ab obiectis formalibus.* And if the fame formall reafo be not applyed by fome meanes fufficient to deriue the effect of that formall reafon to our vnderſtanding, it cannot breed the fame Fayth: As for example, If the reuelation whereupon Fayth is grounded be not at all made knowne to men by fome or other infallible meanes, but eyther only by a knowne lyar, or onely by a probable fpeaker, it cannot breed in them infallible belief. But there is no ordinary infallible meanes by which the diuine reuelation, and the true meaning of it, is made knowne

Greg. Naz.
tract. de fide.

to men, beſide the infallible aurhority of the Church.
Ergo.

Fourthly, Although one haue all perfect vnity in
Fayth, and belief of all points, which the ancient Fathers belieued, but wanteth vnion in ſacred rites and ſacraments, and due ſubordination of obedience with the
viſible Paſtours of the Cath. Church, he cannot be accounted a member of the ſaid Church: for as want of
vnity in Fayth maketh an Heretique, ſo want of vniõ
in Sacraments and due ſubordination of obedience to
the Paſtours of the Church, maketh a Schiſmatique.
Now, it is certayne, that neyther Heretique nor Schiſmatique can be a member of the true Church, nor can
deriue an vninterrupted pedigree of the profeſſours vpward vntill the Apoſtles, or the ancient Orthodox Fathers of the Primitiue Church, as may be ſhewed in
particuler in *Luther* (for example) the great Grand-
Father of all moderne Proteſtants, who when he firſt
left Communion with the Roman Church, did not aſ
ſociate himſelf to any other former viſible Church of
Catholiques or Heretiques, but made a Congregation
of his owne, diſtinguiſhed in nature and name from all
other Congregations in the world.

Laſtly, I ſaid that W. C. hath not ſatisfied *M. Fishers*
queſtion with alleadging his 4. Authours, *Illyricus, D.
Iohn white, D. Reynolds,* & *Amandus Polanus.* For although
Illyricus name men in all ages, and do deſcribe ſome of
their doctrine, and ſome of their acts, yet he neyther
doth, nor can proue ech one of thoſe he nameth to be a
Proteſtant, but rather euidently ſheweth how that all
or moſt of them did differ in diuers points of doctrine
frõ the Engliſh Proteſtãt Church. So likewiſe *Io. White*
nameth only one or two in ech hũdred yeare, but doth
not proue them to be Proteſtants, but plainely confeſ

G ſeth

feth that his meaning is not to iuftify euery one he nameth to haue bene a full Proteftant in euery point;neither doth he tell vs which of them in particuler did agree with Proteftants in all, euen fundamētall points. As for *D. Reynolds* , and *Amandus Polanus* , it is alfo certaine, that they do not(as *M. Fishers* Queſtion requires) name men in all ages, who can be proued & defended to haue held all conformable , and nothing contrary to the 39. Articles of the Proteſtant Engliſh Church.

All which being well confidered , it appeareth, that W. C. who promiſed to diſcouer *Fishers* Folly, hath not diſcouered any great ſtore of wit in his vndertaking to anſwer *Fishers* queſtion, which he is neuer able to anſwere. And if his true name be *William Crashaw*, as is ſuppoſed, one may iuſtly meruayle why he did not rather employ his pen in anſwering a booke called *Pulpit-Babells* written againſt a Sermon of his preached at Paules Croſſe, and printed with the title of Twenty woundes ; in which is diſcouered not only his great folly, but alſo malice in ſeeking to wound the Roman Church with ſo many falſe & groſſe ſlaſiders, as in the aforeſaid booke called *Pulpit-Babells* is made ſo manifeſt, that W. C. himſelf may well be thought(by his neuer offering to defend that Sermon) to be aſhamed of it, & to wiſh that he had neuer printed, nor preached it.

THE

THE VII. CHAPTER.

About a Treatise of the perpetuall Visibility of the true Church.

I PERSVADE my felf, that euery one who confidereth the circumſtances of the Author, Title, time, and occafion of printing this book, will expect to finde in it a moſt ful and complete Anſwer to *M. Fishers* queſtion ; for the Author is ſayd (and by his Armes ſet before is ſhewed)to be the Lord Archbiſhop of *Canterbury*, the Primate of the whole Engliſh Proteſtant Church, a man famous for more then ordinary reading of Hiſtories, and who (as the Preface inſinuateth) hath more trauelled in this Argumēt of ſhewing a perpetual viſible Proteſtant Church, then any other euer did in the Engliſh tongue, who conſequently is moſt likely to want neither will, nor skill to ſet downe Names of Proteſtants in all ages out of good Authors(as *M. Fishers* queſtion required)if any ſuch euer were to be found. The Title is : *The perpetuall Viſibility of the true* (which in this Authors conceipt, is the Proteſtant) *Church*. The tyme, and, as it ſeemeth, the occafion of printing this Booke, was ſhortly after his Lord.ᵖ had vnderſtood, what Queſtion *M. Fisher* had propoſed to his Chaplyn *D. Featly*, and that his Chaplyn had boldly vndertaken to ſhew a perpetuall viſible Proteſtant Church, by naming Proteſtants in all ages out of good Authors .

All theſe Circumſtances, I ſay, confidered, who

would

would not expect to finde in this booke a moft full &
complete Anfwere, fufficient to fatisfy any Proteftants
Confcience, and to ftop M. *Fishers*, or any other Papifts
mouth from euer more asking names of vifible Proteftants, people, & Paftors in all ages. But hauing perufed the Booke, I find not in it any part of a good Anfwere to M. *Fishers* queftion. Firft, for that this booke,
quite cōtrary to the title of perpetuall vifibility, labou-
reth to proue, that the Church needs not, nor muft not
be perpetually vifible, but may, yea muft be fometime
inuifible, and this fo neceffarily, as that thereupon he
frameth this fyllogifme:

The true Church muft fometime be Inuifible:
But the Romifh Church (fayth he) hath byn alwayes
    vifible:
Ergo, Will fhe, nill fhe, fhe is not the true Church.
    2. Although it maketh a fhew of naming Proteftants
in fome ages before Luther, yet it doth not, (as the Iefuits queftion required, and as Catholiques do, in fhewing the vifibility of their Church) fet downe from
Chrift and his Apoftles downeward, or from the prefent tyme vpward vntill the Apoftles and Chrift, a
Catalogue of Names contayning an orderly fucceffion
of lawfully fent Paftors in all ages, teaching the perpetuall vnchanged doctrine of Fayth firft receiued from
Chrift; but recknoneth a diforderly confufed rabble of
Heretiques, who either neuer were lawfully fent Paftours of the Church, or loft their miffion, commiffion,
and authority to teach, by changing the firft receyued
Chriftian Catholique Fayth, & following their owne,
or fome other priuate mens phantafie. And befides, it
falfly challengeth fuch for members of the Proteftant
Church, who neither can agree in doctrine of Fayth
one with another, nor with Proteftants, and therefore
                                                    can

cannot be proued, nor defended to be Proteſtants.

3. The reafons which it alleageth to proue and defend the Church fome tyme to be Inuifible, and fuch as it nameth to be Proteſtants, are moſt weake and infufficient, as will eafily appeare, after I fhall haue explicated the true flate of this queſtion, Whether the true Church be alwayes vifible? And what Catholiques meane by the perpetual vifible Church? And why they require Names of Paſtours, Teachers, and other profeſſours of the firſt receiued Fayth of Chriſt to be ſhewed in all ages out of good Authors? I am the more willing to explicate this as cleerly as I can, partly becaufe I fee the Author of this Booke doth miſtake, and mifreport the true meaning of Catholiques in this point; partly to let it be feene how much it importeth, and how neceffary it is for difcerning which Company of men is the true Church, of which all forts are to learne Fayth neceffary to faluation, and with which all are obliged to retaine Communion and due fubordinatiõ, that the Names of lawfull Paſtours be ſhewed in all ages out of good Authors.

Note therefore firſt, that this Name *Church*, may be taken in diuers fenfes; firſt, for the Company of the Elect, either abfolutly, or with fome fuppofition, to wit, of their being actually called by the preaching of Gods word, and participation of the Sacraments, efpecially Baptifme, to be members of the myſticall body of Chriſt, & of their finally dying in that ſtate. Secõdly for all fuch as are actually iuſt, and liuely members of Chriſts myſticall body, although in Gods forefight all are not to perfeuer to the end in that ſtate. Thirdly, for a Company of men, linked in the profeffion of the true vnchanged Fayth of Chriſt, Communion of right facraments, and fubordination to lawfull Paſtours, whe-

G 3   ther

ther al be predeſtinate or not, & whether al be actually iuſt or not.Now theChurch in the firſt 2. ſenſes is doubtles inuiſible, in regard none cã without ſpeciall reuelationknow certainly who are, or who are not predeſtinate,or actually Iuſt; but in theſe two ſenſes,euery one hath more need(by humble harty prayers and vertuous workes)to endeauour to be,thenby curious diſputation to ſeeke to know who is, and who it not,a member of Gods Church.

In this our diſputation therefore the Church is to be taken in the third ſenſe,and the rather,for that the holy Scriptures and Fathers do ſpeak of the Church in this third ſenſe,whenſoeuer they do (as they often do) appoint people to receiue from the Church, doctrinall Inſtruction,and to haue with the Church ſacramentall Communion,and to yeild to the Church obedientiall ſubordination;in which reſpect the Church muſt needs be at all tymes Viſible , and ſuch, as by diligent ſeeking may be found by all ſortes of men in all ages, and in ſome ſort knowne and belieued in particuler to be that ſeede which our Lord hath Bleſſed, and endued with his ſpirit and word, and by which onely(according to the ordinary Courſe of his prouidence)he intendeth to communicate to all men , who do deſire(as all ought to deſire)inſtruction of Fayth,ſacramentall grace, and direction in all practicall matters neceſſary to ſaluatiõ.

But whereas the Church in this third ſenſe may be taken eyther,1. for the whole Company; or 2. for the more principall part ,to wit, the Paſtours which haue authority to inſtruct, feed, and rule others,to wit, the people who are to receiue of the Paſtors inſtruction of Fayth , food of ſacramentall grace, gouernement and direction, and(when need is) correction in matters concerning manners ; our chiefe queſtion is about the Church in this 2. ſenſe : and in this ſenſe is it, that the

Iſa. 59.

Church

Church hath ben, is, and alwayes shalbe visible euen in
greatest persecutions of Pagans, and amidst the most
thicke mysts of Heresies and Schismes, and ill liues of
Christians, according as we may learne out of that *August. ep.*
saying of S. Austine : *The Church is clouded sometymes* **48.**
with a multitude of scandals, but euen then also she is eminent in
her most firme members. Yea in tyme of Antichrist himself, when the Church may be said most to flye into the
desert, yet euen then she shalbe in some of her principall members, not only visible to the Faythfull, but
euen to her greatest Enemies, who could not persecute (as they will then most terribly) the principall
and most firme members of the Church, if they were
altogether inuisible vnto them. The Church therefore
in this sense is, and must be alwayes visible in some sort
both to friends and enemies, both to the Faythfull and
Infidels ; in some sort, I say, but in what sort it must be
always visible, resteth further to be declared .

Note therefore 2. that Catholiques do not affirme
that the Church must alwayes haue a like manner of
visibility, or at all tymes haue an outward, prosperous,
especially pompous, temporall state of Church-men
possessing Churches and Church-liuings &c. or haue
alwayes an equall number of Pastours and people
actually professing the truth in all places ; For sometymes the water of persecutions may ouerwhelme
many of the Faythfull people, who at other tymes
were spread largely ouer the world, and in number as
the sands of the Sea. Sometymes also the multitude of
cloudes of Heresies, schismes, and other scandalls may
take away from vs the actuall sight euen of many teachers of truth, who at other tymes did gloriously shine
as stars in heauen ; so as in respect of this variety of the
manner of visibility, as well as for other respects, the
Church

Church may be said to be like the Moone. Neuerthelesse these Comparisons must not be so farre stretched,
as that at any tyme the Church should be driuen so
quite out of all kind of Visibility, as any should haue
iust cause to say (as is said in this booke, that some said)
that the Church for sometime was extinct;for althogh
some sentences of scripture alleaged by this Author
against the perpetuall visibility of the Church,seeme to
say,that at some tyme not one member of the Church
is left on earth, or that when the Sonne of man cometh he shall scarse find Fayth on earth;yet these generall sayings are not so to be vnderstood,but that there
must be alwayes(as this Author confesseth) a Church,
and, as I say, a visible Church of Christ, (as we may
learne out of Scripture) against which Hell gates can
neuer preuayle, and with which Christ, and his holy
Spirit wilbe all dayes,vntill the end of the world, and
in which alwayes shalbe Pastours lawfully sent , teaching and baptizing, and performing all other offices
necessary for preseruation of the Faythfull and con-
uersion of Infidels;so as it cannot be, but this Church &
these her Pastors must be at all times visible, both to
Faythfull & Infidels , in such sort as although perhaps
they be not alwayes actually seene by all men,yet they
may be easily found out,and knowne by all who desire to learne of them Fayth necessary to saluation : &
they neither may so hide themselues, nor can be kept so
altogether Inuisible or hid , that men of any age nee-
ding and seeking Instruction of Fayth,cannot by any
meanes get any notice of them.

In this sense therefore it is most certaine that the
Church neuer must,nor may, nor cã be altogether inuisible,but as *Isaias* prophesieth,her gates must be open
continually,and shall not day or night be shut , to the
intent

Matth. 16.
Matt. 28.20.
Ioan. 14.
Eph. 4.

Isa. 66.

intent that the strength of Nations may be brought vnto her, and their kings; And this in regard of the great necessity people haue to enter into the Church, which is for that, as the same Prophet sayth, the Nation and kingdome which shall not serue her, shall perish. Becaufe therefore it is so necessary to know, and enter into the Church, to serue God in her, and her for God, *it is not* (as S. Aug. fayth) *lawfull for any man to be ignorant of her.* And therefore (as the same S. Austen inferreth) *she cannot be hid,* or altogether inuisible, but must in all ages be knowne in the Nations, and in the midst of people; so as all that fee her, shall (or at leaft may, if they will) know her to be that feed(or fociety of men) which our Lord hath Bleffed: Bleffed, I fay, more then any other fociety of men in the world. *Aug. ep.170.* *Ibidem.* *Isa. 61.*

Note 3. that as by this difcou fe we fee, that the true Church must be alwayes fo visible, as that at leaft fome of her principall members must be alwayes eminent & eafy to be knowne, both by friends & enemies, Faythfull and Infidels; fo it cannot be doubted, but that in all ages, the names, or fome things equiualent to names, of fuch eminent knowne men, may be found in hiftoryes yet extant, as well as the Names of men eminent for matters of far leffe moment are found; for (as I once noted before) there cannot be affigned any reafon, eyther of the part of Gods prouidence, or humane diligence, why the Names of men eminent for profeffion of diuine truth, fhould be omitted in hiftoryes, written by Friends or Enemies, or that all fuch Records of hiftoryes, being fo neceffary for the fetting out of the glory of God and his Church, & to confirme the truth of the ancient prophefies, fhould be quite fuppreffed, or that any fuch fuppreffion of Records fo neceffary could be made without any particuler memory left thereof in some or other bookes yet extant in these our dayes.

Now this being so, we may easily see, 1. How weakly this Author proueth, that the Church must be sometymes Inuisible; for sith one place of scripture must not be so interpreted, as to be contradictory to another, and that by some places of Scripture plaine in themselues, and so interpreted by Ancient Fathers; it is euident, that the Church in that sense in which I haue already explicated, cannot be at any tyme altogether Inuisible. It is most certaine, that the other places of scripture alleaged by this Author against the perpetuall visibility of the Church must be so interpreted as they do not proue the Churches absolute Inuisibility at any tyme, but at most a lesse visibility sometymes then at some other tymes; or as meant of the Church taken in the first and second, and not in the 3. sense, of which only our question is vnderstood at this tyme.

2. We may see, how much it importeth, for discerning which is the true Church of which all men must learne true Fayth, that the Names or something equiualent to Names of true Pastours in all ages, be shewed out of good Authors; And how great reason Catholiques haue to require Protestants who pretend to be the true Church, to shew the Names of some eminent visible members of their Church, and especially of their Pastours in all ages; For if indeed their Church be the true Church, of whome are vnderstood the glorious things which were in scripture prophesied of, and promised to the Church, then doubtles it had eminent members, Pastours, & teachers succeeding one another in all ages, whose names & memorable actions, sayings or suffrings may be found in histories yet extant, as the names of such are found whom Roman Catholiques assigne for members of their Church; for sith it much
imports,

imports, that matters of fuch confequence fhould be
knowne to men of all ages, doubtles Gods prouidence
and humane diligence hath not fayled to fet out and
preferue hiftories, contayning memory of fuch principall members of the true Church, & their doctrines &
actions, being neceffary to fhew the truth of diuine
prophefies and promifes made to the true Church, and
to make men difcerne the true, from the falfe Church,
more then in preferuing memories of leffe important
men and matters, which we fee to be yet in hiftoryes
extant in thefe our dayes.

If therefore, I fay, Proteftants will needs pretend to
be the true Church, Catholiques may well vrge them
(as the Fathers vrged the Heretiques of their Ages ma-
king the like pretence) and fay with Tertullian : *Edant*   *Tertul. l. de*
origines Ecclefiarum fuarum, euoluant ordinem Epifcoporum *præfc. contra*
fuorum, ita per fucceffiones decurrentem vfque ad nos &c. Vt il- *hær.*
lorum primus aliquem ex Apoftolis, aut Apoftolicis viris, qui ta-
men cum Apoftolis perfeuerauerit, habuerint authorem & ante-
cefforem. Let the fet forth the origens of their Churches,
let them vnfold the order of their Bifhops, fo running
downe by fucceffions vnto vs, as that the firft of them
had for his Author and Anteceffour fome Apoftle, or
Apoftolicall man who perfeuered with the Apoftles.
Which vninterrupted fucceffion if they cannot fhew,
as they cannot, but Catholiques can, and do; it may appeare euidently to all men, that Proteftants are not, &
Catholiques are, that Bleffed Company vnto which
the prophefies and promifes of Scripture (made to the
true Church) do belong, and that confequently all are
to accompt Catholiques, and not Proteftants, to be the
true Church, of which all muft learne true doctrine of
Fayth neceffary to faluation, and with which all muft
be vnited in Church-Communion, and vnto which

all muſt be ſubiect in due ſubordination. Let vs ſee
therefore whether this great Antiquary and Primate of
Englilh Proteſtants, who is commended for hauing
more trauayled in this argumét, then any other writer
in our Engliſh tongue: Let vs ſee, I ſay, whether he can
bring a ſucceſſion of Proteſtant Paſtours downeward
as *Tertullian* vrgeth, or deriue their pedegree vpward,
1. naming the men. 2. prouing. 3. defending them
to be members of the Proteſt. Church, in ſuch ſort as
M. *Fiſhers* queſtion required.

Firſt, I find, that although he nameth diuers in the
ages before *Luther, Iohn Huſſe* and his followers, *Ziſca* &
his *Thaborites, Wicliff* and his Sectaries, *Dulcinus* and the
Dulciniſts, Waldo and *Waldenſes, Berengarius*, and *Bertram*
&c. yet he neyther maketh ſuch an orderly cōtinuall
Succeſſion of their perſons in all ages, as Catholiques
do in their printed Catalogues, nor ſheweth their
agreement one with another, cr with Proteſtants of
this age in all points of Fayth as Catholiques (*Gualterus*
and others) do ſhew to be in thoſe, whom they name
for mébers of their Church: neyther doth he ſufficiently
* proue and defend them to be Proteſtants againſt the
obiections of Catholiques, as Catholiques, namely L.
D. defendeth S. N. his Appendix againſt the obiections of Proteſtants : neyther doth he ſo much as goe
about to name (and much leſſe to proue or defend) who
among this Company were in all ages lawfully ſent
Paſtors, which are neceſſary to be alwayes in the
Church, as not onely ſcriptures and Fathers, but euen
Proteſtants affirme; who alſo hold, that the only want
of them were a ſufficient argumét to proue the mullity
of the Church, as Catholiques do moſt punctually diſtinguiſh Paſtours from people, and thoſe which were
chiefe Paſtois from other their infeiiours, and can, and
do

Marginal notes:

* Theſe proofs and defenſes which he maketh are in the prece-dent & ſub-ſequent Chapters re-futed.

Iſa. 59. 21.
Act. 20. 28.
Eph. 4. 11. 12.
Aug. in Pſal. 44. Prote-ſtant *Apol.*
Trac. 2. c. 8.
ſect. 1.

do proue and defend their Paſtours in all ages to haue
byn lawfully ſent.

This Booke therefore maketh a moſt inſufficient
Anſwer to *M. Fiſhers* queſtion, in all theſe ſeuerall reſ-
pects, as may be ſeene by any who will compare
what it bringeth for proofe, or defence of thoſe it nameth, with what I haue already ſaid in my Refutation
of the like alledged by *M. Rogers,* or W.C. & that which
I am to ſay againſt his Chaplain *D. Featly,* and others
in the ſubſequent Chapters.

THE VIII. CHAPTER.

About a Booke termed: Luthers Predecef-
ſours: *ſet out by a Nameleſſe Author.*

ONCERNING this idle Páphlet
called *Luthers Predeceſſours,* litle need
be ſayd, more then hath ben all-
ready; for neyther doth it name mē
in all ages, but onely for 200. yeares before Luther, neyther doth it
proue thoſe it nameth to agree with
the preſent Engliſh Proteſtant Church in all the 39.
Articles; neither doth it ſet downe any other ground
to defend them to be Proteſtants, then ſuch as are already, or may be eaſily refuted, or by which ech other
ancient or moderne Heretiques may be defended to
be members of the Proteſtant Church; for as theſe he
nameth agree with Proteſtants in ſome of their *Tenets*
and eſpecially in their oppoſition againſt the Pope &

H 3 the

the Rom. Church;so also do all other both ancient and recent Heretiques, yea Turkes, Iewes, Pagans, and the Deuils themselues.

And as this Author finding these he nameth to agree with Protestants in some kinde of opposition against the Pope, and the Church of Rome, is contented to make a Catalogue of their Names, endeauoring to proue and defend them to be members of the Protestāt Church, although it be manifest that their disagreements from English Protestants, are not onely about small matters, but about matters of great Consequence which touch the very essence, substance, and soule of Protestant religion; as for example about the Article of free Iustification by only Fayth, which was as much oppugned by Wickliff and his followers (who are the men this Author chiefly names), as it was by the ancient Fathers, or yet is by the Pastors of the present Roman Church: So I do not see why he may not also(for that some kind of agreement is found in auncient Heretiques, Turkes, Iewes, Pagans, and Deuils themselues in some points, and especially in their opposition against the Pope and the Church of *Rome*) be content to make a Catalogue of their Names, and with shame inough affirme, proue, and defend them all to be members of the Protestant Church. For if one say, that all these cannot be Protestants, in regard they haue ben condemned by the ancient, and are yet condemned by the present Church; this Authour may say, that it is true, *de facto* they were, and are condemned, but this hindreth not but they may be members of the Protest. Church, supposing that *de Iure* they ought not to haue bene condemned, and their Tenets may be iustified. Now whether *de Iure* anciēt Heretiques, Turkes, Iewes Pagans, and Deuils were so condemned, as that their

Tenets

Tenets cannot be iuftifyed, this Author may doubt ; for although they difagree in mayne points , fome of which touch the effence, fubftance, and foule of the Chriftian Religion, yet they all agree in fome poynts, and namely in the chiefe points in which Proteftants do agree, to wit, in holding one or other kind of oppofition againft the Pope and Roman Church. Why therefore may not all their names be put in one Catalogue, and they all be accounted members of one, and the fame Proteft. Church, as well as Wickliff, and his Followers?

Moreouer, this Author fetteth downe certaine ftrang groundes, which being admitted, I do not fee, but all Heretiques may proue and defend themfelues to be the true Church againft whatfoeuer arguments. For firft, this Authour will haue it fuppofed, that the Church muft be proued and allowed by the doctrine, and not the doctrine authorized by the Church ; which being vnderftood in the Authors fenfe, to wit, that ech particuler man muft firft learne which is true doctrine in all neceffary pointes, by reading Scriptures, and thereby proue, and allow thofe to be the true Church which hould that doctrine in all points which he in particuler iudgeth to be neceffary to be held according to fcripture, without depending vpon the Iudgment & authority of any Church, or expecting to be taught by it, which be Scriptures, which true Tranflation, which true Interpretation, & which be truthes fundamentall & neceffary to be expreffly knowne to all true members of the Church: I do not fee, I fay, but that any Heretique of whatfoeuer fect, (fuppofing this falfe gioud) may (by as good an argument, as that which this Author fo much commendeth, calling it the Argument of Worthy *D. Featly*) proue himfelf, and thofe of his
fect

sect to be the true Church, and that there were visible
Professors of his Sect in all ages, saying, according to
the forme prescribed by this Author: The reformed doctrine which the Church of our Sect holdeth, must
needes haue Professours in all ages, becaufe it is Eternall, for Eternity must needes haue a perpetuall dura-
tion without interruption. Which how foolish an argument it is, euery man that hath but a meane wit, may
eafily fee; for if euery man must be permitted to censure what is Eternall doctrine of Fayth, by onely reading priuatly the holy fcripture, we fhall haue fo many
Eternall doctrines of Fayth, as there are different fancies of men, who will Cenfure all, and not fubmit
themfelues to the authority of any Church; which is in
S. Bernards iudgment, *Intollerable pride,* and in *S. Auftens,*
Infolent madnes. And therefore this Authour muft know,
that although the diuine doctrine in it felfe do not
need to be authorized by the Church, yet in refpect of
our acknowledging it to be diuine, we muft heare and
belieue thofe who are knowne by other markes to be
lawfully fent Paftours of the true Church, as we may
gather out of *S. Paul,* in his Epiftle to the *Rom.* 10.
Ephef. 4.

Secondly, this Author will not be tyed to fhew a
vifible conftituted Church, which may be knowne
by diftinction and fucceffion of Bifhops &c. but will
haue it fufficient that any Company (of Lay-men for
example) be fhewed to haue held (not all points but)
the mayneft doctrines maintayned by him and his affociates : Neyther will he haue it regarded, if thofe he
fheweth haue in former tymes ben *de facto* condemned
by the Church for thofe moft and mayneft doctrines;
but he will haue it fuffice that he fay, *De Iure, they ought*
not to haue ben condemned; and that he fay, *I can Iuftifie*
their

their Tenets : (that is , if he may be allowed to be Iudge of Controuerſies,& not to be bound to heare, obey, or ſubmit his Iudgment to any Church) as indeed euery other Heretique may, and will ſay for men holding ſome doctrines of his ſect (although formerly they haue ben cōdemned by the firſt foure Generall Councels, or by the Ancient Fathers *S. Auſten* , *S. Hierom , S. Epiphanius*) *de Iure* they ought not to haue bene condemned,and I can Iuſtify their *Tenets.*Which Plea if it be good, I do not ſee but it will as well ſerue to vphold all doctrines, condemned by the aforeſaid Ancient Councels and Fathers, as theſe which are condemned by the Councell of *Trent,* or the preſent Paſtours of the Cath. Roman Church .

But by this Authors leaue, he muſt be tyed to ſhew diſtinction and ſucceſſion of Proteſtant Biſhops in all ages,or elſe he cannot ſhew (as *M. Fiſhers* Queſtion requireth) a viſible Proteſtant Church in all ages. For as, not onely ſcriptures and ancient Fathers, but alſo his Worthy *D. Featly,* and other more learned Proteſtants Tract of the grant, Biſhops, or at leaſt prieſts or Paſtours muſt be al- viſibility of wayes in the Church;neither can it be the true Church the Church, of Chriſt,if there be no true Biſhop, prieſt, or lawfully aſſert. 4. ſent Paſtour in it. And therefore it was the vſuall argument of ancient Fathers, to vrge Heretiques to ſhew perpetuall Succeſſion of their Biſhops from Chriſt and his Apoſtles; which if they could not do, they did account them ſufficiently conuinced, not to be the true *Tertul. præ-* Church . So *Tertulliā,* who ſayth: *Edant origines Eccleſia- ſcrip. aduerſ. rum ſuarum &c.* Let them ſet forth the Origens of their *Hæreſ. c. 3ʒ.* Churches, let them vnfold the order of their Biſhops, ſo running by ſucceſſion vnto vs, as that the firſt of them had for his Authour and Anteceſſour, ſome Apoſtle or Apoſtolicall man,who perſeuered with the Apoſtles.

I   See

See alſo *Optatus,* who ſayth : *t eſſ a Cathedra originem reddite, qui vobis vultis ſanctam Eccleſiam vendicare :* Shew yee the beginning of your (Epiſcopall) Chayre, who will challenge to your ſelues the holy Church.

Sith therefore this Author doth not, nor dare not vndertake to ſhew Proteſtant Biſhops, or Paſtours in all ages, we may conclude that he neyther hath ſufficiently anſwered, nor dare gee about to anſwere *M. Fiſhers* queſtion, requiring a viſible Church of Proteſtants to be ſhewed in all ages, by naming, prouing, and defending out of good Authors, ſuch profeſſors thereof in all ages, as may make a continuall viſible Church.

THE IX. CHAPTER.

Concerning D. VVhites Anſwere.

 Ll I can finde in *D. Whites* Booke called : *A Replye to Ieſuit Fiſhers Anſwer to his Maieſlies Propoſitions,* concerning this preſent Queſtion is, firſt this generall bare aſſertion : *In all ages ſome Perſons held the ſubſtantiall Articles of our Proteſtant Religion,*

Pag 19. 140. *both in the Roman and Græcian Church.* But he neyther nameth the men in particuler, neyther doth he giue a Catalogue of all ſubſtantiall Articles, nor a definition, or deſcription well proued out of Scriptures, by which as by a Rule all may know certainly, what is, and what is not a ſubſtantiall Article of Proteſtant Religion.

Secondly, he tels vs, that *the Græcians maintayne ſome Articles in common with the Proteſtants, and that in this We-*
ſterne

fterne part *Waldenfes*, *Thaborites*, the fchollars of *Wickiff* called *Lollards*, *maintayned the fame doctrine in fubstance with the moderne Proteftants*, as appeareth by the *Confefsion of their Fayth &c*. But thefe points in which thefe agreed, eyther are not fubftantiall, or there were other points as much, or more fubftantiall in which they diftered one from another, and all of them from Proteftants; as fhalbe fhewed whenfoeuer D. *White* will make vp his whole Catalogue of Names of thefe, and all others in all ages, with an offer to proue and defend them to be Proteftants; at which tyme alfo the differences which are found among fome of the ancient and moderne Roman Catholiques, may be eafily declared, and proued to be nothing fo great in matter or manner, as are the differences found betwixt the *Gracians* or *Waldenfes*, *Thaborits*, or *Lollards*, from moderne Proteftants, or betwixt moderne Proteftants themfelues: for, all the differences betwixt ancient and moderne Roman Catholiques are onely in matters of practife, or in points of doctrine not defyned, or not knowne to be defined, nor generally held for diuine truth by the vniuerfall Church; neyther is this difagreement maintayned obitinately, but with readines to fubmit fo foone as the Church by her chief Paftour, either alone or with a generall Councell, fhall defyne what is to be held for truth; Wheras the Iarrs betwixt moderne Proteftants on the one fide, and *Gracians* or *Waldenfes*, or *Thaborites* or *Lollards* on the other fide, are about mayne matters defyned by full authority of the Church, or generally held by the Church; and many of thefe moderne Proteftants hold their opinion fo obftinatly that they will not yield, and fubmit it, although the chiefe Paftor, or a whole generall Councell of Paftours, or all other men in the world (befides themfelues) fhould defyne

the

the contrary to be truth.

Thirdly, D. *White* fayth; *If it were fo, that we could not for certaine ages past nominate, or afsigne out of Histories, any ·ther vifible Church befides the Roman and Græcian; yet (fayth ·e) becaufe right Fayth may be preferued in perfons liuing in a orrupt Church, and becaufe God hath promifed there shalbe ·lwayes in the world a Church hauing eyther a larger, or fmal-er number of Profeßors : If Proteftants be able to demouftrate ·hat they maintaine the fame Fayth and Religion, which the holy Apoftles taught, this alone is fufficient to proue, they are the true Church.*

But D. *White* ought not to delude his Reader in this fort, faying, *if it were fo that we could not &c.* infinua-ting as if he could(if he would) nominate in all ages out of Hiftoryes a vifible Proteftant Church, diftinct from the Roman and Græcian, when he knoweth well inough, that he cannot nominate any fuch di-ftinct vifible Proteftant Church ; or els why doth he not nominate it, hauing ben fo much vrged to nomi-nate it? why alfo did he in the firft conference with M. *Fisher* graunt he could not? Secondly, he fhould not tell vs, that Fayth may be preferued in perfons, liuing in a corrupt Church;for it is hard, if not impoffible to ima-gine how fo many right belieuers as by Gods promifes muft be always in the world, efpecially obferuing the precept of Pofitiue and Negatiue profeffion of Fayth, and executing the duties which muft always be per-formed in the true vifible Church, could be preferued in a corrupt Church, both from being corrupted, and from being noted by the reft of that corrupt Church; for eyther they did Communicate in feruice and facra-ments with thefe of the corrupt Church, and fo were corrupted by them by doing the contrary to the nega-tiue precept of profeffion of Fayth; or if they did not,
                                    they

they could not auoyd being noted by their forbearing to communicate with the corrupt Church, as others in like cafe were, & are. Thirdly, when he fayth, if Proteftants be able to demonftrate that they haue the fame fayth which the Apoftles taught, it alone were fufficiét to proue they were the true church; he fhould reméber, that fo may the Arrians, Anabaptifts, and euery other fect of Heretiques fay; If we Arrians, Anabaptifts &c. be able to demonftrate, that we haue the fame Fayth which the Apoftles taught, it alone is fufficient to proue, that we were the true Church. This Conditionall Propofition therefore which the Doctour bringeth for his vpfhot, doth no more proue Proteftants to haue had a continuall vifible Church, of which the queftion now is, then the lyke Conditionall can proue Arrians and Anabaptifts to haue had a continuall vifible Church, which doubtleffe they had not.

If the Doctour iufer, that although he onely fay, If Proteftants be able &c. yet he meaneth to fubfume and fay abfolutly, that Proteftants are able to demonftrate &c. I reply, that fo alfo will Arrians and Anabaptifts fubfume, & not onely fo fay, but will for proof of their peculiar doctrines, bring more feeming playne fentences of fcripture, then are, or can be brought by Proteftants for their peculiar doctrines. It is not therefore inough for the Doctour to fay, eyther conditionally, or abfolutely, The Proteftants are able to demonftrate, that they haue the fame Fayth which the Apoftles taught, for neyther can he truely and cleerly demonftrate, any one Proteftant doctrine to haue ben taught by the Apoftles, & much leffe all Proteftant doctrines; neyther if he could, doth that fufficiently proue, that Proteftants had a continuall vifible Church, in regard more is required to a vifible Church, then only true do-

ctrine;

doctrine; for a ſchiſmaticall Company of lay-men may haue true doctrine, and yet they are not a true viſible Church, in which muſt be Paſtors teaching true doctrine, and adminiſtring ſacraments with due ſubordination of people to Paſtors, and receauing inſtruction and Sacraments at their hands.

D. *White* therefore is moſt deficient in his nominating and aſſigning a continuall viſible Proteſt. Church. It may be, the Doctour being onely aſſiſtant to D. *Featly*, who boldly vndertooke to ſhew Names of Proteſtants in all ages, did not conſent to this vndertaken taske; but if ſo, why did he not then diſclaime, or why would he be aſſiſtant to him at all, when he knew before hand that M. *Fiſher* meant chiefly to vrge this point? & why doth he not now acknowledge plainely (as the truth is)that none can nominate, or aſſigne a continuall viſible Proteſtant Church in all ages, out of good Authors?

This for the preſent ſhall ſuffice for Refutation of what D. *White* ſayth to this point. As for other matters contained in his large-long-expected, two-yeares-laboured, Impertinent *Reply to* M. *Fiſhers* Anſwer to his Maieſties Propoſitions, I hope the world ſhall ſee, ere it be long, very ſufficiently refuted : and therefore I will paſſe to the examination of what D. *Featly* hath ſaid concerning the Queſtion now in hand.

THE

THE X. CHAPTER.

A Reply to *D. Featly* his Anſwere, to *M. Fishers* Queſtion.

OCTOVR *Featly* being the firſt and principall Diſputāt who did in the Conference vndertake to anſwer *M. Fishers* queſtion, & to ſhew (both by Syllogiſme & Induction) the Proteſtant Church to haue ben alwayes viſible, was firſt & principally obliged to name, proue, and defend viſible Proteſtant Paſtours, and people in all Ages, and therefore ſhould haue been the firſt man who did in print anſwere this queſtion: but I finde him the laſt of ſixe or ſeauen. And it ſeemeth he did of purpoſe delay his Anſwere, partly that he might ſee what acceptance & ſucceſſe the Anſwers of others ſhould haue; that if bad, they might beare the blame, and he being (*Felix ille vir quem faciunt aliena pericula cautum*) warned by other mens harmes, might learne by their errours, to make a better anſwer; but if good, he might be more bold to follow their footſteps, and make vſe of their labours: partly alſo, that he might gaine more tyme and leaſure to deliberate vpon the matter, and to make diligent ſearch into libraries, and to read all, or the chief Proteſtant writers who had handled this Queſtion, & that hauing ſeene all that is, or can be ſaid by others, he might adde what he could by his owne wit and ſtudie, and ſo compile a moſt complete Catalogue of Names

of

of Proteftants in all ages with fufficient proofes and defences, or at leaft grounds of proofe and defence fo well fortified, as better could not be expected from any Proteftant.

Wherefore it may be well fuppofed, that if any Proteftant either haue, or can make a good Anfwere to *M. Fishers* Queftion, *D. Featly* hath made it; But in cafe it fhalbe found, that *D. Featly* after fuch a folemne and publick vndertaking, after fo long deliberation, after fuch diligent fearching in libraries, and reading other mens bookes, and finally after fuch ferious ftrayning of his wit in ftudy; hath not, nor cannot make a good Anfwer, by giuing Names of Proteftant Paftours and people fufficiently proued and defended to haue made a vifible Proteftant Church in all Ages: If, I fay, *D. Featly* haue not in his lately printed Booke made fuch an Anfwer, let neuer any man expect, that this Queftion euer will, or can be well anfwered; and thereupon let it be concluded, that the Proteftant Church hath not been alwaies vifible (nor côfequently been) in all ages, in fuch fort as the true Church of Chrift hath been and ought to be ; and confequently that the Proteftant Church is not, nor was not the true Church of Chrift, of which all men muft learne that Fayth and Religion which is neceffary to faluation .

Let vs therefore (omitting all by-matters, which may be found in D. *Featlyes* Booke, (to which fo far as need fhalbe heereafter Anfwer may be made:) let vs, I fay, ferioufly obferue what Anfwere he maketh to *M. Fishers* Queftion requiring Names, proofes, and defences of Vifible Profeffors of the Proteftant Church in all ages out of good Authours.

Firft I obferue, that *D. Featly* hath not performed his promifed Induction of Names, of fuch as he thinketh

keth to be Proteftants in all ages (which fhould be the
firft parte of his Anfwere, according to the Methode
prefcribed by *M. Fisher* ;) which argueth that he cannot
eyther with good confcience or credit, performe what
he promifed. For if he could name men in all ages,
whom he could with good confcience and credit,
proue and defend out of good Authours to haue been
Profeffours of Proteftát Religion, he would(doubtles)
as hauing had moft vrgent Reafons fufficient to moue
him to name them before this tyme, in regard firft, of
his Aduerfaries fo much preffing this point both before,
in, and after the Conference; and that he may ftill expect that neither Papifts mouthes wilbe ftopped , nor
Proteftants confciences well fatisfied, vntill Names of
Proteftants be fet downe in all ages, good proofes
brought out of good Authours, and folid defence made
againft all Obiections .

Secondly, In refpect of fatisfying his owne promife
to make a full Induction, and the promife of the Right
Honourable Earle of Warwick, who faid he fhould
come againe to name Proteftants in all ages.

Thirdly, In refpect of verifying his owne words &
Arguments vttered in the Conference, by which as is
faid in *M. Fishers* letter to the faid Honorable Earle, he
and his affiftant *D. White* are fo far from hauing dif- »
charged themfelues of the great enterprize they vnder- »
tooke, as they ftand more engaged then before to the »
performance of it; for hauing profeffed and acknow- »
ledged that the true Church , or, to vfe their owne »
words, the Church that is fo vifible as the Catholique »
Church ought to be,(and the Church whofe Fayth is »
eternall and vnchanged muft be) is able to Name her »
profeffors in all ages, either for their owne honour, or »
for the fatisfaction of the world, they muft fetdowne »

« Names of their Profeſſours in all ages, or els they ſham-
« fully diſcouer themſelues not to be that true viſible vn-
« changed Church that can name them. Neither will it
ſuffice, that D. Featly ſay (as he ſayth in his Anſwere to
this part of the ſaid letter) when I diſputed thus in the

D Featlyes Conference: The Church, whoſe Fayth is perpetuall
Reply pag. « and vnchaunged, is ſo viſible, or ought to be ſo viſible,
143 « that the Names of the Profeſſours thereof may be ſhe-
» wed in all ages ; I argued not ſo according to my
« owne opinion , but as is expreſly ſet downe in the
Conference (ex Conceſsis.) This Anſwer, I ſay, will not

Relation ſuffice, for according to the Proteſtant Relation of the
called M. Conference, thus did D. Featly diſpute : That Church
Fisher cat- which is ſo viſible as the Catholique Church ought to
ched pag.17 be, and as the Popiſh Church is pretended by M. Fisher
« to be, is ſo viſible, that the Names of the Profeſſors may
« be produced and ſhewed. But the Proteſt. Church is ſo
« viſible, as the Cath. Church ought to be, and as the Popiſh Church is pretended by M. Fisher to be.   Ergo.

The Maior of which Argument, cannot be ſaid to
be ex Conceſsis, for M. Fisher neuer graunted it , but muſt
be held to haue proceeded out of D. Featly his owne
opinion : for M. Fisher denied it , and D. Featly went
about to proue it, by this enſuing ſyllogiſme ſet downe
by the ſame Proteſtant Relatour.

Thus :

« The Church whoſe Fayth is Eternall, & perpetuall,
« and vnchanged, is ſo viſible as the Catholique Church
« ought to be, and the Popiſh Church is pretended by
« M. Fisher to be.
« But the Fayth of the Proteſtant Church is Eternal,
« perpetuall, and vnchanged .   Ergo.

The Maior of which laſt Syllogiſme being by D.
Featly brought to proue the Minor of the former, argueth

gueth, that as it was his owne opinion that the Proteſtant Church was ſo viſible, as the Romiſh Church
was pretended by *M. Fisher*, to wit, ſo viſible as names
of the profeſſours may be ſhewed in all ages: So alſo
it was his owne opinion, that, That Church whoſe
Fayth is Eternall and vnchanged, is ſo viſible as the
Romiſh Church was pretended to be, to wit, ſo viſible that the Names of the profeſſours thereof may be
ſhewed in all ages. D. *Featly* therefore muſt not ſay (as
he doth now ſay) that he did only argue *ex Concesſis*,
and not according to his owne opinion.

Moreouer, if it were not his owne opinion, but only
M. Fishers, that the Church whoſe Fayth is perpetuall
and vnchanged, is ſo viſible that the Names of the Profeſſors may be ſhewed in all ages, as now he would
haue vs thinke; I aske why he did cōtrary to his owne
opinion and Conſcience boldly affirme in the Minor
of the firſt Syllogiſme, that the Proteſt. Church whoſe
Fayth he held to be perpetuall and vnchanged, is ſo
viſible as the Romiſh Church was pretended by *M. Fisher* to be, knowing that *M. Fisher* held the Romiſh
Church to be ſo viſible, as that the Names of her profeſſors, not only may be ſhewed, but ought to be, and
ordinarily are in printed bookes(*Gualterus* in Latin, &
S. N. in his Appendix to his Antidote in Engliſh,)
both ſhewed, and proued throughout all ages? Why
alſo did he againſt his owne opinion and Conſcience,
delude the Auditours in the Conference, not only
with this foreſayd (knowne to be falſe) *Minor* propo-
ſitiō, *The Proteſt. Church is ſo viſible as the Cath. Church ought
to be, and as M. Fisher pretendeth the Rom. Church to be*: but
alſo with offering & vndertaking by a full Inductiō to
ſhew Names of Proteſtāts in all ages, which (as it now
ſeemeth) in his owne opinion and Conſcience he did

not

not then thinke might or could be ſhewed, and yet in
the ſame Proteſtant Relation he is induced, ſaying,
Thus I diſpute : *The Proteſtant Church was ſo viſible, that*
Relation *the Names of thoſe who taught and belieued the doctrine therof*
called Fiſher *may be produced in the firſt hundred yeares, and ſecond, & third,*
catched. pag. *and fourth, and ſo in the reſt.* Ergo. *It was ſo in all ages.*
36.
      Now I aske *D. Featly*, whether this argument was
made out of his owne opinion or not? If it were made
out of his owne opinion, why doth he deny that he argued out of his owne opinion in his Syllogiſmes, in
which no more is affirmed then is in this Induction ?
But if it were made contrary to his owne opinion, &
that in his Conſcience he thought he could not ſhew
names in all ages, what a ſhamleſſe Seducer is he, who
contrary to his owne Opinion and Conſcience, did
then make his Proteſtant Auditours think, and would
yet make his Reader belieue, that he could, and would
name Proteſtants in all ages, ſaying in his late printed
booke: *Proteſtants are nominable, their names may be produ-*
ced; There are Records yet extant, out of which we are able to
make a Catalogue *of Proteſtant Profeſſors* : and yet cōming
to his Catalogue, he only nameth a few for the firſt
two ages. What a ſhamfull Iuggling is this ? firſt in publique Conference (when he ſaw that his owne credit, and the credit of the Proteſtant cauſe did ſo require)
he goeth about to proue, that he can name profeſſors of
the Proteſt. Religion in all ages; but when he is by the
letter written to the Earle of Warwick preſſed to ve-
rifie what he ſaid while he diſputed, (which he
knoweth he cannot do with credit,) then, forſooth,
he telleth, that he did not diſpute according to his
owne opinion. And yet againe perceiuing, that the
world doth expect that Names of Proteſtants in all
ages ſhould be ſet downe according to the Induction
                                                    which

which he began to make in the Conference, & which
the Earle of *Warwicke* in his behalf promised should
be finished, he repeateth his vaine bragge, that he can
name Proteſtants in all ages; but when he cōmeth to
his Catalogue, he only nameth as followeth.

The Beginning of the Catalogue.

For witneſſes of the Truth, of the doctrine we
now profeſſe, and maintaine in the Churh of England,
I alleadge,

In the firſt age, from Chriſts Birth, to the firſt
hundred yeares.

> *Chriſt Ieſus.*
> *The twelue Apoſtles .*
> *S. Iohn Baptiſt .*
> *S. Marke .*
> *S. Luke .*
> *S. Paul,* with his Schollers *Titus , Timothy,*
> and the Churches planted, or watered by
> them .
> *Romans . Corinthians* &c.
> *Clemens* about the yeare 90.
> *Ignatius* about the yeare 100 . with the
> Churches to whom he wrote .
> The *Trallians , Magneſians , Tarſians , Philadel-
> phians.* &c.

In the ſecond age from 100. to 200.

> *Polycarpus .* 140 .
> *Iuſtin Martyr .* 150.
> *Methodius .* 155 .
> *Dionyſius Corinthiacus.* 158 .
> *Hegeſippus.* 160. *S. Irenæus.* 160.
> *Clemens Alexandrinus.* 200 .

Theſe

Thefe be all he nameth for Profeſſours of Proteſtant doctrine maintained in the Church of England; but he neither proceedeth on forward, in giuing Names as he ought according to his promifed Induction; neyther doth he out of good Authors, bring prooſes ſufficient to ſhew any one of theſe he nameth to be Proteſtants, more then may be brought by any other Heretique (as is already ſaid againſt thoſe which *M. Rogers* named;) neither doth he giue any ſufficient grounds, by which he may defend them in better ſort, then any other Heretique may defend them to haue ben profeſſours of his Sect; and he may find in the bookes which were ey-ther written by theſe he nameth, or which make men-tion of them, as plaine and expreſſe places condem-ning ſome or other of the 39. Articles, profeſſed and maintained by the Engliſh Church, as any he can find condemning *Arians*, *Anabaptiſts*, or whatſoeuer other condened Heretiques; neither ca he giue better Anſwer to ſuch places as are againſt Proteſtants, then may, by Arrians for example, or other Heretiques, be giuen to any places which he can out of the ſaid bookes obiect againſt Arrians or other Heretiques, ſuppoſing they may be allowed ſuch libertie (as *D. Featly* taketh to himſelf) in deuiſing grounds ſutable to their opinions.

Moreouer, diuers of theſe named by *D. Featly*, are ex-preſſly condemned by Proteſtâts, far more learned then *D. Featly*, for holding the Româ Fayth, or ſome other oppoſite to the Proteſt. doctrine profeſſed in England, in diuers maine points, as may be ſeen in the Proteſt. Apologie. But he cannot ſhew in the like ſort Catho-lique writers who do condemne any one of them for holding Proteſt. doctrine in any one point, contrary to the Roman Fayth and Religion.

Very idle therefore, and impertinent is this firſt part

of *D. Featlyes* Catalogue, and as idle and impertinent wilbe his proceeding(if euer he will proceed) in it, fo far forth as he fhall name any one of the approued ancient orthodox writers. Thofe other Heterodoxians which his Lord and Maifter in the Booke called, The perpetuall Vifibility of the true Church, nameth & accounteth Proteftants, may be fhewed (euen by confeffion of learned Proteftants) in fome points to haue held the doctrine of the Roman Church, quite oppofite to the prefent Englifh Proteftant Church her doctrine, & therefore neither the one fort, nor other can help him to patch vp a Catalogue of Proteftants, in all ages, who can be proued, and defended to maintayne the doctrine of the Englifh Church; neither can they, and the Englifh Church compofe one, and the fame Proteftant Church; neither confequently can the Proteftant Church be fhewed by an Induction, to haue been vifible in all ages, as the Doctor did vndertake to fhew.

See the Treatife of the Church fet out by W. G, in manner of a Dialogue.

2. I obferue, that *D. Featly* (knowing he cannot with credit name, proue, and defend Proteftants in all ages, in fuch fort as *M. Fifhers* queftion required) vfeth diuers Tergiuerfations, & fhiftes in this his Reply, thinking therby to auoyd difgrace to himfelf, and preiudice to the Proteftant caufe.

Certaine Tergiuerfations vfed of D. Featly.

Firft, he goeth about to perfwade his Reader, that there is no neceffity of producing Names, and that his offer to produce them, is *ex fuperabundanti*, and confequently no difgrace to him, nor preiudice to the Proteftant caufe if they be not produced. But by his leaue, he hauing engaged himfelf to produce names, cannot auoyd

auoyd difgrace if he do not produce them . And if neither he, nor any other do produce Names, the Proteftant caufe cannot auoyde preiudice, as appareth by
M. *Fishers* fiue propofitions aboue rehearfed , by which
is fhewed(and againft M. *Rogers* maintained) that the
Proteftant Church cannot be the true Church of
Chrift, if it haue not had in all ages Paftours teaching,
and people belieuing, whofe names may be fhewed
out of Hiftories Neyther will any wife man belieue
they can be named, if the Names (hauing ben exacted
and promifed) be not now produced.

　　Secondly, *D. Featly* doth confeffe , that the true
Church hath ben hitherto alwaies in fome degree
vifible, as in hiftories yet extant is recorded ; whence
followeth,that the profeffors of the true Church may
in all ages be fhewed in fuch fort as hiftories do record
them: But hiftories do not only record Names Appel-
latiues of true profeffors, or true profeffours in generall,
but alfo Proper Names , at leaft of fome of the moft
eminent in all ages: And therefore if in all ages, Names
of fome Proteftants(eminent either for doing, or fuffering, or faying fome thing which may fhew them to
haue bene members of the Proteftant Church) be not
produced out of hiftories,the Proteftant Church is not
to be accounted the true Church of Chrift.

Reply tou-
ching the vi-
fibility of the
Church.
Affert. 4.

　　Thirdly,if fome proper Names of other forts of Profeffors, who were in ech age, & fome of their actions or
fuffrings , or at leaft fayings(wherby it may be plainly
fhewed to all forts, of what Fayth and profeffion they
were)be recorded, and may be, (and if it be exacted
fhalbe)fhewed in hiftoryes yet extant , which were, &
are preferued by the prouidence of God, and diligence
of the Paftours and people of the true Church, in regard they do one way or other redound to the glory
　　　　　　　　　　　　　　　　　　　　　　　of

of God and good of the Church ; What reafon is there
to imagine, that the fame prouidence of God, and diligence of Paftours & people of the true Church, fhould
not much more carefully haue in like fort preferued the
memory of proper Names of fome or other eminent
profeffors of the true Church,& fome of their actiōs,or
fufferings or fayings,in all ages, whē as this doth moft
greatly redound to the glory of God,and good of the
Church,and may both ferue to fhew clearly, how the
diuine Prophecies and Promifes of the true Church
haue been fulfilled; and may make all forts clerely fee
the difference betwixt lawfully fent Paftours & preachers, whom holy Scriptures commaund all men to
heare,belieue, and obey; and vnfent falfe prophets and
vpftart Heretiques, whom the fame Holy Scriptures
warne all men to auoyd, and not to heare.

*Matth. 18.
17.
Matth. 23. 1;
2. 3.
Luc. 10. 16.
Hebr. 13.17.
Matth. 7. 15;
Tit. 3. 10.*

The difference of which two forts, all (efpecially
vnlearned men) cannot fufficiently difcerne by their
only doctrine;for that(as Vincētius Lyrinenfis noteth)
the falfe prophets and Heretiques can, and vfually do
couer their woluifh foule-killing doctrines, vnder
the fheepes clothing offeeming plaine words and fentences of holy Scriptures, which both in Sermons, &
in written, and in printed Bookes they vfe to cite as
plentifully as true Paftours;neyther cā a man either by
his owne wit, or by hearing Schollers difpute , or by
a pretended priuat fpirit iudge infallibly , which is the
true, which is the falfe fenfe of Scripture , or which
true, which falfe doctrine, efpecially in all points of
Fayth (many of which exceed the capacity of all naturall wit and reafon ;) but muft learne of lawfull
Paftors and teachers,all infallible diuine truth neceffary to faluation , as *S. Paul* fayth; *How shall they belieue
vnles they heare;heare vnleße they preach ; preach vnleße they be*

*Vincent Ly-
rinenf aduer;
fus barcf. c;
36.*

*Rom. 10. 14;
15.*

L   *fent*

fent? Therefore euery man muſt firſt by ſome other
markes find out, who be theſe lawfully-ſent preachers,
before he can diſcerne, whether the doctrine taught
by them be true; and who be falſe Prophets, that he
may auoyd, and not ſo much as heare what they
teach. Now among other markes by which true Paſtours may be diſcerned from falſe Prophets, one chief
is to haue had lawfull Calling, Miſſion, Commiſſion,
and authority to teach, deriued by vninterrupted Succeſſion from the calling, miſſion, commiſſion, and authority to teach, which Chriſt our Lord had from his
Father and gaue to his Apoſtles; which ſucceſſion may
out of Hiſtories be ſhewed (euen to vnlearned men)
to agree only to the Paſtours of the Catholique Roman Church, in ſuch plaine manner as no other ſort of
Chriſtians can with any probability(euen in the Iudgment of the ſame vnlearned men) make a like Clayme
vnto it. For whereas Roman Catholiques can, & do in
printed bookes make a Catalogue, and ſet downe the
Names of their Paſtours in all ages, who ſucceeding
one another, haue lineally deſcended from Chriſt and
his Apoſtles(as may be proued out of good Authours)
without changing any one point of the Fayth held,
and taught, and deliuered to them by their predeceſ-
ſours(as may be eaſily defended, neither can it be contradicted by any ſufficient Inſtance out of the like good
Authours;) no other ſort of Chriſtians, differing in doctrine of Fayth from Roman Catholiques, can make a
lyke Catalogue contayning Names of their Paſtours
in all ages, who ſucceeding one another, haue lineally
deſcended from Chriſt, and his Apoſtles, without
changing of ſome one, or other point of Fayth held,
taught, and deliuered to them by their predeceſſours.
For either they will not be ſo ſhameleſſe, or ſenſeleſſe

Marginal notes: Rom. 10.15. Heb.5.4. Act.13.3. 1.Tim.4.14. 2.Tim.1.6. Matth.28. 18. Ioan. 20.21.

as to fet downe Names of any in all ages, whom they
dare affirme to haue bene profeffours of their Religion
in all ages, but will rather flye to the common fhift of a
pretended Inuifible Church : or if feeing the neceffity
of auoyding this *Charybdis* of an Inuifible Church, they
put away all fhame, fetting downe names of men whō
they pretend to haue been profeffours of their Fayth;
it may be euidently conuinced out of good Authours,
that eyther all, or moft of thofe they name, were fo
farre from being profeffours of their Fayth, as they did
condemne it, and held the contrary in fome or other
point.

All which confidered, *D. Featly* may fee, what preiudice is like to come to his Proteftant Church, by his
not producing Names of Proteftant Paftours in all
ages, and by his not prouing and defending them.

The 2. Tergiuerfation and Shift which *D. Featly* The 2. Ter-
giuerfation.
vfeth is, that he perfifteth in faying he can name Pro-
teftāts in all ages. But this he fayth he will not do, vntill *M. Fisher* anfwere the Challenge which now he
maketh, bidding him produce Names of Roman Catholiques in the firft two ages: which is a moft impertinent, vnneceffary, and vnfeafonable Challenge. Firft
I fay, it is Impertinent, for whether *M. Fisher* euer or
neuer anfwer this Challenge, *D. Featlies* credit and the
life of the Proteftant caufe lyeth bleeding at the ftake,
and needfully requireth that he, or fome other fhould
produce Names of Proteftants in all ages, and proofes
out of good Authors, and that he defend them againft
M. Fishers obiections, as hath ben already fhewed. Secondly, it is not neceffary, that *M. Fisher* fhould in
thofe ages Name Roman Catholiques. For diuers already haue named them, namely *Gualterus* in his *Tabula
Chronographica* in Latin, and S. N. his *Appendix* in Englifh,

L 2

gliſh, and M. *Fiſher* himſelf in his Reply to M. *Wotton* &
M. *White* Miniſters. Thirdly, it is vnſeaſonable to challenge M. *Fiſher* at this time to ſet downe Names of Roman Catholiques; for the due ſeaſon to require this of
M. *Fiſher* only is, (as appeareth by the paper by which
M. *Fiſher* did engage himſelf,)after S. *Humfrey Lynde* , or
his friends, (hall haue named, proued, and defended viſible Proteſtants in all ages , in ſuch ſort as M. *Fiſhers*
queſtion required: Then indeed, but not before, is M. *Fiſher* obliged to name , proue, and defend Roman Catholiques in all ages ; and then with Gods help he doth
intend to name both Paſtours and people in all ages,
which he will proue to be Roman Catholiques , not
by ſuch particuler ſentences of ſcriptures or Fathers,
which being ſubiect to ſeuerall ſenſes, may by the per-
tinacie of Aduerſaries ſeeme not to make a cleare
proofe, but either by the very Confeſſion of learned
Proteſtants themſelues , or by the plaine ſtory of the
liues of ſuch as he nameth , or by ſuch cleere teſtimonies as cannot with any reaſon be denied, to proue that
they were not Proteſtants, but Roman Catholiques.

The third
Tergiuerſa-
tion.   A third Tergiuerſation and (hift vſed by D. *Featly* is ,
that he would perſwad, that this Methode of requiring
Names , it not ſo good as the other which himſelf
would haue followed in the Conference : to wit , by
prouing the Proteſtant Church to haue been viſible,
by a Demonſtration *à Priori.* Two principall Reaſons
he bringeth againſt this Method of requiring Names;
The firſt is , that many men and matters may haue
been, and were, whereof no Names can be ſhewed out
of good Authors, either for that Authors did not write
of all men and matters, or for that all the Records once
written are not now extant. But this reaſon doth not
ſhew this Method in this matter to be good. Firſt,
                                                    for

for that although other men, and matters may haue been, and were, wherof no names are now extant in hiftories; yet fuch men as we treat of in this Queftion, could not haue been doing, faying, or fuffering fuch things as were neceffary to be done, faid, or fuffered by fuch kind of men, but (according to the ordinary courfe partly of Gods Prouidence, partly of humane Diligence,) Names, or fomthing equiualent to Names of fome principall men in all ages, doing, faying, or fuffering fome things by which they may be knowne to haue bene profeffours of the true Fayth & Religion of Chrift, may (doubtles) and are found in fome hiftories or other monuments yet extant. Secondly, whatfoeuer may be of other mē & matters, it is confeffed by D. *Featly,* that the Names of thofe whom he efteemeth Profeffours of the true Religion of Chrift, are yet to be found in all ages in Records yet extant. Therefore he hauing engaged himfelf to name the men, and the credit of the Proteftant caufe needfully requiring them to be named, as is already proued, he cannot by this idle exception, be excufed for his not naming them.

The fecond Reafon which he obiecteth againft this Method of requiring Names, and prouing out of good Authours, that the men named were Proteftants is, that, *Hiftoriæ non faciunt fidem diuinam, fed humanam*; Hiftories do not (to wit immediatly) breed diuine Fayth, but only humane. But he muft remember that alfo *Demonftratio à Priori non facit fidem diuinam, fed fcientiam humanam*; A demonftration doth not (immediatly) breed diuine Fayth, but fcience either altogether, or in part humane: for, euen true Theologicall Demonftrations do not breed (immediatly) an act of diuine Fayth, but of Theologicall fcience, which dependeth partly on Fayth, partly on the light of hu-

L 3 mane

mane reafon, and fo in part is humane, and not altogether fo certainly infallible as Fayth, which only re-
lieth vpon diuine authority, which is moft infallible.
And as a Theologicall Demonftration (if it be a true
one)may by the Act of Theologicall fcience which it
breedeth, difpofe the vnderftanding to an Act of diuine Fayth, while the vnderftanding eleuated by grace
doth reflect and confider the true Conclufion, not as
inferred by the force of the Argument, but as conteyned in the reuealed principles of Fayth: So the confent
of vndeniable Hiftoryes may (by the Act of morally
certaine humane Fayth which they breed) difpofe the
vnderftanding eleuated by grace, to an Act of diuine
Fayth, while the faid vnderftanding doth reflect and
confider the truths fet downe, not now as fet downe
in humane hiftoryes, but as being virtually contayned
in reuealed Principles, to wit, the Prophecies and promifes of Scripture which foretold thofe truthes which
are fet downe in hiftoryes.

Perhaps *D. Featly* will reply faying: Sith a Theologicall demonftration, efpecially *à Priori*, doth breed an
act of Theologicall fcience, which is more certaine
then the act of morally certaine humane Fayth which
is breed by Hiftories, why fhould not the Method of
that demonftration *à Priori* which he vrged in the Conference, be thought a more certaine way; and confequently a better Method to find out the true Fayth, &
by Fayth the true Church, then by requiring Names
out of Hiftoryes? I anfwere, that the Queftion is not
now in generall, what is the beft Method *Speculatiuè*
in it felf, but what was propofed in the Conference, as
being then for that Matter & Cōpany *Practicè* thought
to be the beft Method to make all forts, and efpecially
vnlearned men, (fuch as many of the Auditours were)
and

and namely the old Gentleman for whofe fake the Cōference was made, to fee, whether or no, the Proteftant Church had been in all Ages fo vifible, as Names of the Profeffours might be produced out of good Authours, as *D. Featly* did vndertake to fhew. And this being the queftion, I affirme that the actuall producing of Names, and prouing and defending, as was then required, was the beft Method, and would haue moft fpeedily and moft foüdly fatisfied the Auditours: And the other Method which *D. Featly* aymed at, by entring into particuler Controuerfies, would haue ben endles, and could not haue fatisfyed.

Secondly, I anfwer, that like as *S. Auftin*, when the Manichees promifed to fhew him cleere truth, infteed of thofe Markes which he faid held him in the Church, one of which was that which now is required to be fhewed, to wit, Succeffion of Priefts from the Chayre of *S. Peter*, the Names of whom both *S. Auftin*, and other Fathers do otherwhere particulerly record, and vrge againft Heretiques, who cannot fhew a like Succefsion: Like, as I fay, *S. Auftin* would not in this cafe fuffer himfelf to be drawen from thofe Markes of the Church (which he called *Charifsima vincula,*) by the promife of cleere truth made by the *Manichees*, becaufe he found that among them (*fola perfonat pollicitatio veritatis*) there was but a vaine found of wordes, and a bare promife of truth: So for the like reafon *M. Fisher* had no reafon to permit *D Featly*, vnder pretence of his promifed demonftration *à Priori*, to diuert from the plaine prefcribed method *à pofteriori*, requiring Names of Profeffors to be produced out of good Authours, which *D. Featly* himfelf doth in a fort acknowledge to be a good Method; for thus he fayth. *If we had no other infallible proofe of the true Fayth, then by the perpetuall Vifibility of the Profeffours*

(side notes:) *Auguft. l. contra Epift. Fundamenti c. 4. & 5.*

(side note:) Reply pag. 105.

Profeſſours thereof, I would hold, it as you do, a point of principall Moment to enquire of the viſibility of Profeſſours : But (ſayth he) *ſith we haue another more eaſie, direct, and Infallible meanes to procure it, viz : by comparing the doctrine with the Canonicall Scriptures, you shall giue mee leaue* M. Fisher, rather to follow the Method generally preſcribed & vſed by the auncient Fathers, as I haue shewed, Aſsertion 7. then the other Method preſcribed by you. Thus hee. But if I can ſhew to him firſt, that this other Methode of his, is neither ſo eaſie, direct, infallible, nor vſed by ancient Fathers (in ſuch ſort as he would haue it vſed) but by ancient and recent Heretiques, and only by ſuch; I hope *D. Featly* will giue *M. Fisher* leaue to call him back from his pretended demonſtration *à Priori*, to anſwer the queſtion according to the preſcribed methode *à Posteriori.*

To ſhew therefore firſt, which Method of theſe two is more eaſie, eſpecially to all ſorts of perſons, I deſire the Reader to reflect vpon what is ſayd of theſe two Methods in A. C. his Reflexion vpon the Conference ; where he ſhall find ſo many things needfull for euery one, who would (by his owne reading, hearing, or interpreting ſcripture) find what is the infallible true Fayth (in all points eſpecially,) or how much of this true Fayth muſt of neceſſity be expreſſly knowne by all that are to be ſaued, that it were a madneſſe to expect, that euery one, or indeed any one, ſhould by his owne priuate reading Scriptures, and comparing the doctrines propoſed by ſeuerall ſorts of Chriſtians with the Scriptures, without hearing and belieuing any Preacher, or Church-man knowne to be lawfully ſent by God. All which being, duly, conſidered, I may boldly affirme, that this Method of D. Featlyes is not ſo eaſie as the other preſcribed by M.Fisher, to wit, firſt(by certaine markes cleerly ſet downe in Scripture

and

See the anſwere to the pamphlet called, *Fisher catched &c. cap. 4, §. 3. of the Method.*

and found by hiſtories to agree only to one ſort, to wit, the Roman Church and ſuch as are vnited to her) to acknowledge her Paſtours to be lawfully ſent, to teach true diuine Fayth in all points neceſſary to ſaluation, and conſequently, that euery one may ſecurely, and ought neceſſarily to learne of them Fayth neceſſary to ſaluation.

Secondly, neyther is *D. Featly* his way ſo direct to the finding of the true Church, as *M. Fishers* is, ſuppoſing (as in this Queſtion is ſuppoſed, and may be eaſily proued out of S. Paul) a man cannot (according to the ordinary courſe) haue true diuine infallible Fayth before he haue heard lawfully-ſent preachers of the true Church, and conſequently muſt know firſt by other markes, which is the true Church, of whoſe Paſtours he muſt learne which is the right Fayth, before he can (with infallible certainty) compare the doctrine taught by Paſtors with Scriptures, and therby know them to be true Paſtors. *Rom. 10.14. 15.*

Thirdly, Neither is *D. Featly* his way ſo certayne or infallible, as the manner preſcribed by *M. Fisher.* For when one hath found out in Scriptures and Hiſtoryes (by the help of learned men) which Company haue alwaies viſibly retained without change the firſt receiued Fayth, and conſequently which Company are the true Church (which holy Scriptures do moſt plainly ſhew to haue auctority from God, & aſſiſtance from the promiſed Spirit of truth to teach all truth) one may reſt infallibly aſſured of whatſoeuer is generally taught, or defined by the full authority of the Paſtours of this Church. But after one hath examined the ſeuerall doctrines of others by his priuate comparing them with Scriptures, and ſhall haue concluded with himſelf which ſeemeth to him to agree beſt with Scri- *Matth. 28. 19, 20. Luc. 10, 16. Ioan. 14. 16, Ioan. 16, 13. Ioan. 20, 21. 1. Tim. 4, 14.*

M ptute,

pture, he cannot be infallibly fure that he hath not failed in examining or concluding, and therefore had need to examine this his Examination & Conclufion by a fecond Examination, and this by a third, and this by a fourth *in infinitum,* without euer refting infallibly certaine; for although the text feeme to him cleere, & the matter neceffary to be belieued, yet he may be deceiued, in regard words are not alwayes to be vnderftood in the literall fenfe, neyther is euery matter needfull to be belieued, which by reafon of fome words of Scripture may to this or that man feeme needfull.

Fourthly, Neither did the Auncient Fathers vfe *D. Featlyes* Method, at leaft in that fort as he intendeth it, to wit, leauing euery man to iudge and conclude what is right fenfe, out of his owne reading or hearing the Scripture, without depending vpon the Iudgment of the Church for the fenfe of it. This did not *S. Bafill,* and *S. Gregory Nazianzen,* as is plaine by that which is written of them, to wit, that they ftudied the holy Scriptures, not interpreting according to their owne fenfe, but according to the expofition of their Forefathers. *S. Auftin* did not fay, that euery man muft compare particuler doctrines with particuler texts of Scriptures, and that this was the way not to be deceiued; but he prefcribed this Rule faying: *Quifquis falli metuit &c.* Whofoeuer is affraid to be deceiued by the obfcuritie of this queftion, let him aske the Church, which the holy Scripture without all ambiguity doth demonftrate: wherby he fheweth that the Iudgment of the Paftours of the Church is infallible, euen in matters obfcure, and not cleerly fet downe in Scripture.

Neuertheleffe in one fpeciall cafe, when queftion was, which Company was the Church, and the parties betwixt whom this queftion was, could not agree

S. Bafil.
S. Gregory Nazianzen.

Ruffin Ecclefiaf. Hiftor. l.2. c.9.
Auguft. lib. contra Crefco. c. 31.

of

of any one Church by whofe Iudgment this queftion
fhould be decided; In this one fpeciall Cafe(I fay) *S. Au-*
ftin did prouoke the *Donatifts*(as we d꜕ Proteftáts)to let
the matter be tried by Scriprures; but how? not by cõ-
paring ech particuler point of doctrine with particuler
texts(as Proteftants would haue done)but by fhewing
out of cleere text of Scripture the Markes of the church,
namely,that the Church muft be Catholique, and vifible in all ages,and in all nations (as may be feene in
S. Auften de vnitate Ecclefia,) and applying this marke to
ech Company , he concluded, that not *Donatifts* who
were not vifible in all ages and nations, but Roman
Catholiques only, who haue alwayes been, and are
thus vifible,be the true church of which holy Scripture
fpeaketh. In this fenfe, *S. Auftin* & we with him, fay
truely,that the Church is to be fought in the Scriptures,
& not in any priuate mans Sanctitie or Iuftice. In this
fenfe alfo (and not in D. *Featlyes*) *S. Chryfoftoms* words
(fuppofing they be *S.Chryfoftoms,* & not foylfted into *S.*
Chryfoftoms workes by fome *Arriã*)are to be vnderftood.

　S. Bafill alfo doth acknowledg (as we do) that with
whófoeuer doctrine agreable to holy Scripture fhalbe
found , the truth is alwayes adiudged to be on their
fide; but *S. Bafill* fayth not, that when queftion is,(as is
betwixt vs and Proteftants) whether this,or that doctrine be agreable to Scripture,and whether therefore
they,or we haue truth on our fide, that the beft Method to end this queftion, is to leaue it to euery priuate
man to examine by Scripture, which doctrine is , and
which is not agreable to holie Scriptures , and thereupon to conclude which is the true Church : neither
doth he fay, that we muft belieue euery priuate Doctour,that fhall tell vs, he can(by fuch a demonftration
à Priori,as D.*Feaily* maketh) proue this or that doctrine,

(marginal note:) Note how, and in what manner S. *Auftin* would haue the true Church foûd by Scriptu-res.

(although contrary to that which is vniuersally held
by the Church)to be agreable to Scripture, and therefore men of his Sect to be the true Church. This *S. Ba-*
fill doth not fay, nor any other orthodoxe Father. Wherefore this Method of *D. Featly* is neither *S. Bafills* , nor
S. Chryfoftoms, nor *S. Auftens,* nor any other holy Fathers
Method, but the contrary, to wit, that all priuate men,
(Doctours not excepted)ought to heare, obey, and fubmit their Iudgment to the Tradition, and authority of
the Catholik vniuerfall Church. So as not ancient Fathers, but Heretiques , old and new, and only Here-

Aug. in   tiques, approue *D. Featlyes* Method, or rather he theirs ;
Ioan. Tract.   for hence did Herefies fpring (as *S. Auften* fayth) that
18.   good Scriptures are (by this kind of priuate examina-
                 tion and interpretation) vnderftood not in a right and
                 good fenfe: and that what hath bene once rafhly affir-
                 med, is afterwards obftinatly defended. And that (as *S.*

Cyprian.   *Cyprian* noteth)men do not obey the Prieft of God, nor
Epift. 55. ad do confider that in the Church there is one Prieft and
Cornel.   Iudge in place of Chrift. We do not therefore refufe
                 triall by Scriptures in the right method of the Fathers,
but we difallow *D. Featly* his Hereticall Method of a-
bufing Scripture, and of making fuch demonftrations *à*
Priori out of them, to proue the Proteftants to be the
true Church, as the like may be made by all other Heretiques of whatfoeuer fect, to proue men of their Sect
to be the true Church, as I haue proued againft *M. Ro-*
gers. Neither can *D. Featly* defend his demonftration to
be good , but by fuch grounds as other Heretiques may
defend fuch demonftrations, as they may make in defence of their Herefies to be good.

    And this fhall for the prefent fuffice, for refutation
of *D. Featly* his Method, which being now fhewed
to be neyther fo eafie, nor fo direct , nor fo infallible,
                                                    nor

nor so approued by holy Fathers, as *M. Fishers* Method is, but a Method vsed by Heretiques and only Heretiques; *D. Featly* must leaue this his Method, and if he be as good as his word, he must hold it (as *M. Fisher* doth, and as it is indeed) a point of principall moment, to enquire of the visibility of the Professors of the Christian Religion, who neuer changed the first receiued Fayth, and therby conclude, which is the true Church of which all may and ought to learne, which is, or is not true Fayth. For if it be true, which truth it self hath enforced out of *D. Featlyes* owne pen, *That the Scripture doth shew the holy Catholique Church, both to haue perpetuall vnchanged Fayth, and also to be perpetually visible; and that* (as he further proueth) *it shalbe visible in all ages and Nations, hauing the spirit of God in it, and the word of God preached, and Sacraments ministred by the Pastours of it*: If it also be true, that holy Scriptures haue shewed this to be true by way of prophecie or promise, as appeareth by the textes which *D. Featly* himself citeth for proofe that the Church must be alwaies visible in máner aforesaid: and that histories do witnesse these prophecies and promisses of this perpetuall visibility to haue been hitherto fulfilled, as *D. Whitaker* acknowledgeth saying; *Whatsoeuer the Prophets haue foretould of the propagation, largenes and glory of the Church, Histories do most cleerly witnes.*

Lastly, if it be true that without hystories we could not know these Prophecies to haue been fulfilled in time past, as Doctour *Iohn Whyte* cófesseth, neither conquently should God receiue the glory, nor we the comfort which followeth this knowledge, if histories (or some other thing equiualent) were not extant, in which the fulfilling of these prophecies and promisses of holy Scripture is cleerely witnessed, not only in generall termes, but (as true and good historyes do ordinarily)

Pag. 103.

VVhitaker. lib. 7. contra. Duræum. pag. 472.

D. Iohn Whyte in the Way, pag. 221.

Things past cannot be knowne but by hystories.

M 3 dinarily)

dinarily)by ſetting downe the particuler **Names** of Countryes and Cittíes where, and at leaſt of ſome of the moſt eminent viſible Paſtours & people, of whom this fore-propheſied, and fore-promiſed viſible Church in all ages and Nations did conſiſt : If(i ſay) all this be (as it is)true, it euidently followeth, as *M. Fiſher* vrgeth in his fiue propoſitions; That if Proteſtants be the true viſible Church , then out of Hiſtories Names of their Profeſſors in all ages may be produced; and *è contra,* if their Names cannot be produced, they were not, nor are not the true church, & therefore *D Featly* the Proteſtants Champion, being by promiſe engaged, muſt produce Names of Proteſtants in all ages, or els he doth giue iuſt cauſe to all men to thinke, that the Proteſtant Church is not the true Church .

The 4. Tergiuerſation.

A fourth Tergiuerſation vſed by *D. Featly* is, to referre his Reader to other Proteſtant writers , making it ſeeme, that theſe men haue already ſo ſatisfied the queſtion that more need not be ſaid. But it is certaine that none of the Authours ynto which he doth refer vs ſet downe a competent Catalogue of Names of men, which are, or can be proued, or defended to be Proteſtants according to the Method preſcribed ; and therefore *D. Featly* muſt giue a better, or els his promiſe is not fulfilled .

The 5. Tergiuerſation

A fifth Tergiuerſation and ſhift vſed by *D. Featly* is, that hauing named Chriſt and his Apoſtles , and ſome others of the firſt 200. yeares, he doth not bring any reaſon or proofe to ſhew thoſe he named to be Proteſtants; which ſheweth that he, who was ſo forward to diſpute, did not in the Conference(nor yet doth) ſincerely and ſeriouſly, for only truths ſake, ſeeke to diſpute about Chriſt and his Apoſtles, but did in the Conference make offer to diſpute about Chriſt , only for a

Tergiuer-

Tergiuerfation and fhift to efcape the *Non-plus,* which he faw he fhould haue been put to, if he had proceeded in naming, prouing, and defending Proteftants in all ages out of good Authours, according to the Method prefcribed in *M. Fishers* Paper.

4. I obferue, that *D. Featly* hath fet downe certayne grounds, by which he intendeth to make a fhew of naming, prouing, and defending Proteftants to be in all ages ; which ground I will difcuffe, and fhew to be moft infufficient to fupport the frame of the pretended vifible Proteftants Church in all ages.

D. *Featlyes grounds examined.*

Firft, D. *Featly* would haue it fuffice, that he fhew any Company of Profeffours of the Proteftant Fayth, whether vnited vnder one gouernment, in one Countrey, Kingdome, or Empire, or fcattered through the whole world, and whether they know one another corporally, or not. But by his leaue, this will not fuffice, for that he himfelf acknowledgeth that the Church extends it felf to all that profeffe true Religion, and participate in the pledges of faluation, and that fuch a Church hath euer been, and fhalbe in all ages and Nations, and that it hath the word of God preached, & Sacraments miniftred by Paftors &c. and therfore although it may be that fome one of the church may not corporally know all others who are members of the fame Church; yet there muft be alwayes fome vnion of the members, preaching, and hearing Sermons, miniftring & receauing facraments &c. or els they cannot be properly a Church, or at leaft not that Church of which *M. Fishers* queftion is, to wit, the vifible Church of Chrift, which alwayes hath ben, is, and fhalbe vifible in all ages & natiõs, as D. *Featly* himfelf confeffeth.

D. Featlyes firft ground examined.

Affert. 4.

2. D.

D,Featlyes 2. ground examined.

2. D. Featly would not haue it needfull that the Names of Proteſtants, vnder this denomination, be ſhewed in all ages ; for he confeſſeth that this Name came vp of late (as ſayth he, the Names of Papiſtes, and Ieſuits) and would haue it ſuffice, that Proteſtants in doctrine be ſhewed, vnder whatſoeuer Names. But he muſt remember that there is a great difference betwixt the Name of Papiſt or Ieſuite, and the Name of Proteſtant : for the Names Papiſt and Ieſuite, do not denominate men of a Fayth newly ſprung vp, or different in any leaſt point from the Fayth of the immediatly precedent, or then preſent Church, when thoſe names came firſt vp ; and ſo ſith the leaſt difference in Fayth doth (as it is in Numbers) change the *ſpecies*, or kind of Fayth, it followeth , that either the Proteſtant Church is not the true Church, or the true Church(contrary to(*)confeſſed Scripture) changed her Fayth.

(*) D. Peatly pag. 103. confeſſeth, Scripture to ſhew the Church to haue vnchāged Fayth.

3. D. Featly would haue it ſuffice, that names of men be ſhewed, whoſe Fayth and doctrine are poſitiuely compriſed in, and confined to Scripture, and oppoſitely, as it is repugnant to all errors in Fayth and manners, againſt holy Scripturs, eſpecially againſt the preſent errors of the Church of *Rome*. But this will not ſuffice to end the preſent queſtion and controuerſy betwixt M. *Fiſher* and him , vnles he firſt proue, That all true Fayth is compriſed and confined to Scripture. Secondly that all Proteſtants Fayth is compriſed in Scripture. Thirdly, that the preſent Romiſh Church holdeth errours againſt Scripture. It may be, that D. *Featly* wil offer to proue all theſe points by Scripture ; But it is not inough to make a bold offer , but he muſt actually performe, and muſt before hand tell vs, who ſhall be Iudge , whether in performing this he do alledge true text, true tranſlation, true interpretation, &

D. Featlyes third ground examined.

out

out of all this make an infallible confequence fufficiét
to proue the aforefaid points. There is no reafon that
himfelf fhould be Iudge in his owne cafe, neither is it
reafon, that he affigne for Iudge any other (efpecially
Englifh) Proteftant, or fome other condemned Heretique; & yet if he did, he could hardly proue the whole
and entire Englifh Proteftant Fayth to be comprifed
in Scripture: for at leaft in fome one or other point he
would find a great difference of Iudgment betwixt
himfelf and other Proteftants, efpecially Lutherans,
who though they were the prime and principall (and
fo ought to be deemed the pureft) Proteftants, will
fay, 1. That *S. Iames* his Epiftle, which Englifh Proteftants do belieue to be Scripture, cannot be proued to
be Scripture out of only Scripture. 2. A *Lutheran* will
fay, that the Englifh Proteftant Fayth denying Chrifts
reall and fubftantiall prefence in the Sacrament, is not
comprifed in, but rather oppofite to the Scripture. 3. A
Lutheran wil fay, that the doctrine of the Romã Church
fo far forth as it holdeth reall and fubftantiall prefence
of Chrift in the holy Sacrament, is not an error againft
Scripture, as our Englifh Proteftants hold it to be.

If *D. Featly* affigne no earthly man to be Iudge of
thefe Controuerfies, but leaue it to only Scripture; I
aske, when, or how, thefe and other Controuerfies
wilbe euer ended, when ech man will bring for his
opinion (to him feeming) cleere Scripture, and wil
anfwere (as he thinketh) cleerly all other Texts of
Scripture, though to others feeming cleere for the contrary opinion. If *D. Featly* fay, that the end ought to be
made by force of demonftration out of Scriptures,
which although it do not actually cõuince thofe who
vnderftand not the termes, or who are wilfully obftinate, yet it will enforce affent in euery pioufly difpofed

N   perfon.

perfon I anfwer, that although this may be fo in fomē
mē whofe vnderſtāding is good,& whofe will is well
difpofed, and in fome matters which are cleeie, & may
be cleerly feene by reafon it felfe , or which are already
belieued, or are eafily belieued , and are fo cleerly fet
downe in Scripture as no Chriſtian wil doubt or make
queſtion;yet if we fpeake of the ordinary fort of men ,
and of fome,euen mayne matters, and feeming to be
cleerly expreffed in Scripture ; for example, Real and
Subſtantiall Prefence of Chriſt in the holy Sacrament,
Confubſtantiality of Chriſt with God the Father, and
fuch like which be aboue the reach of reafon , and
which by reafon of other texts of Scripture, or opiniōs
of learned men haue been called in queſtion ; it willbe
hard to make fuch a cleere Demonſtration out of Scripture , as to conuince any Heretique prepoffeffed with
the contrary opinion, efpecially if he once haue by
reading Scripture perfuaded himfelf throughly that he
vnderſtandeth aright what is the true meaning of Gods
word in any one Text which may feeme conformable
to his opinion; for when a man hath once fo fetled errour in his vnderſtanding , and perfuaded himfelf that
he hath warrant of Gods word for his opinion , there
is not any Demonſtration which can be made out of
any other,though feeming moſt cleere, Texts of Scripture fufficiēt to conuince him, but he will ſtill hold the
errour which firſt poffeffed his heart , and will according to it inuent one or other Anfwer to the Text alleadged, or to the argument. And therefore vnleffe D.
Featly can giue fome infallible Rule, by which euery
man may infallibly and eafily know how to vnderſtand the termes of ech text of Scripture in the right
fenfe, fo as to make euery man agree when wordes are
to be taken properly, when figuratiuely, which is im-
                                    poffible

poſſible; it is not poſſible, that by confining men to
pick their Fayth out of only Scripture, or to be iudged
by only Scripture, Controuerſies in matters of Fayth
can be preuented or ended; which might be eaſily preuented or ended, if the auctority of the Pope, or chief
Paſtour, and Councels be admitted, according to the
practiſe of the Apoſtles and Fathers of all ages, to ouer-
ſway priuate mens(though neuer ſo ſeeming holy, or
learned) Iudgements.

4. *D. Featly* will not tye himſelf to ſhew in all ages
Proteſtants, who did renounce all, or directly oppugne
any one particuler doctrine of the Roman Church,
but graunteth that theſe who renounced all thoſe Roman doctrines of Fayth, which he calleth errours, could
not be much before Luther; And therefore he would
haue it ſuffice to the eſſence and ſubſtance of Proteſtants in Fayth and doctrine(whatſoeuer name they be
ſtiled by, as *Becherits, Berengarians, Petrobruſians, Henri-*
cians, Albigenſes, Waldenſes, Dulciniſts, Lollards, Linadamits,
Wiclefiſts, Huſſits, Reformers)that they hold the Proteſtant
Fayth implicitly and virtually, that is to ſay, ſayth he, if
they hold the Scripture for the ſole and entire rule of
Fayth, and conſequently condemne all doctrines of
Fayth againſt, and beſide the holy Scriptures, eſpecially
if they deliuer ſuch poſitions & doctrines, from whence
by neceſſary and infallible Conſequence, ſome particuler error of the Romã Church(although not perhaps
ſprung vp in their tyme) may be refelled.

This ground D. *Featly* hath deuiſed, thereby to giue
himſelf ſcope, and therby hope to name, proue, and defend viſible Proteſtants in all ages, as by a lyke deuiſing
of grounds it is eaſie for any Heretique of whatſoeuer
ſort to proue and defend men of their ſect to haue ben
in all ages. But leaſt D. *Featly* ſhould pleaſe himſelf to

much

much with this his deuice, I will firſt diſproue this
grotid. Secondly I will ſhew,that although this grotid
were true,yet he could not by it truely name & ſotidly
proue and defend Profeſſouts of a viſible Proteſtant
Church in all ages, in ſuch ſort as *M. Fiſhers* queſtion
did require;noɾ at all,vnleſſe he will diſclaime fiom all
theſe which he hath named in the fiiſt 200, yeares, and
will ſet ſuch in their roomes as may be ſet with ſmall
credit, and ſhame inough to the forger of this falſe
ground,and to the great diſgrace oɾ the Proteſtants
Church,ſuppoſing it haue not,as it hath not, any better ground,wherby it can pretend to haue had viſible
Profeſſours in all ages.

For diſproofs of this ground, I need ſay no more,
but that it is a new deuice vnwarranted by Scripture,
or conſent of Fathers,or any ſufficient reaſon : for what
Scripture,or Fathers, or reaſon doth ſhew it to be ſufficient for to make a Proteſtant to hould the Scripture
for the ſole and entire rule of Fayth,eſpecially when all
or almoſt all ſorts of Heretiqnes hold Scripture to be
the ſole rule of Fayth? Secondly, this ground is grounded vpon falſhood, to wit, that Scripture is to be held

2.Theſſ.2.14.

for the ſole and entire Rule of Fayth, ſo as all vnwritten ,although diuine, Traditions are to be excluded

D. Francis
Whyte in the
firſt Confe-
rence with
M. Fisher.

from being any rule or part of the rule of Fayth. This
to be falſe I proue out of *S. Paul,* who ſayth expreſſly
Tenete Traditiones, hold the Traditions, *which you haue
learned,whether by word,or our Epiſtle.* Ergo,there are ſome
diuine Traditions deliuered by word of mouth which
muſt be held by good Chriſtiãs, as well as thoſe which
S. Paul deliuered in his Epiſtle. Neither can *D. Featly*
eſcape by ſaying.as once *D. White* ſaid,that thoſe Traditions which then were vnwritten, were afterwatds
written: for how doth he know that they were afterwards

wards written? It is a principle of Proteſtants, that nothing pertayning to Fayth (as to know whether ther be, or be not ſome diuine vnwritten Traditions, needfull to be belieued by good Chriſtians, greatly pertaineth to Fayth) muſt be affirmed without ſome cleer text, or euident conſequence out of Scripture. But no cleere text, nor euident conſequence out of Scripture telleth, that theſe vnwritten Traditions which *S. Paul* ſpeaketh of in this place (and thoſe other which Chriſt himſelf ſpeaketh of, when he ſaid *multa habeo vobis di-* Ioan. 16. 12. *cere*, I haue many things to ſay to you which you cannot now beare, but the Paraclete the holy Ghoſt when he cometh ſhall teach you all things) were after written in any booke now extant of Canonicall Scripture. *Ergo*, neyther *D. Featly*, nor *D. White* may affirme that theſe, and all other diuine Traditions needful to be belieued (by ſome or other, Paſtours or people) which once were vnwritten, were after written.

The conſent of Fathers for vnwritten Traditions may be ſeene in *Bellarmine*, and *Coxius*, and *Gualterus*, and others. The Reaſons alſo which Bellarmine & others bring are vnanſwerable, and namely this; Proteſtants themſelues do hold it needfull to belieue by diuine Fayth all thoſe particuler bookes, which they account Canonicall, to be diuine Scripture, and euery ſentence and word which is in them to be worthy of diuine & infallible credit. But no cleere text of ſolé Scripture is a rule of it ſelf alone, ſufficient to aſſure that all the ſaid bookes are diuine &c. *Ergo*, either they hold it needfull to belieue theſe bookes to be diuine by diuine Fayth without any diuine rule or ground (which is to ouerthrow diuine Fayth) or they muſt admit an vnwritten rule and ground, by which they may be ſufficiently aſſured that theſe bookes be diuine, and euery

ſentence

fentence and word in them worthy of diuine and infallible credit.

But admitting for arguments fake, that it were a found and true ground, That euery one, and onely thofe, were Proteftants who hold the Scripture to be the fole and entire Rule of Fayth, (and who confequently condemne all doctrines of Fayth which be contrary or befides Scriptures &c.) let vs fee what vfe *D. Featly* can make of this ground. Firft, he cannot by this ground name men in all ages, who did hould the Englifh Proteftant Fayth, and who did not contradict, and condemne any one Article exprefled in the 39. Articles, as M. *Fishers* queftion required:for one may hould Scripture to be the fole rule, and yet condemne fome of the 39. Articles, as is euident by all fuch Proteftants who refufe to fubfcribe to the faid Articles.

Secondly, He cannot by it proue thefe he named, to wit, Chrift and his Apoftles, and the other primitiue Fathers of the firft 200. yeares, or others of fucceeding ages, to be Proteftants. For, to proue this, he muft not only fay, he doth not find in Scripture, and thofe Fathers writings any mention of any Rule of Fayth, befide Scripture, for this were only *Argumentum ab auctoritate negatiua* : which is of no force againft vs, as is already fhewed. Neither muft it fuffice to proue Chrift and the Apoftles, and other primitiue Fathers to be Proteftants, that he can bring fome fentences of Scripture, or thofe Fathers out of which Proteftants vfe to make Arguments againft vnwritten Traditions, or other Roman doctrines, as it did not fuffice to proue Chrift and his Apoftles, and Primitiue Fathers to be Arrians, that fome could, and did bring out of the fame Scriptures and Fathers (to them feeming moft cleere) fentences, out of which they made feeming ftrong Arguments

Supra cap. 5. *againft* M. *Rogers.*

guments againſt the Conſubſtantiality of Chriſt.

If *D. Featly* ſay, that the ſentences with he, & other
Proteſtants bring, are cleere, not only ſeeming cleere;
and the conſequence which they deduce are good, &
not only ſeeming good; I aske, *quo Iudice*? who being
iudge, are the ſentences brought by Proteſtants, cleere,
and their Conſequences good? If this be ſo only in the
Proteſtants owne Iudgment; ſo, if an *Arrian* be iudge,
the ſentences they brought and Conſequences they
made, wilbe iudged cleere and good. But as no reaſon
did permit that *Arrians* ſhould be iudges in their owne
cauſes, but were to be iudged by the Councell of *Nice*,
which partly by Scripture and partly by Tradition
did iuſtly condemne them, as hauing obſerued that
their denying of the Conſubſtantiality of Chriſt, had
a noted Authour, and was at the firſt publication contradicted, and after condemned by the ordinary Paſtors, as a profane Nouelty, and as an Errour contrary
to the common Fayth of the Church; In which like
ſort the *Arrians* could not ſhew the affirmatiue doctrine of Conſubſtantiality, either then, or formerly to
haue had a like noted Author, and to haue been at the
firſt publication contradicted or condemned by a lyke
lawfull Iudgment of ordinary Paſtours, as a nouelty
and an errour contrary to the common Fayth of the
Church: So neyther is it reaſon that Proteſtants ſhould
be iudges in their owne cauſe, but were to be iudged
by the Councell of *Trent*, which did iuſtly condemne
them, partly by Scripture, partly by Tradition, as hauing obſerued that their denying the authority of the
vnwritten diuine Traditions, and other their nouell
negatiue doctrines, had noted Aurhours, and were at
the firſt publication contradicted, and after condemned by the lawfull Iudgment of ordinary Paſtors of
the

the Church for Nouelties and Errors againſt the common Fayth of the Church. In which like ſort Proteſtants cannot ſhew, that any one of our Catholique affirmatiue Doctrines, maintayning the authority of vnwritten diuine Traditions, Tranſubſtantiation, Purgatory, Indulgences &c. had any noted Authors, or were at the firſt publication contradicted & condemned by a like lawfull Iudgment of ordinary Paſtours of the then being church, for errours contrary to the common Fayth of the Church.

The which difference doth ſhew, that our ſaid Catholique doctrines defined in the Councell of *Trent*, as well as thoſe which were defined by the firſt foure generall Councells, were doctrines belieued by the Church in all ages, either expreſly or implicitely, although perhaps this belief was not ſo cleerly expreſſed in the writings of thoſe Fathers who liued before theſe Councells, as was in the Councells themſelues. For although it is not to be doubted, but the Primitiue Fathers hauing receiued the whole truth from the Apoſtles, belieued it entirely as well before the Councells as after, *explicitè*, or *implicitè*, yet we ar not aſſured that all which they thus belieued, is expreſſed in their writings, nor that all which they wrote did come to our hands; but we may be ſure, that (in caſe any thing contrary to the former Fayth of the Church, and not at leaſt implicitely inuolued in ſome other ground of Fayth) had bene taught by any ancient Father or latter writer) neyther gods prouidence, nor the human diligence of Paſtours would euer haue permitted it to haue bene defined in any, eſpecially generall, Councell; neither could it haue come to be publiquely preached & practiſed, but the firſt publiſher would haue ben noted, and his doctrine contradicted and condemned by
lawfull

lawfull authority of Paftours, as we fee (by record of Hyftories) hath bene whenfoeuer any like, or far leffe nouell doctrines haue ben brought in, by any Hereticall Conuenticle, or teacher contrary to the former Fayth of the Church.

It may be that the deuill might fecretly fowe the tares of fome errors in the harts of fome few, or might get them to whifper them fecretly from one to another in corners, before Paftours could take notice; but when once they fhould be publiquely preached or practifed, the Paftours could not be fo Ignorant or negligent, but they muft needs haue perceiued a palpable difference betwixt wheate and tares, betwixt venerable Ancient Fayth, and abhominable nouell errour; Chrift his holy Spirit at leaft would not haue neglected to excite the Paftours (being watchmen placed by him vpon the walls of this *Ierufalem*, and being appointed by him to *Ifa. 62. 6.* gouerne the Church) but would haue made them op- *Act. 20. 28.* pofe themfelues, and refift euery fuch, efpecially groffe Innouation, euen with open reprehenfion and publique Condemnation. Neither is it poffible that Hell gates could by any craft of Sathan fo much haue pre- *Matth. 16.* uailed againft the Church, as by any fuch vniuerfall *18.* Innouations in any age, either quite to take away the *Ofee 2. 19. 20.* Fayth out of the Church, or to make it quite inuifible, *Matth. 5. 14.* or to make all true profeffours fo irreligioufly fecret among themfelues, or fo deepe diffemblers as they neyther would (when the glory of God and good of foules *Rom. 10. 10.* required) difcouer themfelues to be true belieuers, nor could be difcouered by any of the world, to be as they were, or ought to haue ben, men abftayning from Rites & facraments of other different Religions, and hauing *2. Cor. 6. 15.* fome fpeciall rites and facraments of their owne, vnto *1. Cor. 11. 17.* which they reforted fometyme among themfelues. *18.*

O   It

It is therefore a moſt idle dreame to imagine, as Proteſtants imagine, that the Roman Church hauing ben
once the right, and true Church, profeſſing the true
Fayth, did, or could fall ſo inſenſibly (as D. *Featly* his
ſimilituds inſinuate)into ſo many and ſo groſſe ſuppoſed errours publiquely preached and practiſed, without
being noted, contradicted and condemned neere about
the tyme of the firſt publication thereof. For, our queſtion requiring the tyme of the firſt vpriſing of any of
our ſuppoſed errors, is not meant of the firſt inſtant, or
ſecret beginning of any error, but of a morall latitude
of time about the firſt publique preaching and practiſe
of ſome notable errour; which could not haue ben in
the Church, eſpecially for ſo many hundred of yeares, as
thoſe our ſuppoſed errors are ſuppoſed to haue been,
without a ſenſible and publique noting, and condemning of the firſt preacher or practiſer of euery ſuch notable, and (as Proteſtants imagine to be now in the
Romā Church)abhominable Idolatrous errours. Neyther if any ſuch publique noting, and condemning of
the beginner of any ſuch errour had ben, could hyſtories yet extant be altogether ſilent, of time when, place
where, and the Name, or ſome thing equiualent to the
Name of the perſon who was the firſt publiquely noted preacher or practiſer of any ſuch errour, and of them
who noted and contradicted him, at leaſt by ſome probable coniectures, as is vſed in hyſtories in ſome caſes,
wherof the abſolute certainty of time, place, or perſon
is not punctually knowne.

Hence appeareth how vaine is that imagination of
D. *Reynolds*, which D. *Featly* citeth and commendeth.
Hence alſo is made manifeſt, that the whole aggregate
or Congeries of ſimilitudes and inſtances, by which D.
Featly would perſwade that Roman errors ſtole inſen-
ſibly

fibly into the Church, are not only no good proofes, but come nothing neere the explication of the point. For all *D. Featlyes* fimilitudes and inftances are either about matters fecret, or not notable, or of fuch fmall moment as few or none haue, or ought to haue care to note, or contradict, or make mention of them in hyftories; but fuch things as Proteftants account errours in the Roman Church (for exãple, Veneration of images, adoration of the Sacrament with beliefe that Chrift is fubftantially prefent) are publique and notable matters, and of fuch moment, as if they had bene thought errours (efpecially in fuch a high degree, as Proteftants think them) contrary to the Scripture and the Fayth of the Primitiue Church, they could not haue bẽ brought in without being noted by Paftours, who vfually doe, and by their office are bound to note, contradict, and condemne the firft publique introducers of all notable nouelties, and much more all groffe idolatryes and fuperftitions. Cleere therefore it is, that *D. Featly* cannot by this his forefaid ground, proue or defend Chrift, his Apoftles, *Ignatius*, and the other Fathers to be Proteftants, and therefore if he will haue this ground ftand good, he muft blot the names of Chrift and his Apoftles &c. out of his Catalogue, and fo muft either not giue names of Proteftants in all ages, which is to break promife, fhame himfelfe, and ouerthrow his caufe; or with more fhame and finne make a full Induction of all Heretiques old and new; and if that will not ferue, he may adde Satan himfelf the firft Authour of Herefie, and of all Ill.

Act. 20. 28.
Rom. 16. 15.
Tit. 1. 9.

 For fith this forefayd ground doth not define, nor giue a Rule which doth infallibly determine how many, and what Bookes, & what parts of thofe Bookes be diuine Scripture, nor obligeth euery one to any par-

ticuler

ticuler Text, or Tranflation, or Interpretation, and co-
fequently leaueth it free for euery one to choofe what
bookes, and what parts therof he will acount Scripture, and what text, tranflation, and interpretation he
will follow for the rule of his beliefe: I do not fee, but
euery Heretique ould & new, and Satan himfelf may
(in this *larga-manica* manner) confine his Fayth to
only Scripture, and condemne all doctrine contrary or
befides Scripture, and oppofe himfelf againlt all, or at
leaft fome Roman doctrines, accounting them errours;
and then what can hinder him (according to the forefaid ground) from being accounted a fubltantiall Proteftant.

Some may (perhaps) fay, that indeed this may fhew
all thefe to be Proteftants, yet this will not ferue to
make an Induction fufficient to fhew a vifible Proteftant Church in all ages, in regard they want vifible
lawfully-fent Paftours, neither do they agree in vnity
of doctrine, nor haue a fufficient meanes to preferue
men in, or reduce men to vnity & certainty of Fayth,
efpecally in all points, to take away this ftumbling
blocke.

D. Feat lyes
5. Ground
examined.

5. D. *Featly* will not tye himfelf to fhew a confpicuous Church, in which is an apparant Hierarchy of
Paftours, as knowing that Proteftant Paftours are not
affignable in all ages, as Roman Catholique Paftours
are: But he would haue it fuffice, that the Church be
fhewed vifible in any degree, and rather by names Ap-
pellatiues then proper, without any diftinction of Paftours from people, and that euery fmall number in
fome ages of obfcure and latent true belieuers, may
ferue, efpecially in Antichrifts dayes, whom he fuppofeth to be already come. For eftablifhing of which
ground, firft he affirmeth, that the militant Church is
                                                      not

not alwayes equally vifible, which to be trne no man
doubteth. 2. He fayth that the Malignāt Church is oft
times more vifible, confpicuous, and ample then the
true Church, & confequently eminent vifibility, amplitude, and fplendour is no ceitaine Note of the true
Church.

But in this he muft giue me leaue to vfe fome diftinction; for if by Malignant Church he vnderftand the
multitude of Pagans, Iewes, Turkes, Heretiques, and
wicked men, compared with thofe who be right belieuers and vertuous liuers ; there is no doubt but in this
refpect the true Church being taken ftrictly either for
the elect only, or only for vertuous profeffours of the
true Fayth, is not fo ample and confpicuous, but may *Luc.* 12, 31.
be called *Pufillus Grex*, a litle flock; and at fome times
neere the end of the world there fhalbe a great fcarci-
ty of fuch right belieuers and vertuous liuers ; But in *Luc.* 18. 8.
this fenfe, we do not now vnderftand the Church, nor *Matth.* 24.
do compare it with the Malignant Church in the for- 11.
faid fenfe, for we fpeak of the Church as it doth extend
it felf to all Profeffours of the true vnchanged Fayth of
Chrift (whether they be elect or not, of vertuous lyfe
or not,) who are vnited in profeffion of Fayth, Communion of Sacraments, and fubordination vnto lawfull Paftours ; Nor do we compare it with Pagans,
Iewes, or Turks, or other abfolute Infidels, or with
Heretiques, or Schifmatiques of all forts iointly, but
with Hereriques or Schifmatiques of whatfoeuer feuerall Sect, but fay, that being thus confidered and compared, it is more vifible and ample then any Hereticall
or fchifmaticall Sects which confift of branches cut off
that great vine, *Quæ crefcendo vbique diffufa eft*, as *S. Auften* *Aug. l. de*
fpeaketh, and are partes diuided from the whole body *Paftoribus.*
of the Cath. Church, which is therefore called *Catho-*
lique

O 3

lique, becaufe although at firſt it was litle, yet it grew, and was, καθ' ὅλον , *fecundum totum* , fpread in fome fort, euen in the Apoſtles dayes, and much more in fucceſſion of tymes ouer the whole world, and is to contynue in all Nations; of which fee *S. Auſten lib. de vnitate Ecclefiæ,* who fheweth that this Church is more confpicuous and ample, then any Herefy, in regard it is found one and the fame in whatfoeuer places and times wherein fuch Herefies are, which commonly are only in fome particuler Countryes, as it were in corners of the world, & in fome particuler ages, but are not found in all places and times, in which the fame vnchanged Catholique Church is found .

So as although multitude alone, or vifibility alone be no fufficient marke of the true Church; yet taking the Church for all profeſſours of vnchanged Fayth (as *D. Featly* granteth it is taken in this queſtion) and comparing it both in place and tyme with the profeſſours of whatfoeuer particuler Herefie or Schifme, ancient or prefent , it is found more confpicuous and ample then any of them , euen Arrian Heretiques and Græcian Schifmatiques not excepted. And therfore as *S. Auſten* hauing proued this Marke out of Scriptures to agree to the true Church of Chriſt, did by it conuince that the Donatiſts could not be , and that the Church fpread ouer the world, which then communicated as now it doth with the Church and Pope of Rome, was the onely true Church of Chriſt : So may I, by the fame Mark, conuince euery iudicious and pioufly difpofed man, That Proteſtants of whatfoeuer one Sect, who fprung vp of late , and are only in few Countryes of one and the fame fect, cannot be the true Church; and that the Church which hath ben, and yet is one and the fame in all places and ages, and which is vifibly fpread
ouer

Aug. l. de vnitate Ecclefiæ c. 2.

Aſſert. 5.

Auguſtin. l. de Vnitate Ecclefiæ.

ouer the world, and vnited with the Church of **Rome**,
is the onely true Church of Christ.

Perhaps some will say, that *S. Auftin* did proue well
againft the Donatifts, who held the Church confined
as it were to Africa, not only *de facto*, but also *de iure*,
so as none befides them who liued in that Countrey,
had any right to be members of the Church : But Proteftants although *de facto* they hold themselues to be the
pureft members of the Church, yet they do not exclude
others (although holding different not onely rites but
also doctrines, fo long as the points be not maine and
fundamentall) from being mēbers of the same Church.

I answere, 1. That although some difference may
be affigned betwixt Donatifts and Proteftants, as also
may be betwixt Englifh Parlamentary Proteftants, &
other feuerall fects of *Linadamits, Petrobrufians, Dulcinifts,
Becharits, Berengarians, Albigenfes, Waldenfes, Wiclefifts, Lollards, Huffits, Lutherans, French Hugenots* &c. Yet I do not
fee, what fundamētall or mayne points of Fayth were
denied by Donatifts, at leaft at their firft feparation,
more then is by fome, or all thefe other Sects. For the
chiefe Error of the *Donatifts*, againft which *S. Auftin* in
the book *de vnitate Ecclefia* doth difpute, is, That they
did feparate themselues for the fuppofed faults of others
for which they accounted the vifible Catholique
Church fpread ouer the world, not to be the true
Church; not denying (for ought I know) that Chrifts
Church had ben, or ought *de Iure* to be fpread ouer the
world, but that *de facto* through faults of men it was
perifhed, and only remayned in men of their Sect;
which Errour is cōmon to them, and either all or moft
of thefe forefaid Sects challenged by *D. Featly* to be
Proteftants in doctrine; for why elfe did thefe forena-
med Sects feparate themselues from the Communion
of

of the vniuerfall precedent, or then prefent vifible Catholique Church fpred ouer the world, making a new Congregation of their owne, if they did not deeme it *de facto*, through faults of men corrupted, and not to be the true Chriftian Church? Nay, why did fome of them exprefly terme it an Antichriftian Church, and the chief vifible head of it the Pope, Antichrift? *Quæ conuentio Chrifti ad Belial?* How could they hauing this opinion of it, iudge it to be the true Church of Chrift, more then Donatifts did?

2. Cor. 6. 15.

The forefaid Argument therefore which *S. Auftin* made againft Donatifts, muft needs be of force againft all fuch Rigid Proteftants, as alfo whatfoeuer fect of Heretiques, who held the vniuerfall vifible Church, through faults of men to haue ben fo corrupted, as that it ceafed to be the true vifible Church. And although it do not feeme to côclude fo directly againft other more moderate Proteftants who are content to account that the Romã Catholique Church did not erre in fundamentall points, and confequently did, & doth remaine ftill the true Church, although corrupted with fome errours; yet indirectly it preffeth thefe men alfo, thewing, that fith there is one, and but one vniuerfall vifible Church, fpread ouer the world, if the Roman Church and the reft which ioyne with it, be ftill the true Church, Proteftants could haue no neceffary and iuft caufe to feparate from it, nor can they be the true Church, which is but one, fo long as they remaine feparate from the Communion of it.

So as, whether Proteftants hold the Rom. Church to erre fundamentally or no, *S. Auftens* Argument in his book *de vnitate Ecclefiæ*, muft needs be as forcible againft them, as it was againft the *Donatifts*; for there were alfo, euen then, fo moderate *Donatifts*, as that they thought

thought it no hindrance of faluation, whether one
were of the Roman Communion, or of the parte of
Donatus, fo long as both ferued one God and Chrift:
But *S. Auften* would not endure they fhould fo thinke, *Auguft. ep.*
but fhewed that it was needfull that, *in vnitate colatur* 48.
vnus Deus, God being one, muft be worfhiped in vnity,
and not in fchifme and feparation. And fo to the luke-
warme Ambidexters of our dayes, who thinke faluation may be had by men of diuers Fayths, fo long as
they erre not fundamentally, I may fay: *In vnitate fidei*
coli debet vnus Deus: fith there is but one God & one *Leo fer. de*
Fayth, (and as *S. Leo* fayth, *Nifi vna fit fides, non eft*: vn- *Natiu.*
les it be one, it is no Fayth) one God muft be wor-
fhipped in the vnity of Fayth, and not in any fect or
Herefie; which is one of the workes of the flefh, of *Gal. 5. 21.*
which *S. Paul* abfolutely pronounceth, *Qui talia agunt*
&c. Thofe which do fuch things, fhall not attaine the
kingdome of God.

For although in the materiall obiect of Fayth the
diftinction of points fundamentall and not fundamen- Note when
tall, may haue fome good vfe in other refpects, to wit, the diftin-
eyther to fhew that fome poynts of Fayth are more ne- ction of
ceffary to be exprefly knowne, or to fhew that befides damentall &
thofe points of the reuealed doctrine which are gene- not Funda-
rally belieued or defined by full authority of the Pa- mentall may
ftours of the Church, there are other neyther generally be vfefull,
belieued nor defined; in which latter, being not yet di- when not.
ligently digefted, nor confirmed by full authority of
the Church, as *S. Auften* fpeaketh, in which an erring *Aug fer. 14.*
Difputer is to be tolerated, to wit, fo long as he doth *de Verbis*
with humility and charity, without pryde or obftina- *Apoftoli c. 12.*
cie, or feparation of himfelf from Church-vnity, peaceably hould his opinion, and doth *implicite* belieue all
the reuealed truth, and fubmitteth his Iudgment to

the authority of the Church, being ready to belieue as
he shall vnderstand it belieueth, or shall by full auctority define to be necessary to be belieued, or to be a
matter of Fayth: In these respects I say, the distinction
of points fundamentall, and not fundamentall in the
material obiect of Fayth, may haue good vse. And
some points may be called fundamentall, & some not
fundamentall, and some may be said to be the foundation, or to pertaine to the foundation of the Church;
some Superstructions builded vpon the foundation;
some may be called *Regulæ fidei*; other *Quæstiuncula diuina
legis*; some such as the most learned and best defenders
of the Catholique Fayth may dissent in (*salua fidei Com-
page*); others, such as cannot be denied or doubtfully
disputed of, without dissoluing the iuncture of Fayth,
and shaking the foundation of the Apostolicall doctrine, and of the Church it selfe, and poysoning the
bowels and surprizing the very vitalls of Chrifts mysticall body: Yet in respect of Sects & Heresies (which
S. *Paul* reckoneth among the workes of the flesh, and
of which he pronounceth vniuersally without distinction, that those who do such things shall not attaine
the kingdome of God) this distinction hath no vse.

For whatsoeuer the materiall obiect be, fundamentall or not fundamentall, great or litle, yea the least
word or syllable of diuine truth, so it be knowne to be
generally belieued, or authoritatiuely defined by the
Church to be diuine Fayth; it is a damnable sinne to
hould Heresie or Errour against it. For, such an Heresy
or Errour, although only doubtfully disputed, or rashly
affirmed, and much more if it be proudly and obsti-
natly defended against the knowne Fayth and autho-
ritatiue definition of the Church, is opposit both to the
formall obiect of diuine Fayth, to wit, diuine reuelation

Gal. 5. 20. 21.

The reason
why the
least Heresy
is a damna-
ble sinne.

tion, and to the authority of ordinary Paſtours , by
which as by a neceſſary condition appointed of God,
the reuealed truth and diuine reuelation is applyed,&
propoſed,and made knowne vnto vs,and ſo it doth in
effect giue the lye to God and his Truth,and to his authorized officers the Paſtors of the Church, of whom
he hath ſaid: *He that heareth you,heareth me, he that deſpiſeth* Luc. 10.10,
you deſpiſeth me , and reſiſteth authority of Prelats and Rom.13.2.
Superiours,and in them Gods ordination, and ſo by *S.*
Pauls cenſure deſerueth damnation.

Hence it is , that the ancient Fathers did not examine whether the materiall obiect, in which Hereſie
or Error was obſtinatly held againſt the knowne Fayth
or definition of the Church,were fundamentall or not
fundamentall,maine or of ſmall moment,great or litle,
expreſly and cleerly ſet downe in Scripture or not; but
although it were but in one word,or ſyllable oppoſite
to any point generally belieued or authoritatiuely defined by the Church , they condemned and anathema-
tized it,and caſt the defendours of it out of the vnitie of
the Church,and pronounced that whoſoeuer held it
(to wit aduiſedly, and eſpecially ſo obſtinatly as to
make by it a ſect,or ſchiſme,or diuiſion,or(as by a drop
of poyſon)infection in the ſimple Fayth of the Church)
could not while he ſo continued, be in ſtate of ſaluation: and that although he gaue his body to burne for
Chriſt, yet he could not therby be ſaued ; neither were
that burning (as many Ignorants imagine,) *Corona* Cyprian. de
martyrij, the crowne of Martyrdome, *ſed pœna perfidiæ,* vnitate Ec-
but the iuſt puniſhment of infidelity. cleſiæ c. 14.

Hence alſo we may ſee the reaſon why *S. Auſten* in
his Booke of Hereſies (hauing reckoned vp many Er- Aug.de Hæo
rours , ſome of which are about very ſmall matters,) reſ.in fine.
pronoũceth, that whoſoeuer holdeth any one of them,

or any other Herefy (without any diftinction of points
fundamentall, or not fundamentall) he cannot be a
Catholique Chriftian, nor (as the fame *S.Auften* otherwhere, or another of the Fathers fayth)can he haue God
his Father, who hath not the Church his mother; or (as
I add)who will not fubmit his opinion to the Church
as a good child ought to do, efpecially hauing heard

Matth.18.17.

Chrift his Father threaten , *If he will not heare the Church,*
let him be to thee as an heathen and Publican; as if he fhould
fay, let him not be accounted a child of the Church,
nor confequently of God .

Laftly, Hence we may gather a cleere reafon of the

**The reafon
of difference
betweenthe
diuerfity of
opinions
betwixt Ca-
tholiques
one the one
fyde,and the
diuerfity of
doctrines of
Heretiques
againft the
Church and
betwixt
themfelues.**

differéce betwixt the difagreements about fome poynts
of doctrine, which was of old among fome of the Orthodoxe Fathers,and is now among the learnedeft and
beft defenders of the Cath. Fayth on the one fide; and
the knowne confeffed diffenfion in doctrine betwixt
moderne Proteftants, againft both ancient Fathers and
vpftart Heretiques of former ages, yea betwixt Englifh
Proteftants, and thofe Proteftants of other Countryes
whether *Lutherans* or *Caluinifts* , on the other fide ; for
the former were not about any doctrines generally
belieued, or authoritatiuely defined by the Church, and
confequently, could not be damnable Herefies , but at
moft errours excufable by reafó of their *implicite* Fayth,
and humble readines to fubmit all to the Iudgment
of the Church , and charitable care in the meane tyme
to keep peace and vnity , without fchifme or feparation from Church-Communion : But the latter are
about doctrines which are knowne to haue ben generally belieued , or authoritatiuely defined by the
Church , and therefore they are damnable Herefies,
and the profeffours of thofe feuerall fects are accounted
Heretiques, not only by the cenfure of the ancient Fathers

thers, and of the prefent Roman Church, but alfo by one another.

As for example, *Luther* doth ferioufly cenfure the *Zuinglian* Sacramentaries to be Heretiques, fo as they cannot for their agreements in other points be accounted to make one and the fame Church, eyther with ancient Fathers or with one another, in regard, as one ill Herbe doth fpoyle a whole pot of pottage, and as to break one commandement is fufficient to make one loofe Charity which is the end of all commaundements, and in fome fort to be guilty of the breach of all the reft of the Commaundements : So one Herefie in any one poynt is fufficient to deftroy, or take away all true diuine Fayth about all other points. Nay *S. Na-zianzen* is fo far from excufing any that holdeth fome Herefy by his agreement in all matters of more moment, that he fayth there is nothing more perillous then thofe Heretiques, who running vprightly in all the reft, with one word, as with a drop of poyfon, do infect the fimple Fayth of our Lord. But hauing alread y againft W. C. difputed more at large, to fhew, that obftinate Errour in any litle point of Fayth deftroyeth all Fayth, I need not now fay any more, to fhew, that the *Berengarians, Waldenfes, Wiclefifts, Hufsits,* and other condemned Heretiques (with whom our moderne Proteftants would gladly be linked in fundamentall points) cannot make one, and the fame Church, although it fhould be graunted, that they did not fo grofly erre in fome points, as fome write they did. And although they concurred in far more points with Proteftants of this age then can be proued, it feemeth that D. *Featly* fufpected that much of this which hath bin already faid, would be obiected againft him, and that therefore he had need of fome other grounds

Luther. aduer.
Art. Louan.
Thef. 17.

1. Tim. 1, 5.
Iacob. 2, 10.

Nazianzen.
orat. de mode-
rat. in difput.

to help him out, in cafe he be notable to name many,
or any in euery age, whom he can proue and defend to
haue ben Proteftants. And therfore,

6. Sixtly, he would haue it belieued, that paucity
of true belieuers, and obfcurity and latencie of the true
Church, protefting againft the corruption and idolatry in later ages thereof, is moft cleerly foretould in
Scripture: As if, forfooth, the true vifible Church which
(as himfelf granteth) according to *S. Auften*, is foretould
by Scripture moft cleerly to confift of a vifible multitude of right belieuers in all ages and nations, could by
the fame Scriptures be cleerly foretould to be reduced
to a *Paucity, obfcurity, & latency* of right belieuers, I know
not whom, *protefting*, I know not where, *againft*, I know
not what, *Corruption and Idolatry, comming in*, I know not
how long agoe, *in the latter ages of the Church*, which I
know not when they wilbe. Certainly, if any fuch
cleere prophecie had been, it is lyke the Donatifts
would haue efpied it, and made vfe of it, rather then as

they did of that obfcure place in the Canticles, *Indica*
mihi vbi pafcis, vbi cubas in meridie. Neither would it haue
hindered, that this was prophecied onely for the latter
ages of the Church; for they might, & doubtles would
haue imagined, that their ages (in which they thought
that all the reft befides themfelues fell into Corruption
and Idolatry, at leaft by communicating with fome,
which as they thought were fallen) had ben one of the
latter ages of the Church, in which the Sonne of man
(being fhortly after to come, as *S. Gregory* thought he

would haue come neere his dayes) there were to be a
falling away of many, and Fayth fcarce to be found
&c. as now. D. *Featly* imagineth to haue happened diuers hundred yeares paft, although for any thing he
knoweth, the comming of Chrift may be diuers hundreds

dreds of yeares yet to come, neere vnto which tyme
thofe prophecies which he mentioneth,are to be fulfilled in a far different fort then he interpreteth, as
doubtles they fhall, if ancient Fathers expofitions may
(as reafon is) be preferred before *D. Featlyes* fancies.

For whereas he will needs imagine the prophecies
which are about Antichrift to agree to the Pope, or rather fucceffion of all thofe Popes which haue been in
many hunreds of yeares paft, at leaft from the yeare
of our Lord 1000. in which he thinketh the Deuill
being before bound, was let loofe, interpreting the
1000. yeares mentioned *Apoc.* 20. to be vnderftood li-
terally and precifely for fo many yeares after the birth
of chrift,although the text doth not tell,that the 1000.
yeares are to begin from the birth of Chrift, but after I
know not how many other things be done, which in
the former Chapters are fignified;and although the ancient Fathers will tell vs, that in Scripture the number
1000. is not alwayes taken for that precife number,
but fometymes for leffe tyme, & fometymes for more,
(as may be feene by *S. Greg. lib.* 9. *Moral. c.* 2.) Yet he
that is fo precife in his interpretation of the 1000.
yeares, can fo enlarge the litle feafon which the holy
Text limiteth for the deuils remayning loofe, and the
tyme of the reigne of Antichrift, which the Ancient
Fathers out of plaine words of the text do fay to be
only three yeares and a halfe, that he will allow it, to
fignifie fo many hundreds of yeares, as he imagineth
the Pope to haue ben Antichrift. Wherby it doth euidently appeare,that he doth not tye himfelf, either to
the words of the text, or to the interpretation of the
ancient Fathers; according to which the prophecy of
Antichrift cannot be thought yet fulfilled, (and much
leffe can it be fulfilled in the Pope,) but according to
the

the cuftome of Heretiques, ftretcheth out or reftraineth
the wordes of the text as may beft fuite with his owne
preconceipts, perfwading himfelf, and making fimple
people belieue that he followeth the Scriptures themfelues, when indeed he followeth his owne, & other
mens erroneous phantafies, coloured with the wordes,
but deftitute of the fenfe of the holy Scriptures: in
which fort the deuill himfelf did not want his *Scriptum
eft,* to oppofe againft Chrift, and therefore no meruayle
if his Minifters do not want their *Scriptum eft,* to oppofe
againft Chrifts true Church.

But let vs imagine (yet alwayes remembring it is an
imagination) that all D. *Featlyes* dreames of prophecy
fulfilled in the Pope and Papifts, had ben truthes, and
that Papifts could not fo much as feigne fuch like prophecies to be fulfilled in Proteftants; why doth D.
Featly tell vs of fuch a paucity, and obfcurity, and latency of the true Church to haue bene foretould in
thofe latter ages in which Antichrift was to perfecute
the Church? Could fuch a great and vniuerfall perfecution of true Chriftians (as is foretold wilbe in the
true Antichrifts dayes) haue bene in any of thefe by-
paft Popes dayes, and yet none but a few, obfcure, latent right belieuers be then extant in the world? Or
could fuch few, obfcure, latent right belieuers proteft
againft the corruption and idolatry of Antichrift, and
yet remaine obfcure and latent, both from the corrupted people and Idolators of that age, and from being
mentioned in hiftories written by fome friends or enemies of the fame or other fuccceding ages? or durft men
write hiftoryes of other matters leffe needfull to be
knowne, and as much or more difpleafing to Popes of
thofe dayes, namely of fome perfonal priuate faults of
the Popes themfelues, and durft they not for the honour

nour of God and truth, make fo much as any obfcure
mention of Idolatrous doctrines publiquely taught or
preached by Popes, contrary to the former Fayth of
the Church (if any fuch had been,) or of proteftations
(againft fuch fuppofed corruptions & Idolatries) made
by fuch, and fuch few obfcure and latent belieuers? It
feemeth that thefe their fuppofed proteftations were as
obfcure & latent as the fuppofed belieuers themfelues,
that is, either no fuch were at all, or were fo obfcure &
latent as no men knew them, nor confequently did, or
could write of them; And therefore it is meruayle, how
D. *Featly* hath notice of them, vnles by reuelation, or
rather by a dreame.

If he fay, that God hath had many true feruants &
worfhippers of him in fecret, whofe names cannot be
produced : I anfwere, that we do not require, that the
Names of all Gods feruants be produced, but fome of
the moft eminent, as doubtles fome alwaies were
knowne eminently in euery age, and (as euen D. *Featly*
confeffeth) may be found in hiftoryes yet extant; and fo
by hiftoryes we can fhew, that euen then, when *Elias*
complained that he was left alone, there were in Ifrael
fome, whofe names eyther proper, or appellatiue may
be giuen, and euident proofe brought that they were
true worfhipers of God. As for example, *Abdias* & thofe
hundred Prophets which he hid; and in Iuda, and at
Hierufalem there was at the fame tyme a publique vifible profeffion of true Religion. And although it be
true, that fome ages be more barren of good writers
then others, yet Gods prouidence and humane diligéce
hath not ben deficient in making and preferuing Records, fufficient to fhew fome in all ages, who were, &
are certainely knowne to haue bene gods feruants. As
on the other fide, fome or other are knowne by the

3. *Reg.*18.4.
2. *Paralip.*19.

Q   fame

same Records yet extant, who were one way or other
their opposits and therin the Deuils inftruments ; neither could Hell-gates, that is, the deuill and all his inftruments, euer fo preuaile againft Chrift, and his
Church, by burning Records, or corrupting them, or
keeping them from view, or by any other meanes, as to
make the Church of Chrift either ceafe to be, or not to
be as a citty built vpon a Hill, which cannot be hid,
or not alwayes vifible.

Let not therefore D. *Featly* with his obfcure, falfly
applyed, & not yet fulfilled Prophefies of the Church
in the dayes of Antichrift, deceiue his Reader, or diuert him from the prefent queftion of the perpetuall
vifibility of the true Church; but acknowledging(as he
doth)that there be cleere and truely applied prophefies
and promifes which foretell the Church her perpetual
vifibility and vnchanged Fayth in all ages and Natiõs,
and that there are yet extant Hiftoryes teftifying the
anfwerable fulfulling of thofe prophefies and promifes.
Let him fet afide all his forefaid Tergiuerfations and
fhifts, and all his newly deuifed grounds fet downe in
his treatife of the Vifible Church, in the diftinctions &
affertions,fo far forth as by this my Refutation he may
fee them to be impertinent and infufficient; and let
him fairely and honeftly without further delaye, performe his promifed induction of Names of fuch in all
ages,as he thinketh to haue bene vifible Proteftants, &
out of hyftories of the fame,or neere adioyning ages,in
which ech man he nameth liued, let him particulerly
fhew, that they faid, or did, or fuffered fome thing,
wherby it may cleerly appeare that they were Proteftants,that is to fay, differed in fome points from the
Roman Fayth, which Proteftants hold to be contrary
to Scriptures, and that they did explicitely, or implicitely

Matth. 16.18.
Luc. 1. 33.
Matt. 5.14.

Affert. 4.

tely hold all the 39. Articles of the Englifh Proteftant Church, without contradicting and condemning any one of them. Which while he doth not, the world may iuftly fufpect, or rather certainely know, that, *The Pro-teftant Church hath not ben alwayes vifible, as the Cath. Roman Church is shewed by Gualterus, in his Tabula Chronographica, and others, to haue ben; & that therefore, The Roman Church is, and the Proteftant Church is not, that One, Holy, Catholique, Apoftolique, alwaies Vifible, Vnchanged, and Infallible Church, fore-prophefied and fore-promifed in Scripture, of which all may, and ought to learne Fayth necefarie to Saluation.*

THE XI. CHAPTER.

About D. Vshers Sermon, preached before his Maiefty. 20 of Iune. 1624.

ALTHOVGH I might let this Sermō paffe as hauing already giuen fuffi-ciēt grounds to make any iudicious perfō fee, that it hath not fufficiētly anfwered the Iefuits queftion: Yet in regard I vnderftand, that fome make much account of *D. Vsher*, and thinke this his Sermon to containe a better Anfwer, then is found in other mens writings; I haue thought it not amiffe to examine what he fayth, fo far forth as concerneth this Queftion.

First, I find that he doth not name Men in all ages, who holding as Proteftants do, contrary to the Rom.

Church

Church, did not contradict and condemne any of the
39. Articles of the present Englith Proteftant Church
which doth excommunicate all who deny any part of
the faid Articles: And therefore he cannot be faid to
haue fhewed fuch a cotinually vifible Proteft. Church,
as is requifite to fatisfie *M. Fisher* the Iefuits queftion.

Secondly I find, that he graunteth, that the Roman
Church is the Temple of God, and that Rom. Catholiques may be faued, fuppofing they be not ignorant of
the Articles of the creed &c. Which I defire to be noted
as being a free Confeffion made in a publique Sermon
by an Aduerfary fo eminent, who would not haue
fhewed fo much fauour to Roman Catholiques, as to
grant them hope of faluation, if truth it felf did not inforce him to it.

Thirdly I find, that with this forefaid true confeffion
he hath mixed diuers falfhoods worthy of fpeciall obferuation. The firft falfhood which I think fit heere to
note, is, that he requireth no more Fayth to be neceffary to the conftitution of the Catholique Church of
Chrift, then is exacted to be profeffed at the Baptifme
of euery particuler Chriftian, or at moft, then is expreffed in the *Nicen, Conftantinopolitan*, or *Roman* Creed.
This to be falfe appeareth, 1. by *S. Athanafius* his Creed
where it is faid, Whofoeuer wilbe faued it is neceffary
that he hold the Catholique Fayth; which vnles euery
one hold whole(*id eft* entire)and inuiolate(*id eft*, in the
right fenfe) without doubt he fhall perifh for euer. But
more pertaineth to Cath. Fayth and the right fenfe of
it, then is exacted to be profeffed at Baptifme, or is expreffed in the *Nicen, Conftantinopolitan,* or *Roman* Creed.
Ergo.

2. Befides the inftruction giuen at Baptifme(which
is the firft entrance into the Church) there be many
things

things both fpeculatiue and practicall which are needfull to be learned, to the intent that ech man may do
his duty according to that eftate and office which he
hath in the Church: In which (fuppofing commodity
of Inftructours) ignorance cannot excufe, but as *S.Paul* 1. *Cor.* 1, 14.
fayth, *qui ignorat ignorabitur*, he that (through his owne 38.
negligence) doth not know his duty, fhall not be
knowne, or approued by Almighty God.

3. The whole Canon of the holy Scripture is in
fome fort (efpecially according to the doctrine of Proteftants) neceffary to be in the Church; and at leaft
fuch as be Doctors and Paftors, and efpecially Bifhops
(who muft alwayes be in the Church)had need to vn- *Eph.*4.11, 12.
derftand fo much of the right fenfe of them, as they
may exhort in holfome doctrine, & reproue thofe who *Act.*20.28.
contradict the truth, that fo they may preferue themfelues and their hearers in the right Fayth, and reduce *Tit.*1.9.
others frō errors againft Fayth. Therfore more knowledge of the true Fayth is neceffary, for the conftitution
of Chrifts Church, then is exacted to be profeffed at
Baptifme, or is expreffed in the *Nicen, Conftantinopolitan*
or *Roman* Creed.

The 2. falfhood is, that he holdeth no more to be
properly Catholique Fayth, befide that firft foundation
which is exacted to be profeffed at baptifme, or which
is expreffed in the Roman Creed.

This to be falfe appareth, for that to make a doctrine
of Fayth Catholique, it is not neceffary, that it haue
ben exprefly belieued by al Chriftian mē, or of al Chri-
ftian(efpecially Heretical) Churches in the world, in
all places and tymes; for then, the whole foundation it
felf expreffed in the Rom. and Conftant.Creed fhould *Sermon pag.*
not be properly Catholique Fayth: for euen *D.Vsher* 28. & 29.
himfelf granteth, that fome part hereof was belieued by
Q 3   fome

some Catholiques onely implicitely, and it is certaine that some Articles of it are not belieued in the right sense by some, especially Heretiques. But to make a doctrine of Fayth Catholique, it sufficeth that all Catholique Christian Churches, and men in all tymes & places did belieue it explicitely or implicitely, in which sort the whole reuealed Truth contayned in Scriptures and vnwritten diuine Traditions, duely propounded for such by full authority of the Catholique Church, or the Pastors thereof, do pertayne to Cath. Fayth so properly, that whosoeuer denyeth any the least point of the sayd reuealed truth with pertinacy (that is, after he know it to haue been duely propounded for diuine truth by the Cath. Church or the Pastours thereof) he is properly an Heretique, and the doctrine is properly Heresy, as is insinuated by *S. Austen* when he sayth: *Qui in Ecclesia morbidum aliquid sapit, si correptus (id est, ab Ecclesia*

Aug. contra Manichæos citatur in C. Qui in Ecclesia 24. q.3. & sumitur ex Epistola 162.

vel eius Pastoribus) vt sanum sapiat , contumaciter resistit, sit Hæreticus, & foras exiens inter inimicos numeratur: He who being once in the Church holdeth some vnsound opinion, if being admonished (to wit, by the Church or her Pastours) to hold found doctrine, doth contumaciously resist, is made an Heretique, and going out of the Church becometh an enemy. Therfore not onely the first foundation professed at Baptisme, or expressed in the Roman Creed, but all reuealed Truth duely propounded by the Pastours of the Church, doth properly belong to the Catholique Fayth ; for all of it is implicitely belieued by all Catholique Churches, & Catholique men, women, and children of all ages and countryes, in that they belieue in God the Father Almighty, and in Christ Iesus his Sonne, true God and man our Sauiour; and in the Holy Ghost, 3. Persons & one God; who in, and by one Holy Catholique and

Apo-

Apoftolique Church teacheth all truth pertayning to
Chriftian Religion, for in thefe Articles rightly belieued and vnderftood, all other reuealed Verities which
euer haue bene, or fhalbe duely propounded by full authority of the Catholique Church & her Paftours, are
implicitely contained, and virtually belieued.

The 3. falfhood is, that he accounteth no more to
be neceffary to the vnity of Fayth, which *S. Paul* requi- *Eph. 4. 5.*
reth when he faith; One Lord, One Fayth, one Ba-
ptifme, but that all agree in fome fort in belieuing and
profeffing thofe common truths which are exacted to
be profeffed at baptifme, or are expreffed in the Roman
Creed. This to be falfe may appeare, in that *S. Paul* doth
not limit the vnity of Fayth onely to thofe common
Truths, but fimply requireth Vnity of diuine Fayth
(which extendeth it felf to all reuealed Truth,) and
exhorteth, or rather exacteth that all Faythfull men be
of one mind, fenfe, and fentence, at leaft in matters of
Fayth, which requireth that not onely all the fame entire reuealed truths be belieued *explicitè* or *implicitè* by
ech Chriftian, which are belieued by the reft (fo as no
diuifions and fects be among them about any matter of *Iren. l. 1. c. 3.*
Fayth,) but alfo as *Irenæus* explicateth, that all the fayd
truths be belieued by all the Church in one like manner, as if it had but one heart, which cannot be, vnles
ech man *explicitè* or *implicitè* belieue ech particuler truth
in one and the fame right fenfe, and for one & the fame
right formall reafon of diuine reuelation, infallibly
propounded and applyed to his vnderftanding, by the
confonant voyce of lawfully-fent Paftours and preachers of the true Church, who by fucceffion from the
Apoftles and Chrift himfelf receiued, & neuer loft authority and Commiffion, to teach the firft deliuered
truth.

Hence

Hence followeth, that not onely such maine errours which in D.*Vshers* sense ouerthrow, or endanger the foundation, but abfolutly all errours contrary to reuealed truth obſtinately maintained after knowledge of the Church her common Fayth, or definition of her Paſtors, are cōtrary to the vnity of ſoule-ſauing Fayth, and are damnable Hereſies; in regard whoſoeuer do hold them, in effect giue the lye to God and his Church, and consequently ſo much as is on their part, take away all infallible authority of God ſpeaking in, and by his Church; which being taken away, or denyed, or deliberatly doubted of in any one point, all diuine infallible Fayth is deſtroyed, as I haue already proued againſt W. C. Hence further followeth, that although one ſhould belieue no Errour but the whole entiere truth in the ſame right ſenſe in which all other good Chriſtians do, yet not for the ſame diuine ſupernaturalll reaſon of diuine reuelation ſufficiently applyed to him by lawfully-ſent Paſtors and preachers, but for ſome other reaſon naturall or humane; ſuch a man cannot be ſaid to haue vnity of Fayth with other Chriſtians, nor indeed any diuine Fayth, but onely an humane knowledge, or belief of thoſe truths; which is not ſufficient to ſaluation.

The fourth falſhood is, that he maketh all Chriſtian Churches, to wit, the Roman, the Reformed, the Græcian, the Ægyptian, the Æthiopian, and all others (though moſt mainely diſagreeing in ſome articles, & in the ſenſe of others, and in the formall reaſon for which any of them are belieued) to make one and the ſame Cathol. Church: This to be falſe, appeareth by that which is already ſayd, for theſe haue not among them that entiere, inuiolate, one, and the ſame Catholique Fayth which is neceſſary to the Conſtitution of

one

one and the fame Catholique Church. For all the fayd Churches (except the Roman, and fuch as agree in fayth with her) do hould fome or other Errors, contrary to the firft receiued Chriftian Fayth. And in thofe Articles in which they feeme to agree they do not hold one, and the fame fenfe which other Churches hold, neyther do they belieue any one Article precifely, for one and the fame formall reafon of diuine reuelation, fufficiently propofed by lawfully-fent Paftours which fome of thefe Churches neuer had, and thofe which once had, loft by falling into notorious Herefy, or fchifme and feparation from that Catholique body of vnited Chriftians, which once was, & yet is fpred ouer the whole world, while thefe diuided partes remaine confined to certayne Countryes, or corners of the world.

The fifth falfhood is, that he excufeth all the aforefaid Churches who hould errours againft the reuealed truth by ignorance (fuppofing the Ignorance be not of the foundation) as if whatfoeuer kind of Ignorance of the error in points not fundamentall were fufficient to excufe. This to be falfe appeareth, for that euery errour againft whatfoeuer part of the reuealed truth propofed fufficiently by the Paftours of the true Church, is damnable finne, as hath ben already proued; and not euery kind of Ignorance, but onely inuincible Ignorance excufeth from finne; which Inuincible Ignorance although fome particuler men may haue ha , yet all the forefaid Churches cannot be prefumea to haue, in regard they haue had notice of the Roman religion, being moft ancient and conftant, and therby haue had iuft caufe to doubt their owne not to haue bene fo ancient and conftant.

The fixth falfhood is, that he diftinguifheth the

R   Papacy

Papacy from the Roman Church, (as the Apoſtle doth diſtinguiſh Antichriſt from the Temple of God wherin he ſitteth) affirming the Papacy, or the Pope & his Prieſts to teach Errours, wrenching the foundation, which the people through Ignorance do not know, nor belieue.

This to be falſe appeareth, for the Pope, Prieſts, and people make but one, and the ſame Roman Church, and therefore cannot be ſo diſtinguiſhed as Antichriſt is from the Temple of God : neither can people without Prieſts be properly called the Roman Church; for *S. Cyprian* defineth the Church, *Plebs ſacerdoti adunata, Grex Paſtori adhærens :* people vnited to their Prieſt, a flock cleauing to their Paſtour. Neither doth the Pope and his Prieſts teach any point of Fayth, which the people, yea euery one of the Cath. people doth not *explicitè* or *implicitè* belieue. Neither is there any one point of Fayth taught by the Pope and his Prieſts which is contrary to, but ſtandeth well with the foundation, as all learned Catholiques know, and the vnlearned belieue; neither can *D. Vsher*, or any Proteſtant euer proue, that eyther Tranſubſtantiatiō, or any other point of Roman doctrine doth either deſtroy, or ouerthrow, or wrench, or weaken the leaſt Article of the Creed which he calleth the foundation, or any other part of the entiere reuealed truth, propoſed by the Church; all which being the truth of Chriſt (the onely foundation) may worthily be ſaid to be a part of the fo ndation : and thoſe onely doctrines which priuate men build vpon this foundation by their owne priuate ſtudy or diſcourſe of wit, are properly to be called ſuperſtructures; which if they be like gold, ſiluer, and pretious ſtones, that is, ſolid, and of good value, the builder ſhall receiue his reward; If they be ſtuble &c.

light

Cyprian Epiſt. 69.

i. Cor. 3. 11. 12.

light and of small worth, the builder shall suffer losse,
yet shalbe saued as by fire. But if the doctrine be contrary to any part of the sayd reuealed truth, it is so far
from being a building vpon the foundation of Christ
speaking in, and by his Catholique Church, as that it
ouerthroweth the foundation so much as in him lieth,
and endeauoreth to lay another foundation, to wit,
the Idoll of this, or that mans phantasie, coloured ouer
with the words, and seeming (but not true sense) of
Scriptures, which is the proper and common damnable
crime of all Heretiques, of whom *S. Austen* sayth wel:
Omnes haretici qui in auctoritate recipiunt scripturas, ipsas sibi *Aug.Epist.*
videntur sectari, cùm suos sectentur errores: All Heretiques *222.*
who receiue the auctority of Scriptures, do seeme to
themselues to follow the Scriptures, when (leauing the
true sense of Scriptures, which is the sense of Christ and
his Church, or of Christ speaking in, & by his Church)
they follow their owne erroneous phantasies: the reason whereof is, becaufe they haue not so much humility as to submit, and conforme their conceipts and
Iudgments to the words and sense of Christ, declared
by the lawfully-sent Pastours of the Church, of whom
he sayth: He that heareth you, heareth me; but through *Luc.10. 16,*
pride, high esteeme, and vayne complacence of their
owne witts and Iudgments, and contempt of the au-
thority of the Pastours of the Church, they conuert all *Aug l.3. de*
the words and mysteries which they find in holy Scri- *bapt cont.*
ptures vnto their owne phantasticall Imaginations, & *Donat.c.19.*
make them (as fooles do bells) found in their eares and
mindes conformable to their owne erroneous preconceipts.

Sith therefore *D.Vsher*, and other learned Protestants
do graunt, that the Romā Church doth hold the foundation, and build vpon it, either as we say gold, siluer, &

pretious

pretious ftones, i. folid and worthy both fpeculatiue &
piacticall doctrines; or at worft, as Proteftants fay,
wood, hay, and ftuble, i. vnneceffary or vnprofitable,
but not damnable fpeculations and obferuations; and
doth not(as all Heretiques ordinarily do) endeauour to
lay a new foundation, to wit the Idoll of any priuate
mans phantafies or nouel opinions, contrary to the former Fayth of the Church , but teacheth that ech priuate man(yea the Pope as a priuate man) ought to fubmit and conforme his priuate conceipts or Iudgments
to the wordes and fenfe of Chrift fpeaking in, and by
the generall Confent of lawfull Paftours, and definitions of generall Councels , which, if any fhould neglect to do , (although it were the Pope himfelf) and
fhould proudly oppofe and prefer his priuate opinion
before the words and fenfe of Chrift made knowne by
vnanime confent of Paftours , or definition of fome
one or other lawfully confirmed generall Councels,
he is (either *ipfo facto*, or by the authority of the Church
may, and muft be) depofed from all Ecclefiafticall di-
gnity, and excommunicated, and caft out of the Communion of the Cath. Church.

Sith I fay this is fo, I meruaile what reafon *D. Vsher*,
or any other Proteftants can haue to thinke, or call the
Pope Antichrift, or to compare the power of the Pope
ouer the Church, to Antichrifts fitting in the Temple
of God, or to hold Rome at this prefent to be that Babylon, out of which Gods people are commaunded to
depart; or to be like a Peft-houfe by reafon of preteded
peftiferous errours, or additions of new doctrines contrary to the firft receiued and generally belieued foundation of Fayth. For if this were fo, how chaunce that
the Authour of the fuppofed peftiferous errours or additions is not particulerly named, or defcribed in Hi-
ftory,

ſtory, nor the tyme when, and the place where ech Errour was firſt publiſhed, and the manner how it came
to be ſpread (as Roman doctrines are) ouer the world;
and what particuler Paſtours , or Doctours did firſt
note, contradict, and condemne it, and the Author of
it, as is ordinarily done when other pernicious Errours
did but offer to creep into the Church ? Or how could
Gods people continue Gods people (eſpecially for ſo
many hundred yeares, as Proteſtants imagine the Pope
or rather the ſucceſſion of Popes to haue ben Antichriſt, and *Rome Babylon*) who did (contrary to the ſuppoſed commaundement of God, bidding them goe out
of her) not onely liue in the ſayd Citty where the ſuppoſed Antichriſt did dwell and raigne , but alſo did
linke themſelues to him in the profeſſion of the ſame
Fayth, Communion of the ſame Sacraments, and obedience to his authority? If (as *D. Vsher* ſeemeth to ſay)
Ignorance being a great bleſſing of God, did excuſe
them from offending God, and from ceaſing to be
gods people, why may not the like bleſſed Ignorance
haue bene permitted to continue in this our age as wel
as in former ages ? Why did Luther, and his vnbleſſed
Aſſociats endeauour to take away that bleſſing of God
with bringing men out of their Ignorance into ſuch a
pernicious knowledge, as might cauſe or giue occaſion
to the ruine of ſo many ſoules ? Why do they not yet
allow men to adhere to the Roman Church (as they
haue reaſon who cannot find any other Church ſo ancient and conſtant in profeſſion of Chriſtian religion,)
but both by perſwaſion and perſecution ſeeke to draw
them from it, who be as Ignorant of any Errour in
Fayth to be profeſſed by it, as any of our anceſtours
were, and are moſt firmely perſwaded, that it teacheth
nothing but truth .

R 3   But

But the truth is, that the Pope is not Antichrist fitting in the Temple of God, neither is Rome that Babylon out of which gods people muſt depart, neither is the propheſy of Antichriſt his ſitting in the Temple of God ſo meant, that Gods people ſhall generally, eſpecially for ſo long a tyme, ſubmit themſelues vnto him, in regard it is certaine, that Gods people ſhalbe generally perſecuted by Antichriſt, by reaſon they do not ſubiect themſelues vnto him. And howſoeuer the commandement which biddeth Gods people goe out of Babylon, be vnderſtood to preſuppoſe gods people for ſome tyme to be in the ſame citty or place, where Antichriſt ſhall ſit and haue his throne, yet it is certaine that all Gods people (remayning Gods people) neuer ſhall, nor can linke themſelues with Antichriſt in the profeſſion of his Fayth, and Communion of his ſacraments, and obedience to his lawes; neither muſt they ſo goe out from any place or citty as to depart (as Proteſtants did) from, and proteſt againſt the vnity of the onely continually viſible Catholique Church, vnder whatſoeuer pretence of reformation of errours in Fayth (which cā neuer be needfull in regard Hell-gates ſhall neuer ſo preuaile, as to make the vniuerſall viſible Church erre in any point of Fayth) or reformation of mens manners, which may be better done by remayning in Church-vnity with them, then by making a ſchiſme or ſeparation from them.

Let Proteſtants therefore reflect vpon, and ponder this their conceipt of the Popes being Antichriſt, and themſelues being the people which by gods commaundement departed out of Babylon, when they proteſted againſt the Roman Church and Religion; whereas others their anceſtours being Gods people as well as they, did for ſo many hundred yeares liue and die in

the

the said Roman Church and Religion, and therein obtained (as *D. Vsher* granteth) saluation. Let Protestants I say, consider how these two can stand togeather: That these our ancestors were Gods people while they did (as they did in life and death) adhere to the Pope & his priests, and beleeued and professed *explicitè*, or *implicitè* the entire Fayth taught by the Pope and his priests, and participated sacraments ministred by the Pope and his priests, and obeyed lawes made by the same Pope and his priests; And that Protestants also are Gods people while they first made, and yet continue such a horrible schisme and separation from the whole Church which adhereth to the said Pope and his priests, renouncing their Fayth, refusing their sacraments, reiecting their lawes, and persecuting with losse of goods, liberty & life, such as remaine vnited to the Pope and his priests: Certainely, if God be (as most certainely he is) altogether immutable, and still one and the same, he cannot be pleased with people of so contrary conditions, with men so much halting on both sides, and seruing two so oppofite Maisters, and professing two so different Religions.

3. *Reg.* 18. 21. *Matth.* 6. 24.

Wherefore I conclude, that if our Ancestors were gods people (as *D Vsher* granteth) then Protestants are not. Which sentence I pronounce (not absolutly of this, or that man in particuler but) of Protestants considered as such, and liuing, and dying such, without actual or virtual repentance, and according to the ordinary course of gods prouidence; for whether by inuincible Ignorance, and extraordinarie prouidence, God can saue some who in the sight of men die out of the ordinary way of saluation, is another question which I leaue to gods extraordinarie power & mercy; vpon which no man ought to presume, but euery one

ought

ought to take the ordinary and onely safe way of saluation, which is to adioyne himself to the onely continually visible Roman Catholique Church, in which our ancestors liuing and dying (euen by Confession of Aduersaryes) haue ben gods people and are saued, and out of which being the onely true Catholique Church (by the constant profession of all ancient and present Catholique Doctours) none are, or can, so liuing and dying, be saued.

THE XII. CHAPTER.

Containing a Confutation of the Pamphlet called, *The protestant Kalendar.*

A LTHOVGH I haue already in the precedent Chapters giuen sufficient grounds, by which euery Iudicious man may gather that this Kalendar doth neyther satisfy M. *Fishers* Question, nor sufficiently answere that argument, by which he, and other Catholiques proue Protestants not to be the true Church of Christ: *Videlicet.*

Matth. 28.
Mar. 16.
Rom. 10.
Eph. 4.
Heb. 11.

The true Church of Christ hath had in all ages Visible, and lawfully-sent Pastours teaching. and people belieuing that one, infallible, entiere Fayth, which Christ and his Apostles taught to be necessary to saluation .

But Protestants haue not had in all ages such Pastours, and people .

Therfore, Protestants are not the true Church of Christ.

Neuerthe-

Neuerthelcſſe for that the Methode heerof maketh
a faire ſhew, and may ſeeme in the eyes of the ſimple
to anſwere directly to the Argument and Queſtion
aforeſaid; I haue thought it not amiſſe to examine what
it ſayth, and to ſhew briefly & plainely that it neither
ſatisfyeth the Queſtion, nor anſwereth the Argument.

First I perceiue the Authour of this Kalendar would
gladly if he durſt deny, or doubt of the *Maior* Propoſition of the Argument. For thus he ſayth: *Concerning their* Pag. 4.
Tenet *of the perpetuall Viſibility of the Church, in ſuch ſenſe*
as they take it, how infirme it is, I referre the Reader to the
learned Treatiſes of the moſt Reuerend & Iudicious Deuines of
our Church, who haue purpoſely written of this Argument. And
he citeth in the margent, *The Lord Archb. of Cant. Treatiſe,*
Of perpetual Viſibility; *D. Feild*, Of the Church; *D.*
Whyte, in the Way to the Church.

But it ſeemeth this Kalendar-maker himſelf durſt
not ſtand peremptorily vpon this deniall, as hauing
ſeene how weakely theſe his Reuerend and Iudicious
Deuines haue oppugned, and how ſtrongly others
both Catholiques and Proteſtants(*)haue proued perpetual Viſibility of the Church in the ſenſe of Catho- (*) D. Featly
liques, briefly ſet downe in the maior Propoſition of *of the viſibi-*
the argument, and more largely explicated in the 7. *lity of the*
Chapter of this Booke, vnto which I referre the Rea- *Church.*
der, who ſhall deſire more full ſatisfactiō in this point. *Aſſert.* 4.
And I wil returne to the Kalendar, whoſe Authour
not daring to ſtand vpon this propoſition ſayth thus:
I rather bend my ſelf to refute the Minor *propoſition wherein* Pag. 4.
they deny, that we of the Proteſtant Church can ſhew any ſuch
ſucceſsion, or Viſibility of our Church and religion in former
times, and that ſo much the rather, becauſe Gregory of Valentia *peremptorily maintaineth, that this is a point that puzzelleth*
vs extreemely, and that we are not able to ſhew any company of
S *people*

people which in times paft was knowne in the world to hold that forme of doctrine and religion which we haue brought in. By which words we may fee what the drift of the whole Kalendar is, and that he meaneth to bend all his battery againft this our Minor Propofition, without medling at all with the Maior, the truth of which he feemeth to admit, when he fayth thus:

Pag. 1. & 2. It cannot be denyed (which *Tertullian* doth auerre) that the antiquity of Religion doth much ferue to teftify the verity thereof, and the longer line it hath had of continuance, the more it claimes our obferuance, and tyes vs to obedience. The Heathen *Hefiode* could fay νόμος ἀρχαῖος; ἄριϛος, The old law is beft: and the beft, & moft deuine of all the philofophers Plato, οἱ παλαιοὶ κρείττονς ἡ ἐγγυτέρω τῶν θεῶν οἰκοῦντες: The ancients are beft, as comming neereft vnto God: and it is a rule among the Lawyers, *Qui prior eft tempore, potior eft iure:* He that is firft in time is chiefeft in right. Hence it is that *Bildad* aduifeth *Iob.* 8. 8. 9. Inquire I pray thee of the former ages, prepare thee for the fearch of their Fathers, for we are but of yefterday, and know nothing, becaufe our dayes vpon earth are but a fhadow: Shall not they teach thee & tell thee? And *Ierem.* 6. 16. Thus fayth the Lord: Stand yee in the wayes, and aske for the old path, where is the good way, and walke therein, and yee fhall find reft to your foules. And in the *Song of Moyfes Deut.* 32. 7. Remember the dayes of old, confider the yeares of many generations : aske thy Father and he fhall fhew thee, thine Elders and they will tel thee.

All which words (being the Kalendars) I haue thought fit to recite, that it may be feene that the Kalendar-maker doth agree with vs in holding, that Chriftian religion to be trueft which is moft ancient &

of

of longeſt continuance, and which by many generations can ſhew (as it were) the pedegree of the profeſſours thereof from Sonne to Father, ſtill vpwards to
Chriſt the vndoubted viſible authour of the true Chriſtian Fayth and Church.

So as now it remaineth (according to the intent of
M. Fiſhers Queſtion) that the Iſſue be tryed whether profeſſours of Proteſtancy can (as Profeſſours of Roman
Catholique Fayth(*) can) name and proue out of good
authours, a moſt ancient and continuall ſncceſſion of
their Paſtours teaching, and people belieuing in all ages
one and the ſame vnchãged entire Fayth which Chriſt
and his Apoſtles taught and deliuered to the Church
from generation to generation by Viſible lawfully-
ſent Paſtours. For this is the point, which as *Valentia*
ſayth, hitherto hath extreemely puzzeled Proteſtants:
and this is the point which *M. Fisher*, and *M. Sweet* hauing propoſed to *D. White*, and *D. Featly* almoſt two
yeares agoe, neither then, nor after was by them, or any
other, nor euer wilbe well anſwered. Yet ſith this Kalendar promiſeth a more Methodicall Anſwere then
hitherto hath bene giuen, I will briefly examine, and
paſſe my Cenſure vpon it, after I haue reduced to the
Readers memory, what anſwere *M. Fishers* Queſtion
requireth.

It is therefore to be obſerued, that *M. Fishers* Queſtion
requireth Names of men to be ſhewed in all Ages (out
of good Authours) who can be proued and defended
to be members of the Proteſtant Church; that is to ſay, men
teaching and belieuing doctrine of Fayth, different
from ſome part of the Fayth of the Catholique Roman
Church, and agreeing in all the 39. Articles which the
Engliſh Proteſtant Church doth account ſo neceſſarie
to be held by euery good Proteſtant, as that it doth ex-

S 2   communi-

Booke of ca-
nons can. 5.
communicate *ipſo facto* euery one, who ſhall hold any
part of them to be erroneous, ſuperſtitious, or ſuch as
he cannot with a good côſcience ſubſcribe vnto. Now
this being obſerued, it wilbe moſt eaſy to ſee, that this
Kalendar doth not giue a good anſwere to M. *Fiſhers*
Queſtion.

Firſt, for that theſe which be named, are men moſt
different in Fayth and religion, one from another, and
not any one of them can be well proued and defended
to haue agreed with the preſent Engliſh Church in the
39. Articles aforeſaid, & conſequently they cannot be
accounted to be of one and the ſame Church with it,

Rom. 10.
Eph. 4.
but rather to be excommunicated by it.

Aug. l. de
vtil.cred.c.17.
Iren.l. 4.c.4.
Tertullian
lib.de præſ-
cript.
(*)VVillet
ſynopſis pag.
69. & 71.
VVhitaker.
cont. Durân
l.3.pag.249.
Lobechius in
Diſputat.
Theolog.pag.
213.ſect. 44.
(*) Iewell de-
fence of the
Apology pa.
43.Oſiander
centur. 3.
pag. 329.
Secondly, in many of the ages there is not any one
named who can be proued and defended to haue bene
a lawfully-ſent Paſtour, or to haue had immediately,
or mediately lawfull Ordination, and Iuriſdiction,
miſſion, and commiſſion to teach Gods Word, and miniſter Sacraments, at leaſt in that ſenſe and manner
which is preſcribed in the aforeſaid 39. Articles, which
defect is ſo eſſential that this onely is ſufficient to ſhew
Proteſtants not to be the true Church of Chriſt(deſcribed in Scriptures, and Fathers) which muſt ſo neceſſarily haue in it, in all ages, lawfully-ſent Paſtours, as that
the onely want of them (euen by confeſſion of learned
(*)Proteſtants) maketh a nullity of the Church.

Thirdly, Some of theſe which be nameth held ſome
or other ſo groſſe errours, as that learned Proteſtants
(*)being aſhamed to heare them accounted members
of the Proteſtant Church, haue expreſſely diſclaimed
from them, ſaying, *they are none of ours.* Likewyſe, ſome
of theſe which he here nameth held expreſly doctrine
contrary to the chiefe Articles of Proteſtancy, and namely to the Article of *Iuſtification by onely Fayth,* which

is

is reputed to be the moſt ſubſtantiall point, and as it *Act. 4. 32.* were the very ſoule of the Proteſtant Fayth & Church. *Rom. 15. 6.* If therefore (according to the Iudgement of Scriptures *Iren. l. 1. c. 3.* and ancient Fathers) there muſt be ſo great vnity of *Leo. ſer. 6. de* Fayth in the church, as if the whole multitude had but *Natiu. Do-* one hart and one ſoule wherewith they belieue, and *mini. Hieron.* one mouth with which they preach, and that the leaſt *in cap. 3. So-* diſunity (by Errour of Fayth obſtinately mainteined) *phon. Na-* infecteth and deſtroyeth Fayth and caſteth the main- *ʒianʒen. orat.* tainers out of the Church ; it cannot poſſibly be , that *de Pace.* men ſo different in Fayth (eſpecially in ſo chiefe *Magnam* and ſubſtantial matters) can be of one and the ſame *ſibi videbat* Proteſtant Fayth & Church, vnles the Proteſtāt Fayth *aſſumpſiſſe* and Church do (as *S. Leo* teſtifyeth old Heatheniſh *religionem,* Rome did)eſteeme her ſelf very religious in that ſhe re- *dum nullam* fuſed not to imbrace in her boſome all falſe opinions *reſpueret* of whatſoeuer ſect or religion . *falſitatem.*

Leo. ſer. 1. in Natiu. Apo-ſtol. Petri & Pauli.

Fourthly, There are many named in this Kalendar for Proteſtants(without any reaſon, or authour, onely for hauing had ſome oppoſition (though in matters of fact)againſt the Pope, or for reprouing ſome vices ob-ſerued in the Pope) who are otherwayes knowne to haue profeſſed themſelues Roman Catholiques, and to haue held the Roman Catholique Fayth, and to haue deteſted all oppoſite doctrines vntil their dying day .

Fifthly, All, or moſt of the ancient Orthodoxe Fa-thers are named for Proteſtants, and yet they all held Communion with the Pope, and did acknowledge his Primacy and vniuerſall Authority(as appeareth by the writings of the chief of them yet extant) to be groun-ded in the Holy Goſpel it ſelf; and beſydes (euen by confeſſion of learned Proteſtants) ſome of them (both in this point and in ſome others) held expreſſely con-trary to the doctrine of Proteſtants cōtained in the 39.

S 3 Articles

Articles , and haue cenſured ſome of the points contained in theſe articles with the infamous note of an-
ciently condemned Hereſy, as may be ſeene in *S. Epi-*
phanius, and *S. Auguſtine* their Catalogues of Hereſies.

Laſtly, This Kalendar nameth Chriſt and his Apoſtles for Proteſtants, but neither doth, nor can proue it;
for among all thoſe Texts which he hath quoted, there
is not one which plainely proueth any one point of
Proteſtant doctrine, or diſproueth any one point of the
Catholique Roman Fayth , as ſhall be ſhewed when-
ſoeuer need ſhalbe , or when any one ſhalbe in particuler inſiſted vpon and vrged. In the meane time, if any
man ſhall deſire to ſee a more large and particuler confutation of this Kalendar, let him read the *Three Conuer-*
ſions of England, and the *Examen of Fox his Kalender,* the *Pro-*
teſtants Apology, and other Catholique Authours , in
which he ſhall ſee particulerly exemplifyed many of
thoſe things, which here for breuity ſake, I haue onely
in generall termes barely mentioned .

The end of the firſt Part.

A
REPLY
TO D· VVHITE,
and Doctour Featly.

THE SECOND PART.

In which is shewed, that the Cath. Roman Church
can Name, Proue, and Defend Visible Professours
of her Fayth, in all Ages.

AND THAT,

She only, and such as agree in Fayth with her, is the True,
Visible, Catholique Church, out of which there
is no Saluation.

Your Fayth is renowned in the whole World. Rom. 1. 8.

Permissu Superiorum, M. DC. XXV.

THE FIRST CHAPTER.

In which is shewed, that the Roman Church hath had Visible Professours, whose Names may be shewed in all Ages.

IN the precedent Chapters I haue shewed, that none of the aforesaid Protestant writers haue answered, nor can answer *M. Fishers* question, requiring Names of Visible Protestants in all ages to be set downe, with such proofes out of good Authours as may make it appeare that the Protest. Church hath ben so visibly spread ouer the world, as the Scriptures and Orthodox Fathers (euen by the Confession of learned Protestants themselues) do describe the true Church of Christ, of which all are to learne that one, Infallible, diuine Fayth which the same Scriptures and Fathers do signifie to be necessary for all who desire to please God and to attaine saluation. I haue also giuen groundes by which in lyke manner may be shewed, That no other sort of Christians differing in doctrine from the Roman Church, can name, proue, & defend visible Professours of their peculiar Fayth, to haue ben visibly spread ouer the world, in such sort as Christs Church

D. Featly of the visibility of the Church. Assert. 4.
Rom. 10. 14
15.
Eph. 4. 11. 12.
Heb. 11. 6.

T

Church ought to be in all ages.

　Whence I may conclude, that the Roman Church onely, and such as agree with it in doctrine of Fayh, is the true visible Church of Christ, of which all people may, and ought to learne Fayth necessary to saluation; for sith it is certaine that there hath bene according to the Prophecies of Scripture, a true Church of Christ which hath had visible Professours spread ouer the world in all ages, and no other hath been; it must needes follow, that the Roman is this same Church whose Professours Names are in all ages mentioned in hystories.

　Now, although this may suffice to proue the Roman Catholique Church to be the onely true Church of Christ, of which all are to learne Fayth necessary to saluation; yet if any one desire more full satisfaction, & wish to see Names of Roman Catholiques in all ages proued, & defended out of good Authours, let him read *Gualterus his Tabula Chronographica*, or *Coxius his Thesaurus*, or S. N. *his Appendix to the Antidote*, or M. *Fishers Reply* to M. *Wotton* and M. *White*.

　Secondly, let him consider, that Protestants neyther haue, nor can out of good Authours confute the Catalogues which these our Authours make, nor confront them with the like Catalogue of Protestants.

　Thirdly, let him remember that Protestants confesse, that the Romaine Church hath had visible Professours in all Ages, and that it hauing in the Apostles dayes receiued the true Fayth, did not alter it for the first 600. yeares. And although some Protestāts affirme, that Rome altered Religion after the first 600. yeares, yet they cannot proue this by naming the Authour of the Alteration, neyther can they shew out of good Records, that any Pope, or other, brought in any one
point

point of doctrine which was noted, contradicted, and condemned by vnanime conſent of Paſtours, eyther of the precedent or the then preſent Church, as we can Name the firſt Authours of diuers Nouelties and Hereſies brought in by Proteſtants, which at the firſt publication were noted, contradicted, and at laſt condemned by the ordinary Paſtours for Errours, contrarie to Scriptures and the common Fayth of the Church.

Fourthly, let him obſerue, that whereas the chief points which Proteſtants do account Errours in the Proteſt. Church, are Tranſubſtantiation, and Sacrifice of the Maſſe, Honour and Inuocation of Saints, Veneration of Images, & Sacred Reliques, Free will, & poſſibility of obſeruing Gods Comaunndements, Merit of workes, vnlawfulnes of mariage in Prieſts and Religious, faſting and abſtinence, Sacrament of pennáce & prieſtly Abſolution, Purgatory and prayer for the dead, Primacie of S. Peter and his ſucceſſors, Authority of the Church, and her Traditions. The aforeſaid *Gualterus*, and other our Catholique Authours, do out of Scriptures, Fathers, and Councels proue, all theſe not to be Errours or nouell inuentions, but to haue ben expreſſed in Scriptures and Fathers, or virtually contayned in principles of the formerly receiued common Fayth of the ancient Church.

Laſtly, If all this will not perſwade him that Chriſt and his Apoſtles, *S. Ignatius,* and the reſt of the Orthodox Fathers Doctors and Paſtours ſet downe by *Gualterus* and others, can be proued and defended to be of the ſame Fayth and Religion which the preſent Roman Church profeſſeth, let him ponder, and weigh the force of this Argument.

All ſuch are Roman Catholiques, and not Proteſtants in doctrine, who do *explicitè,* or *implicitè* hold the

autho-

authority of S. Peter, and the Popes his fucceffors in
fuch fort, as Roman Catholiques hold at this day.

But Chrift and his Apoftles, *Ignatius*, and all the
Orthodox Fathers of all both the firft, 2.3. and all other
ages, did *explicitè* or *implicitè* hold the authority of S.
Peter and the Popes his fucceffours, in fuch fort as Roman Catholiques hold it at this day.

Ergo, Chrift and his Apoftles, *Ignatius*, and all the Orthodox Fathers are Roman Catholiques.

The Maior I proue : becaufe the chiefe thing which
makes the Roman Catholiques diftinguifhed from all
other forts of Chriftians, is, that all, and onely they,
hold the authority of S. Peter and the Pope, eyther
alone or with a generall Councell, to be fupreme vnder Chrift, and infallible in defining Controuerfies of
Fayth, and in declaring what is to be belieued by
Fayth, and in this refpect they are called Papifts, who
in holding this, virtually hold all, and do not condemne any other point of the Roman Fayth, fo long as
they do firmely hold this

The Minor I proue thus :

If the words which Chrift fayd, and the Euangelifts
wrote in the Gofpell, do fignify (according to the explication of many of the graueft and moft learned Orthodoxe writers, without any contradiction of others,)
that to S. Peter and his Succeffours was giuen the fayd
fupreme and infallible authority ; then , doubtles,
Chrift and his Apoftles, *Ignatius*, and all other Orthodox Fathers did *explicitè* or *implicitè* hold the authority
of S. Peter and the Popes his fucceffors, in fuch fort as
Roman Catholiques do at this day hold;neither can it
be faid, that they did condemne any other point of
Roman Fayth,fith all other points are virtually contained in this one point.

But

But fo it is, tuat the words which Chrift and the
Euangelifts wrot in the Gofpell do fignifie (according
to the explication of many of the graueft and moft
learned Orthodox writers, without contradiction of
others) that to S. Peter and his Succeffois was giuen
the faid fupreme and infallible authority. *Ergo.*

If the fequele of this laft Maior be doubted, I aske
what other rule can be affigned, by which the true fi-
gnification of Chrifts words and confequently the effect may be certainely knowne vnto vs?

This laft *Minor* is fhewed at large by our Catholique Authors, *Gualterus* in his *Tabulæ Chronographica,*
verit. 11. *in fingulis Centurijs. Coxius Tom.* 1. *Thefauri,* and
others.

Some may perhaps object that although Chrift, his
apoftles, and the orthodox Fathers held this authority
in fuch fort as the prefent Romã Church doth, yet how
fhal we know that they did not hold contrary to the
Roman Church in fome other points of her Fayth? I
anfwere, that euery point of Rom. Fayth is fo connected which the aforefaid fupreme and infallible authority of S. Peter and his fucceffours, in defining matters
of Fayth, either alone or with the reft of the Paftours
fpread abroad in the world, or gathered together in a
general Councell, as that whatfoeuer point of reuealed
truth is duely propofed by that authority, it is to be accounted a point of Catholique Rom. Fayth; and whatfoeuer point (although in it felf a reuealed truth) is not
actually or virtually propofed duely to vs by that authority, it is not to be accounted a point of Fayth : So
that whofoeuer holdeth that authority, in fuch fort as
it is held by the prefent Rom. Church (as Chrift our
Sauiour, the Apoftles, and all orthodox Fathers held it)
cannot be faid to condemne any point of Fayth which

T 3   the

the prefent Rom. Church holdeth, but at leaft *implicitè* holdeth all, in holding this authority.

Now to defend Chrift and his Apoftles, *Ignatius*, and all Orthodox Fathers to be Rom. Catholiques and not Proteftants, is a moft eafie matter, if one obferue thefe few Rules.

The firft is, That one may be a Rom. Catholique, although he do not exprefly fet downe in writing euery point of Rom. Fayth. By this rule we may fee, how weakely thofe argue who fay ; Chrift & his Apoftles, and the Fathers of the firft 300. yeares, do not expreffe in their writings this, or that point which is defined in the Councell of *Trent*: *Ergo*, they are no Rom. Catholiques. The which Confequence being grounded on Negatiue authority, is of no force, vnles it be firft proued, that euery Rom. Catholique hath exprefly fet downe in writing all points of his Fayth, or held no more inwardly in hart, then he expreffed in outward words or writing, which cannot be proued.

The fecond Rule is, That one may be a Roman Catholique, although fomething faid or written by him, feeme to contradict fome point of Roman Fayth; for words may feeme to haue another fenfe then was intended by the fpeaker or writer. Therefore they argue weakely, who (out of fentences of Fathers and Scriptures, which onely feeme to contradict fome point of Roman doctrine,) conclude that Chrift or his Apoftles, or thofe Fathers were no Rom. Catholiques; and much more weakely, or rather wickedly, do fome Proteftants alledge S. Hierome, or any other of the Fathers to proue the Pope Antichrift, or Rome Chriftian Catholique, to be Babylon fpoken of in the Apocalyps.

D. Iames his catalogue fet downe by D. Featly is anfwered.

The third Rule is, That one may be a Rom. Catholique

lique, although he be proued to haue held some opiniõ
contrary to that which is truth, and which is the Fayth
of the Rom. Church; so long as the matter was not
knowue to him to be contrary to truth, or to the generall Fayth, or definition of the Church. By this Rule
some ancient Fathers, namely *S. Cyprian,* and some later
writers, did not cease to be Rom. Catholiques, by holding some opinions contrary to the truth, and contrary
to that which the Rom. Church now generally holdeth, or hath defined to be a point of Fayth; so long as
the matter was not knowne to them to be contrary to
truth, nor contrary to the common Fayth of the Rom.
Church. Those therefore argue weakely, who out of
some opinions found in Orthodox Authours, contrary
to some point defined in the Councell of Trent, endeauour to proue those Authours to be no Rom. Catholiques; for this Consequence is not good, vnles
withall it be proued, that the matter was in those Authors dayes defined, or generally held as a point of
Fayth by the Church, and knowne to these Authours
to haue ben so defined or held, at such tyme as they
held those erronious opinions. Out of which Rules
I conclude, That sith Christ our Sauiour, his Apostles,
S. Ignatius, and the rest of the Orthodox Fathers cannot
be proued to haue held any opinion which themselues
did know to be contrary to truth, or contrary to the
generall Fayth, or definition of the Church, they cannot be proued to be no Rom. Catholiques, or to haue
had a Fayth different from the Fayth of the Catholique Roman Church.

THE

THE II. CHAPTER.

In which is shewed, that out of the Catholique
Roman Church there is no Saluation.

I MIGHT briefly proue the Intent of this
Chapter by this short Syllogisme:
Out of the Catholique Church there
is no saluation .
But, onely the Roman , & such as liue
in vnity thereof , is the Catholique Church .
Ergo.
The *Maior* is a principle not to be denied, or if it be,
it may be easily proued .
The *Minor* I proue :
The Catholique Church, out of which is no saluation, is that continually visible Church, of which Isaias
prophecieth saying: *Thy gates shalbe opened continually*, day
» and night they shal not be shut, that the strength of
» Nations may be brought vnto thee and their kings,
» for the Nation and kingdome which shall not serue
» thee, shall perish .
But as appeareth in the precedent Chapters of this
my Reply, onely the Rom. Church , and those which
liue in vnity with her, hath ben this continually visible Church, of which the Prophet speaketh.
Therefore the Rom. Church, & such as liue in vnity
with her, is the Cath. Church , out of which is no saluation .
Secondly, I may vrge all wise Protestants with this
morall

moral Argument. In that Church only is faluation to
be hoped for by wife men, in which all, not onely
friends, but alfo the beft learned Aduerfaries grant faluation may be had; for in matters of fo great moment as
is eternall faluation, wife men ought to place their
hope onely in the fecureft way, and not aduenture
vpon the vncertainty of their owne, or other priuate and partiall mens opinions.

But it is farre more fecure to liue and dye in the
Rom. Church, in which (as appeareth by a Booke
called *The Grand-Iury*) both all friends, and the beft
learned Proteftants her Aduerfaryes graunt faluation
may be had,) then to liue, and die in the Proteftant
Church, in which none but partially affected men, to
wit Proteftants themfelues, doe promife faluation.

Ergo, all wife men ought to place hope of faluation,
only in liuing and dying in the Rom. Cath. Church.

But becaufe thefe proofes are but fhort, and will not
perhaps perfwade euery man to belieue fo fharp and
feuere a fentence, to wit: That out of the vnity of the
Rom. Church there is no faluation; I haue thought
good to adioyne vnto thefe fhort proofes, this enfuing
larger difcourfe.

*A Difcourfe, in which is shewed, by Reafons
drawne out of Scriptures and Fathers,
That out of the Vnity of the Roman
Cath. Church, there is no faluation.*

ALTHOVGH it be moft certaine, that we haue
a moft mercifull Lord and God, who as *S. Paul*
fayth, *would haue all men to be faued, and to come to the know-*
ledge,

1. *Tim.* 2. 4.

V

2. Pet. 3. 9.

Aug. serm. 15.

ledge of truth, and as *S. Peter* sayth, *would haue none to perish:* yet he wil not saue vs, except our selues freely concurre with his grace, according to that of *S. Austen, Qui fecit te sine te, non saluabit te sine te.* The reason whereof is, for that as it pertaineth to the sweetenesse of Gods prouidence to concurre with euery creature according to the nature of it, and to bring it to the naturall end by proportionable naturall meanes ; so it belongeth to the same sweetnes of Prouidence, that he doe not force or necessitate man being a free creature, but bring him freely to his supernaturall end of eternall saluation, by free vse of some or other proportionable supernaturall meanes.

That man may freely cooperate to his saluation, it is needfull that he know his supernaturall end, & meanes that lead therûto.

2. To bring man freely to his supernaturall end, by the free vse of supernaturall meanes, it is necessarily required that men should haue some or other knowledge of the said end, and meanes. The reason whereof is, because *nihil volitum, quod non est præcognitum*, nothing can be freely intended as an end, or chosen as a fit meanes which is not in some sort knowne: and sith no naturall knowledge of man is either proportionable, and fit or sufficient to moue the will to supernaturall desires and endeauours requisite to the attayning of mans supernaturall end by supernaturall meanes, it is necessary that he haue supernaturall, at least obscure, knowledg of the said end and meanes.

3. This supernaturall, euen obscure, knowledge of mans supernaturall end, and supernaturall meanes leading therevnto, cannot be had by any man vnles God do (either immediatly or mediatly) reueale to him to what end he hath supernaturally ordayned him, & by what supernaturall freely vsed meanes he may attaine this end. The reason hereof is, because none can know the secret counsells of God, besides the spirit of God, &

such

such to whom it pleaseth him to reueale them. But to know to what supernaturall end man is ordayned, and by what supernaturall meanes it may be attayned, is a secret counsell of God. 1. Cor. 2. 10. 11

4. Besides this reuelation of Gods part, it it necessary that a man of his part doe giue supernaturall and infallible assent to this reuelation, and to the truth of the thing reuealed; so as at least in an obscure manner he may heereby haue in his soule some supernaturall, firme, and infallible knowledg, proportionable to the Reuelation, and the truth reuealed, and sufficient to moue the will firmely to intend this supernaturall end and effectually to vse the meanes. The reason of this is, for that if a man doe not giue any assent, no knowledge is bred in man by the Reuelation. And if the assent he giueth be only probable, it is not proportionable to the Reuelation which is infallible : neither is it sufficient to moue the will to intend the supernaturall end so firmely, as is requisit to ouercome so many difficulties, and to vndergoe the labours and paines which are requisite, to choose prudently, & to execute diligently and constantly such things as are necessary for the attayning of the said end, in regard we see that our slack will is slowly inough moued by infallible assent giuen to the diuine Reuelation, and therfore would be much more slow, if the Vnderstanding did onely assent probably vnto it.

Besides gods reuelation it is required that man yeld firme and infallible assent to the truth reuealed.

That a man may yield firme and infallible assent to the reuealed Truth, it is needfull that the reuelation be sufficiently applyed to him by some infallible meanes appointed by God.

5. That a man may giue firme infallible supernaturall assent to the diuine Reuelation and the truth of the things reuealed, it is not enough, 1. That the thing Reuealed be most true in it selfe ; or 2. That the Reuelation of that truth was once made, and is yet extant in some or other mans memory, or in some written or printed booke: But it is needfull that it be sufficiently

propoun-

propounded, and applyed in particuler to euerie man
who is to giue infallible supernaturall assent vnto it,
by some or other infallible supernaturall meanes,
appointed by God, and this also such as is in some sort
proportionable to the capacity of ech man who is to
assent by meanes of it. The reason is, for the truth of
the thing reuealed , and the reuelation being aboue
reach of all reason, one that neuer heard , or by any
other meanes vnderstood any thing of the thing reuealed or the reuelation, could not assent at all; & if he
only heard of it by a knowne lyar, or only by a probable speaker, he could not giue infallible, but (at most)
probable assent vnto it. Therefor that a man may giue
supernaturall infallible assent to reuealed truth, it is necessary, that besides the truth of the thing, and besides
the reuelation, both the one and the other be aplied to
him in particuler by some or other supernaturall infallible meanes, proportionable to the reuelation, and to
the truth reuealed, and to the person to whom it is in
particuler applied, not only in the enlightning *ex parte
Intellectus,* of the part of the vnderstanding, which giueth him ability to vnderstand it, but also *ex parte Obiecti,* of the part of the obiect , that it may be fit to be
vnderstood by that particuler man : like as it is not
inough to see a Colour, that there be a true Colour,

The Meanes and perfect eyesight, but that the Colour must also by
which God a conuenient meanes and approximation, or a propor-
hath appoin- tionable nearenesse, be duly proposed to this particuler
ted to apply mans eyesight .
the diuine
reuelation is   6. This infallible supernaturall meanes aforesaid by
the teaching which the thing reuealed, and the reuelation it selfe is
of lawfully- duely proposed,and applied in particuler to euery man
sent Pastours who is to giue infallible assent vnto them,is according
& Doctours to the ordinary course (as appeareth by the holy Scriptures)

tures) no other but the teaching, not only of the prophets and Apoſtles, but alſo of the ſucceeding Paſtours and Doƈtours and Lawfully-ſent preachers of the true viſible Catholique Church, by which only (as appeareth by Hiſtories) all Nations haue hitherto beene conuerted, and being conuerted haue beene in all ages inſtruƈted, and taught ſo, as they belieued infallibly things reuealed, and the reuelation which without this teaching they neuer ſhould haue belieued, nor ſhould yet belieue infallibly although the things reuealed and the reuelation were, and yet are in themſelues moſt certaine and infallibly true. The which doubtles, moued *S. Auſten* to ſay, *Ego Euangelio* (not only *non credidiſſem*, but) *non crederem, niſi me authoritas Eccleſiæ commoueret.* I (not only had not belieued, but) could not ſhould not, or would not belieue the Goſpell it ſelf, if the authority of the Church did not moue me.

7. This Church, whoſe Paſtours are by Gods appointment to propoſe vnto all men the Reuelation & the things reuealed, is no other then the viſible Catholique Roman Church, that is to ſay, That viſible company of men ſpred ouer the whole worlde, who profeſſe the ſame Fayth, vſe the ſame Sacraments, and liue in obedience vnder viſible Paſtours, eſpecially the chiefe Paſtour of the Roman Church, who being S. Peters ſucceſſor, hath by Chriſts appointment chiefe power and authority next vnder Chriſt himſelfe ouer the whole Chriſtian world. This I proue by theſe Arguments.

The firſt Argument.

If there was, is, and muſt be in all ages a viſible Church ſpread ouer the world, hauing in it viſible lawfully-ſent Paſtours & Doƈtours, whō by Gods appointmēt all muſt heare, belieue, obay, & with whome

Rom. 10. 14.
15.
Eph. 4.11.12.

Aug. contra Ep. Funda-menti.
The Paſtours and Doƈtours appointed to propound and apply the diuine reuelation, are the Paſtours and Doƈtours of the Roman Church.
Matth.16.18.
19.
Luc. 22.32.
Ioan.21.17.
Iſa.59.21.
iſa.60.11.
Mattk.28.
19 20.
Luc. 10.16.
Heb.13.17.
Rom. 10.14.
15.
Eph.4.11.12.

V 3   all

all muſt be ioyned in vnity; and no other ſuch was beſides thoſe of the Catholique Roman Church. Then the Catholique Roman Church hath bene, & is ſpread ouer the world, & hath lawfull viſible Paſtours whom all muſt heare, belieue, and obey, and with whom all muſt be ioyned (actually) in Church-vnity.

But there was, is, and muſt be in all ages ſuch a viſible Church, hauing ſuch Paſtours &c. and no other ſuch different from the Catholique Roman Church was in all ages, as appeareth by hyſtories. *Ergo.*

The Conſequence of the *Maior* is cleere; for if one ſuch Church hath been, is, and muſt be in all ages, & no other hath bene beſide one, to wit the Catholique Roman Church; It followeth euidently that this one, and no other different from it, or not conected with it, was, and is ſuch a Church.

The *Minor* hath 2. parts; The firſt, to wit, That there was, is, and muſt be in all ages ſuch a viſible Church, hauing ſuch Paſtours &c. may be proued out of teſtimonies of (a) Scriptures and Fathers.

The 2. part (to wit, no other was different from the Catholique Roman Church) cannot be denied, or if any doe deny it, he muſt aſſigne another, naming the men in all ages out of good Authours, and prouing and defending them to haue belieued all articles of the true Fayth, and to haue duely vſed all the right Sacraments, and to haue liued in vnity, and to haue obayed lawfull Paſtours, as the true Church ought, which neuer was yet, nor euer can be aſſigned.

The ſecond Argument.

If the Roman Church was once a Church which had the priuiledge of hauing lawfully-ſent Paſtours & Doctours, whom all good Chriſtians were bound to heare, belieue, & obey, and communicate with; & did

neuer

(a) Iſa. 59. v. 21.
Iſa. 60. Iſa. 61 v. 9. Math. 5. v. 14, 15. 16. Math. 19. v. 17.
Math. 23. v. 32. Math. 28. 19. 20.
Luc. 10. v. 16. Rom. 10. v. 14. Eph. 4. v. 12. 13. 14.
1. Tim. 3. v. 16.
S. Cyp. lib. 4. ep. 9. & lib. de vnitate Ecl.
Baſil. conſtit. monaſt. c. 22.
Iren. l. 4. cap. 43. Cyril. catech. 18.
Aug. lib 1. contra Creſcon. cap. 33. ep. 170. contra Fauſt. c. 13.

neuer loofe that priuiledge, fhe is ftill fuch a Church which hath that priuiledge. But the Roman Church was once fuch a Church, neither did fhe euer loofe that priuiledge. *Ergo.*

The Confequence of this Maior is cleere; for what-foeuer Church, once had fuch a priuiledge, and neuer loft it, muft needs ftill haue it

The Minor hath 2. parts, The firft is, that the Roman Church once was fuch &c. This appeareth by te-ftimonies of (b) Scripture and Fathers, and is further confirmed by authority of his Maiefty, who faid, That the Roman Church is the mother Church from which we ought no further to depart, then fhe hath departed from her felfe. *See Conference at Hampton-Court* .

The 2. part of the Minor is, that the Roman Church neuer loft this her priuiledge. This I proue.

If the Roman Church euer loft her priuiledg fpoken of by Scripturs and Fathers, eyther this was by her fal-ling into fome euident damnable herefy or fchifme, & feparation of her felfe from the Catholique vifible Church, or by lawfull fentence of Excommunication or depriuation of her priuiledg pronounced by fome Generall Coûcell, or fome particuler lawfull Superior to the Roman Church.

But fhe neuer loft her priuiledge by any of thefe waies, or any other way that can be affigned. *Ergo.*

If any deny the Confequence of this laft Maior, it pertaineth to him to affigne fome other way of loofing priuiledges. If any deny the laft *Minor*, he is obliged to fhew out of good hyftories when, and by whome, and what euident damnable herefy, or fchifme, or fepara-tion from the vifible Catholique Church, was brought into the Roman Church, and what Lawfull Generall Councell, or particuler lawfull Superiour did excom-

municate

(b)Ro.1.v.8.
Cypr.l.1.ep.
3.
Hieron.ep.57.
& Apol. 3.
cap.4. aduerf.
Ruffin. Alfo
Apol.1.c.1.
Iren.l. 3.c.3.
Aug. de vtil.
cred. cap.17.
& ep. 165.
& contra ep.
Fund.cap.4.

municate her, or depriue her of her priuiledges for such
herefy, schisme, or some other iust cause. For if any such
notorious change had beene in Rome, deseruing such
a sentence, these circumstances would haue bene, and
being would haue bene noted by the rest of the Christian world, and record thereof, being of so great importance for discouerie of diuine truth and discerning
which is the true Church, would partly by diuine prouidence, and partly by humane diligence haue bene
preserued in the true Church, as of such like and lesser
matters records haue bene, and are yet preserued; so as
we may say, if such a change of religion, and therby
losse of priuiledge hath bene, hystories yet extant must
needs make some, at least obscure, mention thereof:
wherefore no mention being (as none is) it followeth
that no such change, or losse of priuiledge was.

8. Hence I conclude, that sith 1. None can be saued according to the ordinary course besides those (I spake of
such as haue free vse of reason) who freely concurre to
their owne saluation; & 2. none can freely cocurre who
haue not supernaturall, at least obscure, knowledge or
belief of mans supernaturall end, and such supernaturall
meanes as by the law of God are necessary to the attayning of it; and 3. none can haue this knowledge or belief, but such as giue supernaturall infallible assent to
truth reuealed by God; and 4. none can giue supernaturall infallible assent to those reuealed truths but
such as heare, & beliue the teaching of the Pastours, doctours & teachers of the true visible catholique church;
and 5. those Pastours are no other but those of the Catholique Roman Church which in tymes past (as appeareth by hystories) hath conuerted Nations and instructed people, in all ages, in the Fayth of Christ:
Hence (I say) I conclude, that none can attaine eternall

salu-

saluation but such as giue infallible assent to reuealed truth, by hearing belieuing & obaying the teaching of visible Pastours Doctours and lawfully-sent preachers of the Catholique Roman Church, vnles it please God to vse some extraordinary meanes; which no mã ought to presume vpon, especially when he knoweth or may know, and hath or may haue the foresaid ordinary meanes; as no man ought to presume to be preserued in corporal health by lyfe extraordinary and miraculous meanes, when he hath, or may haue ordinary meanes.

9. Hence it followeth that no Pagan, no Turke, no Iew, no Heretique or Schismatique of whatsoeuer sect or schisme, if he so liue & dye in his Infidelity, or Heresy, or schisme can (according to the ordinary course) be saued: for although it may be that some of all these sorts may through inuincible ignorance be excused from actuall sinne of their Negatiue Infidelity, consisting in not hearing or belieuing the ordinary visible Pastours, and also of their Positiue imbracing this, or that particuler sort of Infidelity, or heresy, or schisme, yet if they haue not infallible diuine Fayth, & therby sufficient knowledge of their supernaturall end, and meanes leading to it, they cannot as they ought freely concurre to the attayning of it, nor consequently can they attaine it. But infallible diuine Fayth they cannot haue otherwise (according to the ordinary course) then *Eph.* 4. 11. 12. by hearing Pastours, Doctours, and preachers lawfully- *Rom.* 10. 14. sent, who are those only of the Roman Church, & not 15. any other who by some infidelity, or Heresy, or schisme either neuer had, or haue lost their lawful Mission, and consequently commission, to teach infallible diuine reuealed truth necessary to saluation.

Moreouer, besides supernaturall Fayth there is required that euery one haue supernaturall hope of attai-

X   ning

ning the end aforesaid, wherby his will being made
strong, may be encouraged to vse all meanes necessary
for attayning the said end: for if, *qui arat, debet in spe arare,*
a man would neuer take paines to plow the ground
but with hope to reape fruit, who wilbe found willing to take so great paines, as are necessary to please
God and to attayne saluation, if he haue not firme hope
that this or that being done or endured, doth please
God and helpe to saluation ? Now, who (besides the
foresaid Pastours of the true Church) can giue him infallible certainety that such, and such things please God
and help to saluation, and therby breed in him most
supernaturall hope, able to make him do and endure all
with perseuerance till death, which is prescribed as necessary to saluation by the law of God? It is true that by
naturall courage strenghtned with hope, proposed by
nature or suggested by instigation of the deuill, some
Infidels or Heretiques may doe and endure much, but
nothing neere that which Gods seruants are by Gods
law in some cases commanded to do, or endure : for
example to deny themselues, to take all crosses and imi-
tate Christ, which things cannot be done or hoped
for, but by grace ouercoming nature; and the ordinary meanes of getting and preseruing this grace is
eyther by right vse of Sacraments, or by acts of supernaturall vertues grounded in supernaturall Fayth, which
ordinarily cannot be had out of the actuall or virtuall
vnity of the Catholique Roman Church.

Besides, if one had diuine supernaturall Fayth and
hope by extraordinary supernaturall meanes, yet he
cannot be saued vnlesse he also haue diuine supernaturall charity, which none can haue who committeth or
consenteth to those who commit any deadly sinne,
especially of Schisme, and Separation of himselfe and
others

1.Cor. 9. 10.

Matth. 16. 24.

others from the Fayth vnity or obedience of the Catholique Roman Church and the Pastours thereof:for as S Paul teacheth if one haue all Fayth so as he can remoue mountaines, yet haue not Charity, it doth not profit to saluatiõ; neyther is it sufficient that one say he loueth God:for as *S.Iohn* sayth,he that sayth he knoweth God and yet keepeth not his commandements, he is a lyar; and he that breaketh any one commandement (sayth *S.Iames*) is guilty of all. Now, one of Gods commandements is to loue our brother or neighbour : This commandement,sayth *S.Iohn*, we haue from God, that he that loueth God must also loue his brothers;and the same *S.Iohn* sayth,he that loueth not his brother whom he seeth, how can he loue God whom he seeth not? Now,if he that doth not loue his brother or neighbour, or doth hate any one man, cannot loue God but committeth deadly sinne,remaineth in death, and is to be acconnted as a murtherer in the sight of God, how much more he that loueth not, but deuideth himselfe from Fayth and communion of sacraments and Rites and obedience of the whole fraternity and brotherhood of the visible Catholique Church,out of which (being the house of the lyuing God, the orderly vnited army and spirituall kingdom,and mysticall body of Christ) none can partake Christs spirit, nor consequently be his;nor consequently if he so liue & die be saued, sith besides I E S V S Christ, there is no other Name vnder heauen in, and by which men must be saued.

1.Cor. 13. 2.

1.Ioan. 2. 4.

Iacob. 2.10.
Ioan 4. 21.

Ibidem 20.

1.Ioan.3; 15.

1.Tim. 3 16.
Cant. 6. 9.
Eph. 1. 23.
Aug. tract.
27. in Ioan.

Act.4. 12.

One may obiect and say, It seemeth by this discourse that we doe vncharitable damne all, besides such as are actuall members of the visible Roman Church, which are but few in comparison of the rest in the world. It seemeth also incredible that our most mercifull Lord (who firſt created all ſorts, yea all men, and will of his part haue all ſaued, and who after ſent I E S V S Chriſt his ſonne to be Sauiour of the whole world) would haue ſo few ſaued. I anſwere. 1. That we ſay not, that any are damned out of any deſire, or wiſh that any man ſhould incurre damnation (which were indeed moſt vncharitable)but we only forewarne men of their perill, letting them know that damnation is threatned by Scripture, & Fathers, and Reaſon grounded thereupon to all who will not heare, beleiue, and obay, and communicate in Sacraments and Church-Rites with ſuch whō God hath appointed to be the ordinary meanes, by which Fayth, and hope, & charity, and the grace of God and other vertues neceſſarie to ſaluation, are to be communicated vnto vs; of which peril to forwarne men, is ſo far from being vncharitable, as it is an act of charity, eſpecially being done (as we doe it) with intent, that they may not fall into damnation for want of knowledge of the ordinary way of ſaluation, by raſh preſuming of extraordinary wayes, which no man may ſafely rely on, while he neglecteth the ordinary way; in regard it is not Almightie Gods vſuall manner to help any by extraordinary meanes when they may, but through pride, willfulnes, or negligence will not know, & help theſelues by ordinary meanes. So as to forewarne men, I ſay, in this ſort of their peril, is a moſt neceſſary act of charity, and to neglect to doe this when need is, or to doe the cōtrarie, by promiſing ſecurity where none is, were a moſt damnable neglect, or an act againſt charity, as to neglect to forwarne men whom they ſee going out of the ſafe High-way into a by-way in which is peril of Robbers, or to tell them they may eſcape robbing although they goe out of the ſafe High-way into certaine perillous wayes, is

euidently

euidently againſt charity and humanity.

2. I anſwere, that we doe not ſay, that all are damned who are not actuall members of the viſible Catholique Roman Church, but eyther ſuch as neyther now are, nor euer in this life wilbe actuall nor virtuall members thereof, for in effect we onely ſay the ordinary neceſſary meanes of ſaluation is diuine ſupernaturall Fayth, hope, charity, and the grace of God, and other ſupernaturall vertues preſcribed by the law of God, and that none can haue theſe vertues (according to the ordinary courſe) but ſuch as heare, belieue, obay, and communicate in ſacraments and rites (in act or deſire, explicitely, or implicitely) with thoſe whom God hath appointed to be the ordinarily lawfully-ſent Paſtours and Doctours, by whoſe miniſtery (and not otherwayes ordinarily) theſe aforeſaid vertues are infuſed, bred, increaſed, and continued in vs; & that theſe ordinary Paſtours are no where found out of the vnity of the Catholique Roman Church, in regard others that ſhalbe aſſigned, either were neuer lawfully ſent, or if they once were, they loſt their lawfull miſſiõ and commiſſion (and conſequently want the aſſiſtance of Chriſts ſpirit, & vigour to communicate it, and by it Gods grace to others) by falling into Infidelity, Hereſy, or ſchiſme, or by vnlawfully conſenting with, or adhereing to any ſuch ſociety of men, who by Infidelity, Hereſy, or ſchiſme haue ſeparated themſelues, or are by iuſt ſentence ſeparated from the Communion of the Catholique Roman Church, or wittingly, willingly, and obſtinatly doe in any ſort refuſe to heare, belieue, obay, and communicate with the ſaid Roman Church.

3. I anſwer, that this doctrine doth not make the number of thoſe which be ſaued leſſe then is deſcribed

X 3   in

in holy Scriptures ; for firſt holy Scripture telleth vs,
that few in compariſon of the whole world are to be
ſaued, *multi vocati, pauci electi, nolite timere puſillus Grex.* It is

Luc. 12. 32.
Matth. 20. 16.

true, that almighty God of his part would haue all ſaued, Chriſt our Lord of his part alſo hath left meanes
ſufficient to ſaue all, and all men either immediatly, or
mediatly haue one time or other, grace offered vnto
them, either by ordinary or extraordinary meaṇes ſufficient (ſuppoſing they put no obſtacle but freely cor-
reſpond to diuine inſpirations) to draw them at leaſt by
degrees to ſufficient ſupernaturall knowledge of diuine truth, and ſo at laſt to Iuſtifying Grace, ſo as the
cauſe why ſo few are ſaued, is the fault of men, not
want of Gods mercy, or Chriſts merits.

4. The number of ſuch as are ſaued may be, according to this doctrine, very many, yea as many as are
deſcribed *Apoc.* 7. For the Roman Church is not contained as ſome imagine within the walles or particuler

Apoc. 7. 4.

Dioceſſe of the Citty of Rome, or the Popes temporall
dominions, or the weſterne Patriarchy: but ſtretcheth it
ſelfe ouer the whole world where any Catholique
Chriſtians are, all which doe belieue the ſame Fayth,
communicate in the ſame Sacraments and Rites, and
liue vnder obedience of lawfull Paſtours, who are
ſubordinat to the Biſhop of *Rome,* being vnder Chriſt
the chief Paſtour. And beſides whatſoeuer other, whether liuing among Pagans, Turks, Iewes, or Heretiques, or Schiſmatiques, who through inuincible ignorance know not, or knowing cannot haue the benefit of the ordinary helpes of Paſtours, are on the one
ſide excuſed from actuall ſinne of their Errours and
outward ſeparation from the Roman Catholique
Church: And who on the other ſide are by Gods
goodneſſe extraordinarily illuminated with ſupernaturall

turall Fayth, and endued with hope and charity, as I
doubt not but manie are; all thefe I fay, although
not being actuall members of the Roman Church, yet
(in regard they are fo difpofed in mind, that if they
knew and had the ordinary meanes and helpe of Paftours and Doctours of the Roman church to teach
them what further is to be belieued and practifed, they
would belieue and practife it for abtaining Gods fa-
uor and eternall faluation) they may be, and are ac-
ccunted virtuall members of the Roman Church, &
fo may be faued. As likewife Catechumens and perfons
excommunicate (fuppofing they dye with a like good
inward difpofition, defire, and endeauour of being
vnited to the Church by baptifme and abfolution)may
be, and are accounted virtuall members of the fame
Church. But if on the one fide, they fhould by inuincible Ignorance, or impoffibility be excufed from
actuall finne of Infidelity, Errour, and fchifme; yet on
the other fide (through the demerit of their other
finnes, committed againft the light of reafon and diuine infpirations which almighty God doth vfually
impart to all men, at one tyme or other) they fhould
not be illuminated (as it is to be doubted moft Pagans, Turks, Iewes, Heretiques and fchifmatiques are
not) or if being illuminated with inward fupernaturall Fayth, they doe not cooperate with it to the at-
taining of hope and charity, and repentance, & other
neceffarie vertues, or if they be malicioufly, and obftinatly bent againft, or groffely negligent in feeking to
know, or knowing careleffe to heare, belieue, & obay
the ordinarie Paftours :

Thefe men doubtles, as being through their owne
fault depriued of the ordinary meanes of faluation
which they might, and ought to haue had by hearing
and

and belieuing ordinary Paſtours, cannot in reaſon preſume to be ſaued by extraordinary helpes of Grace, (which are not to be expected when ordinary may be had) for we muſt not expect miracles without neceſſity, but may iuſtly feare, or rather be ſure that ſuch men if they perſeuer in this ſtate of mynd vntill death, cannot attaine ſaluation. And therfore no man who teareth God and is carefull of his ſoules health, will ſuffer his mynd eyther to be maliciouſly and obſtinatly bent againſt Roman Catholique Paſtours, or negligent in hearing, belieuing and obaying, and vniting himſelfe with the ſaid ordinary Paſtours, but ſhould and ought firſt hartily deſire, and pray to God to ſend him ſome meanes wherby he may be rightly informed in truth neceſſary to ſaluation, and alſo doe his further beſt endeuors to find, with reſolution to follow, thoſe whō he may learne to be ordinary Paſtours and lawfully-ſent preachers, whom God hath appointed to teach the ſaid reuealed entire truth, without expecting that God himſelfe ſhould extraordinarily appeare, or make an angell appeare vnto him to giue him inſtruction, which inſtruction alſo were like to be no other, then to ſend him to the ſaid ordinary teachers; as appeareth in the example of *Cornelius*, and *S. Paul*, vnto whom although it pleaſed Chriſt our Lord extraordinarly to appeare, to the one by an Angell, to the other by himſelfe, yet for particuler inſtruction he wiſheth *Cornelius* to

Act. 10. 5.
Act. 9. 8.
ſend for *S. Peter*, & *S. Paul* to goe into the Citty, where *Ananias* was ſent to him to teach and baptize him.

2. It may be obiected, that it ſeemeth it may ſuffice that a man doth agree with the Roman Church in ſome chiefe heads or fundamentall points of doctrine, as in belieuing the Holy Trinity, Chriſt crucified &c. although in other points he hold contrary: for if one
haue

haue but foe much actuall supernaturall Fayth as may
breed hope, and charity, and repentance &c. and so
much submission and obedience in hearing and belieuing ordinary Paftours in thefe fundamentall points,
and in taking baptifme of them, the cafe may be put that
he may be faued although he doe not actually belieue
any more, but hould opinion contrary to the reft of
the doctrine of the Roman Church: And although alfo
he receaue no other Sacraments, nor thinke it neceffary to receaue any other, nor to obay any other commandement of the ordinary Paftours ; as for example
if one being onely inftructed in the faid fundamentall
points, & only taught that it is neceffary to be baptized,
and hereupon actually doth belieue, and is effectually
baptized, and after that prefently dyeth or liueth where
he neuer heares more inftruction, and for want of inftruction fimply thinketh no more to be neceffary,
nor any other thing taught by the Roman Church co-
cerning other articles to be true, but being asked pofi-
tiuely fayth(according to that he knoweth by the only
light of nature)that it is falfe :

Such a man doubtles, by reafon of inuincible ignorance finneth not in this, and on the other fide he feemeth to haue had meanes fufficient of faluation, according to that of our Sauiour, *Qui crediderit & baptizatus
fueris faluus erit:* why therfore may not Proteftants and *Marc. 16. 16.*
other Heretiques and fchifmatiques be faued who hold
the faid fundamentall points and be baptized, and liue
either where they haue noe inftruction, or not fufficient to make them belieue other points of Roman
Fayth, or to fee it neceffary to receaue any other facraments, yea although fymple(as they haue beene taught
by their preachers)they thinke Roman Fayth in other
points to be falfe? I anfwere, that fuch an extraordinary

cafe

cafe may be put, or at leaſt imagined in which ſuch a
one as is deſcribed in the obiection, may haue ſuch inuincible ignorance as he may be ſaued. But this caſe of
hauing ſuch inuincible Ignorance is extraordinary, &
muſt not be made a Rule for any to rely vpõ ordinarily,
eſpecially when there are ſo many occaſions & meanes
to get knowledge & ſo few mẽ (in cõpariſon) foũd who
either outwardly haue not heard, or by diuine inſpiration do not inwardly, at leaſt ſometimes , ſuſpect or
doubt that it is not ſufficient onely to belieue ſome few
principall points of Fayth, and only to be baptized;
for both in Holy Scriptures, and other bookes and ſer-
mons, and in ordinary ſpeaches more is ſpoken of, and
the liues and examples of other Chriſtians of ſeuerall
ſorts giue occaſion of doubt or queſtion , that ſome-
thing more is to be belieued or practiſed : neyther is
there any reaſon , or authority ſufficient to aſſure, that
there needs no more, for firſt (theſe matters being ſupernaturall) naturall reaſon cannot tell that any part is neceſſary, or if ſo much, why not more ?

   And for authority, wheras ſome hould more, ſome
leſſe to be fundamentall , or abſolutly neceſſary to be
knowne and belieued expreſſely, eyther *neceſsitate me-*
dij or *præcepti*, no man ought to aduenture his ſaluation
vpon the authority of any one, or ſome few, eſpecially
tam pauci, tam noui, tam turbulenti, ſo few, ſo new, ſo tur-
bulent Preachers, who doe teach this libertine *Larga-*
manica-doctrine, that it is ſufficient to belieue a few fundamentall points and that one may in all other things
(although reuealed by God, and propoſed to be belieued by full authority of the Catholique Church) belieue what he liſt, or not belieue any of them , ſuppoſing he can ſo frame his conſcience (as is moſt eaſy for
ſuch who make noe conſcience of not hearing , and
                                                  believing

belieuing and obaying the teaching of the Church :)
No man, I fay, ought to aduenture his faluation vpon
fo fleight and vncertaine authority, efpecially when
with looking a little about him into the Chriftian
world, or by asking, he may fynd far greater authority
affirming it to be needfull to belieue *explicitè* or *implicitè* all reuealed truth, propofed by full authority of the
Church, without doubting or denying any one point;
the which he may find to be affirmed by the greateft
authority in this world, to wit, by the authority of the
moft glorious, moft ancient, moft vniuerfall and conftant confent of the Paftours and Doctours, and other
profeffors of the Catholique Romã Church, of whom
euery one that doubteth, ought to learne what is, and
what is not to be belieued by diuine Fayth to be reuealed truth; alfo what part of it is, and what is not fo
held for a point fundamentall, or neceffary to be
knowne, and belieued expreffely *necefsitate medij,* or
præcepti , by euery one, what by thofe who haue como-
dity of inftructors, what by thofe which want it, what
by thofe of more capacity, and what by thofe of leffe,
what by Paftours, what by people &c. for according to
thefe differences of perfons and other circumftances,
more or leffe of the reuealed truth is neceffary to be expreffely knowne and belieued vnder paine of damnation, as Deuines do commonly hould , who alfo do all
conftantly affirme, that it is not lawfull for any Prieft,
or layman learned or vnlearned to deny obftinatly, or
deliberatly doubt of any part of the faid reuealed truth,
being by the true Church fufficiently propofed, notified, & made known to be a truth reuealed by God, in
regard this were in effect to giue God and his Church
the lye , and proudly to oppofe and preferre a priuate
mans Iudgment and will, before, or againft the Iudg-

Y 2

ment

ment and will of God, and his true Church; which to
doe aduiſedly, and eſpetially with contempte or con-
tumacy, muſt needs be a damnable ſynne, although
the matter in which this is done be neuer ſo ſmall. For
our Sauiour who commaundeth vs to heare, belieue, &
obay the Church, doth not limit his commaund only
to matters fundamentall, or of chiefe moment, but without all limitation or diſtinction of matters, he ex-
Matth. 23. 2. preſſely ſayth, *Omnia quacumque dixerint vobis ſeruate &*
facite, obſerue and doe all things whatſoeuer they ſay
vnto you, that is, little and great, and euen in matters of
fact done againſt any of our brethren; and therfore *à*
fortiori, in things done immediatly againſt God himſelfe
Matth. 18. 17. or his Church, Chriſt our Sauiour indefinitely and without all reſtriction ſayth, He that will not heare the
Church, let him be to thee as a heathen and publican;
whoſe ſtate being damnable, the ſtate of him who ſhall
in manner aforeſaid not heare, or belieue, and obay the
Church muſt needs be alſo damnable, ſo long as without repentance he continueth in that wilfull not
hearing, belieuing, and obaying the Church. In regard
of the Church that may be truely ſaid, which is ſaid of
ſome particuler members of it; *It is not you which ſpeake,*
Matth. 10. 20. *but the ſpirit of your Father which ſpeaketh in you,* ſo that
the Church may ſay (as *Moyſes* ſaid) to thoſe who re-
bell or murmure againſt it, *your murmuring is not againſt*
vs, but againſt God our Lord : But to rebell and murmure
Exod. 16. 8. againſt God deliberately with contempt, and comtu-
maciouſly, muſt needs be damnable ſinne. *Ergo,* not to
heare, belieue, and obay, but rebell & murmure againſt
the Church in manner aforeſaid, muſt needs be damnable ſinne.

3. It may be obiected, ſaying; It may be ſhewed that
the Church of *Rome* hath giuen iuſt cauſt of Proteſtants

stants schisme or separation, or that at least now that
the separation is made, it is the fault of the Church of
Rome, that vnion is not procured, for there were many
Errours not only of fact, but also of Fayth, and for Errours of Fayth it is necessary to separate. I answere. First
with *S. Austen*, that there cánot be any iust cause for any
particuler man, or any particuler Church to separate it
selfe from the whole visible Catholique Church, and if
not to separate at first, much lesse to continue the separation: for if to separate be ill, it is much worse to continue in it. If one act of fornication be (as it is) damnable
much more damnable is it to liue many yeares in a state
of fornication, or in any other great sinne, especially of
schisme. The reason of this my answere is, for that Errour in Fayth cannot be in the whole Church ; and for
any other Errour it is not a necessary, or iust cause to
make men separate from the Church, in regard all necessarie reformation may stand with Church-vnity;
neyther can there be any correction (as *S. Irenæus* calleth it) or reformation (which cannot stád with Church
vnity) so great a good as to counterpoize the euill of
schisme, for schisme being a renting or tearing of one
part of the Church from the other, doth necessarily
make one of those parts to be no part of Christs mysticall body, which is but one(*vnum corpus*) nor consequently informed with Carists spirit, which being one
(*vnus spiritus*) is not found out of Christs mysticall body:
But to make any part of the Church to become noe
part of the mysticall body of Christ, and consequently
to be depriued of his spirit and grace, and consequently
not to be his, is a greater euill thē can be counterpoized
by any good which can come of any such reformation
as breaketh Church-vnity; for noe such reformation
can giue the life of Christs spirit to any that wanteth it,

*Aug. ep. 48.
ad Vincent.*

Eph. 4. 4.

*Aug. tract.
27. in Ioan.*

Y 2   but

but at most some more pretended perfection of life to
those which already haue the life of Chrifts fpirit,
which is not fo great a good, as the life it felfe which
fchifme taketh away from one of thofe parts which
doth rent and teare themfelues from Church-Communion.

2. I anfwer, that it is certaine that the Roman Church
did not rent herfelfe from the Proteftant Church, in
regard fhe neuer was vnited vnto it, neyther was there
any Proteftant Church before Luther and others, who
being once members of the Roman Church, did confeffedly make a rent, feparation, and departure, or going
out from it; the which being done vnder pretence of
reformation demanded, and not graunted, I aske whether this reformation demanded and not graunted was
in doctrine or manners? if only in manners, it was not a
fufficient caufe, as is already faid, neyther was it needfull or fit to make a fchifme, efpecially fuch a horrible
fchifme, as was made for procuring Reformation of
manners, efpecially when it might be better made by
remaining in Church-vnity with fuch as needed to be
reformed, who would more eafily heare good admo-
nition of brethren liuing in vnity, then of thofe who
haue made themfelues ftrangers and oppofit by feparation. If it be faid that reformation needed in doctrine, I
aske whether in doctrine of Fayth neceffary to faluation, or in doctrine not neceffary? 1. For doctrine not
neceffary, fchifmes (efpecially fuch a one at this) doubtles
ought not to haue bene made, in regard Schifme is a
greater euill then can be recompenfed with any doctrine not neceffary to faluation. 2. If it be faid that the
caufe why Proteftants did feparate themfelues, was for
that the Roman Church did erre in doctrine neceffary
to faluation; I aske, firft what particuler doctrines thefe
be?

Caluin con-
feffeth it *l.ep.
ap.141.*

be?For either they are, 1. certaine grosse Errours, slaunderoufly obiected by Proteftants, but not held by any Roman Catholique;or 2. fome opinions found in fome particuler mens writings, but not held vniuerfally nor defined by the Church; or laftly doctrines defined in the Councell of *Trent*. For doctrines of the firft and fecond kind, Proteftants had no reafon to feparate themfelues from the Romã Church, for that thofe(not being her doctrines, nor held by her, nor any way neceffary to be held by any who will hould cõmunion with her) could not be any iuft caufe to moue any to feparate from her, but rather to ioyne with her in detefting the former,as fhe alwayes did and doth,and correcting the latter kind,as fhe fometymes doth, eyther by burning their books, or by razing out the Errours out of their bookes,or by writing againft them. And for doctrines of the third kind which are accounted damnable Errours of the Roman Church, I aske in whofe Iudgment they be accounted damnable Errours? If onely in priuat particuler Iudgmẽts of her aduerfaries or rebellious children, it is againft all reafon, that this their priuate Iudgment fhould be preferred before the common Iudgment of their confeffed mother the Romã Church; and it is fo farre from being a fufficient caufe of making a rebellion againft her,or a fchifme or feparation from her,as it is to be reputed with S. *Bernard intollerable pride,* and with S. *Auftin,* moft *infolent madneffe,* to oppofe any priuat mans Iudgment,or difpute againft that which is iudged or generally practifed by the Church. If Proteftants fay they hould them to be Errours not vpõ their owne priuate Iudgment, but eyther for that they find them not in Scriptures, or ancient Councels and Fathers of the firft 600. yeares, or for that they find them (tò wit in their priuate Iudgment) to be contrary to

Ber. fer. 3. de refur. Aug. epift. 118.

Scriptures

Scriptures and Fathers. I anfwere.

First, that this is still to reduce all to their priuate finding, or not finding. 2. I anfwere, that it is not neceffary that euery point of Fayth be found expreffely, and in particuler in Scriptures or writtings of Fathers, by the priuate Iudgment of euery particular man, but that it be propofed as a truth reuealed, & made knowne to vs eyther by written or vnwritten Traditions, fo that although fome points *of Trent-doctrine* be not loud expreffely, plainely, and in particular in Scriptures, Councels and Fathers (as also diuers points which Proteftants doe belieue and teach, are not found in Scriptures, Councels and Fathers) yet there is not any one point defined in the Councell of *Trent* contrary, but conformable to, and conteyned in, and may by good confequence be deduced out of Scriptures, Councels and Fathers, immediatly or mediatly; which is fufficient, (for to require that euery point fhould be proued immediatly out of fome particuler fentence of Fathers Councels, or text of Scriptures, by a good fyllogifme which doth demonftratiuely conclude that particuler point, is not neceffary:) neyther can our Proteftants fo proue diuers points of their doctrine fet downe in their 39. Articles which their Minifters fubfcribe vnto, and are obliged to hould. For although Proteftants (as all other Heretiques, old and new, vfe to doe) alleadge ordinarily (in their Sermons, Homilies, Catechifmes books of articles, and other books) quotations of places and fometymes words of Scriptures or Fathers which make the fimple people belieue that their doctrine is conformable to, contained in, and immediatly deduced out of fuch fentences & texts as are quoted, and whofe words are alleadged; yet let any man not partially affected, & hauing skyll in Diuinity and Logick examine

and

and he will neuer find, that there is any one euident Confequence, or immediate Syllogifticall, efpecially demonftratiue, Proofe of any one point held by them againft vs Catholiques, which is, or can be made out of any text of Scripture, or fentences of approued Fathers; and he will further difcouer, that in moft of the allegations, eyther the text is corrupted by falfe tranflation, or peruerted by falfe interpretation, or the inference is not good, or our doctrine is ignorantly or malicioufly mifreported, and confequently the text mifapplied, or the matter affirmed and proued is either impertinent or not denied by vs, or may, *mutatis mutandis*, be as well vrged againft Proteftants, as againft vs: the which obferuation may ferue for a generall anfwere to moft of the books which are at this day fet out by Proteftants.

If Proteftats in this cafe appeale from the Iudgment of the Church, eyther to the Letter of Scripture, or to conference of one place of Scripture with another, although the Church be not bound to admit this their appeale no more then the temporall Prince or Common welth is bound to admit a like appeale made by rebellious fubiects or other malefactours from the authority of their Iudgment to the letter of the Law, or conference of places of the law-bookes, which being permitted, no theef that hath wit would be hanged; yet we are fo confident of the Church her caufe, as we dare try Cotrouerfies between her and Proteftants by the very letter of Scripture, or conference of places; allwayes fuppofed that in fine the priuate Iudgment of Proteftants in their owne caufe may not be preferred (as no reafon will permit) before the Iudgment of the Church, but that the Iudgment of the Church (as the Iudgment of the Prince or Common Welth vfeth euen in her owne cafe) may pronounce the definitiue fen-

tence frō which there ought to be no appeale; but as our
Sauiour said, *Qui Ecclesiam non audierit sit tibi sicut Ethnicus*
& Publicanus, It one shall not heare and obay the Iudgment of the Church, let him be to thee as an heathen &
publican; which spiritually is as ill, or worse then that
which was appointed in Deuteronomy, *Qui superbierit*
&c. he that shall be proud, and shall not obay the sentence of the chiefe Priest, by the decree of the Iudge let
him die the death.

Matt. 18. 17.

Deut. 17. 12.

If lastly Protestants shall plead against this finall
Church-Iudgment the testimony of their inward
priuate spirit, I answere, that first sith the spirit of God
was promised to the Catholique Church, and not to
any priuat man, or company of men separate (as Protestants are) from the said Church, this their Plea cannot
be good. 2. Whatsoeuer Protestants can say to make
their Plea good against the Catholique Church, may
be said by Anabaptists, and whatsoeuer other Heretiques, who did, or shall separate themselues from the
Protestant Church. As therefore Protestants would
answere (notwithstanding whatsoeuer is alleaged)
that such a pretended spirit in Anabaptists cannot be
good, the like answere they may, *potiori iure*, expect
from Catholiques, who deny this their pretended spirit (though neuer so sensibly felt, or seemingly cōfirmed
by words of Scriptures) to be the true spirit of God, it
being rather the spirit of the prince of Darkenes trans-
figuring himselfe into an Angell of light, and couering
his false senses with seeming words of true Scriptures.

The which to be so, may partly be made plaine by
the want of Humility, Obedience Concord, Vnity
which be effects of a good spirit, and by the contrary
qualities of pride, disobedience, discord and other effects

fects of an ill spirit; but most clearly by that rule of
discerning spirits giuen by *S. Iohn, Nos ex Deo sumus &c.* 1. *Ioan,* 4. 6.
We are of God, he that heareth vs is of God, he that is
not of God, doth not heare vs, for according to this rule
we are assured that euery spirit is of God, which heareth
belieueth, and obeyeth the Church of God; and on the
contrary part, that spirit is not of God which doth not
heare, belieue, and obey the visible Catholique Church
which is certainely knowne to be of God, and to haue
in it the true spirit of God, in regard it hath in it an vninterrupted continuall succession of Pastours and Doctours vniuersally spread ouer the whole world, and
consenting one with another, and with their predecessours in the first receaued and neuer-chaunged doctrine of Christ; for this, and no other company hath
in it the spirit of God, and vnto this and no other com-   *Matt.* 28. 20.
pany doth Christ our Lord and God promise his owne   *Ioan.* 14. 16.
presence, and the Holy Ghost his assistance all dayes,
and for euer, euen vntill the consummation of the   *Rom.* 1. 8.
world. And therefore sith it appeareth by Scriptures   *Irenæus lib.* 3.
and Fathers, that the Roman Church was once in pos-   *c.* 3. *Cypriaa.*
session of this priuiledge, and by hystories that she ne-   *epist.* 18. *in*
uer made chaunge of the first receaued doctrine,   *edit. Morelii.*
nor otherwise lost this her priuiledg, as is already
proued;

I may certainely conclude, that she, and those that are
ioyned with her, may say with *S. Iohn, Nos ex Deo sumus,*
we are of God, he that heareth vs is of God, he that
is not of God doth not heare vs; In this we know
the spirit of truth, and the spirit of Errour: and here-
vpon may subsume.

But Protestants do not heare vs.

Therefore, we know that they are not of God, and
that their pretended spirit is not the promised spirit

of

of truth, but the spirit of Errour; and that the spirit of
sauing Truth is onely in those, who in all humility,
obedience, concord, and vnity of hart & spirit actually
adhere to the Catholique Roman Church, and consequently, that there is no saluation out of the Vnity of
the Catholique Roman Church.

FINIS.